T5-BBG-670

*"OUT OF SMALLE BEGININGS . . ."*

# *"OUT OF SMALLE BEGININGS..."*

## An Economic History of Harvard College in the Puritan Period (1636 to 1712)

MARGERY SOMERS FOSTER

THE BELKNAP PRESS OF
HARVARD UNIVERSITY PRESS
Cambridge, Massachusetts
1962

*Distributed in Great Britain by Oxford University Press, London*

---

*Library of Congress Catalog Card Number 62–13266*

*Printed in the United States of America*

*To the memory of my mother and father,*
*who would have been as much entertained*
*by this investigation as I have been*

# *PREFACE*

Over the centuries, as Professor Robert Ulich and others have pointed out, universities have been founded in answer to a felt need of the time. If that need is felt by those in a position to back up the feeling with action, a university is founded; if not, it is stillborn or shortly dies. Who felt the need for a college in the microcosm of Massachusetts Bay in the seventeenth century? What did they do about it? Were they successful? These are among the questions we can ask about Puritan Harvard. Though new questions have arisen since the Puritan Period, these persist today — these and many subsidiary questions: President Henry Dunster did not worry in 1643 about the deteriorating value of Boston real estate as an investment, but Dunster was considerably troubled by the deterioration of the quality of the wampumpeage accepted as toll for the College's Charlestown Ferry; no McCarthy was trying to intimidate the faculty of the seventeenth-century Harvard, but a Puritan General Court's support was important, and the College's attitude in both instances greatly influenced its economic as well as its intellectual future.

The object of this study is to describe the economic situation of Harvard College in the Puritan Period, and to show how general economic factors of the period influenced the College, as well as how factors other than economic affected Harvard's economics. Where possible I should like to show the origins of present-day practices and to determine which elements are continuing and which are either transitory or new. The major purpose is to try to throw light on 1962 colleges.

The obvious point of attack for an economic study of an institution in the twentieth century is the institution's financial statements, which lead into all phases of its conduct. The plan of this study is therefore based on the arrangement of a financial statement and the questions one would ask about it. This plan seems worthwhile despite the fact that some continuity of the story is lost and some repetition occurs in the effort to organize the data in this way. (For example, government grants appear in receipts, again when disbursed as salary, and once more under growth of assets.)

But for Puritan Harvard adequate financial statements were not available and so we are forced to build them. We carry the study in detail to July 1712, the date of the last list of assets in our period which is supported by source material in contemporary financial journals. Some few additional facts are included up to 1715, when after twenty years the Brattles gave up the Treasurership.

Chapters I and II give the general political and social background and an introduction to the characters, and tell of the type and adequacy of available records. These first two chapters show some over-all figures which begin to establish a scale for our period, and Chapter III attempts to set the economic stage and evaluate the figures in real economic terms. Chapter IV deals with income from students, Chapter V with income from governments, and Chapter VI with various categories of gifts, income from endowment, and a summary of all income. Chapter VII tells of disbursements, and Chapter VIII of the growth of assets. Chapter IX makes some general observations which fall far short of meeting the original broad objectives but nonetheless pick up some of the outstanding insights of earlier chapters.

There is room for much more work on this subject in this period, but it is not probable that the major outline of the financial picture will change from the one presented here. There is additional supporting detail in my thesis (1958), "The Economic History of Harvard College in the Puritan Period," available in the Radcliffe and Harvard University Archives. The thesis explains the use and interpretation of the records; it also gives a complete record of gifts, which is available nowhere else and is included here only in summary.

The many quotations from documents of the Puritan Period retain the original spelling and capitalization. I have expanded all obvious abbreviations (excepting dwt. [pennyweight]), brought down all superior letters, and replaced old form letters by their modern counterparts — such as "th" for "y," "I" for the long-tailed "J," "u" for "v," and "v" for "u." Dates are in modern form. The designation of pounds, shillings, and pence is here uniformly "£ *s.* *d.*" even inside quotations, whatever symbol was originally used, and £, *s.*, and *d.* refer to Massachusetts currency unless otherwise stated.

I should like to express my gratitude first and most of all for the suggestions and helpful guidance of Professor Seymour E. Harris. It was he who first proposed this subject; he led me to undertake an entirely enjoyable investigation which combines my original Radcliffe objective — to study the economics of education under him — with a long-standing interest of mine and my family's — American colonial history. A more knowledgeable and considerate mentor could not have been found. Mr. Harris is working on a long-range analysis of Harvard's economics which will put this early phase of the College's history into suitable perspective.

I am much indebted to Professor Bernard Bailyn for both his courses in American history and his continuing interest in this project. Dean Bernice Brown Cronkhite, Dean Wilma Kerby-Miller, and Professor Arthur Cole have continuously encouraged the undertaking. Professor Raymond de Roover read and criticized the material on accounting, a summary of which shows in this volume. Miss Ruth Crandall's valuable material is acknowledged in the text. Numberless teachers, colleagues, and other friends have contributed to my thinking and borne with my gross unsociability during the course of the work.

No one could write on this subject without acknowledging a debt to Professor Samuel Eliot Morison, the official tercentenary historian of the University, the heir of the generations of Harvard historians who preceded him. His books, *The Founding of Harvard College* and *Harvard College in the Seventeenth Century*, represent years of research from which any historical work on Harvard can start. Professor Morison generously gave me the freedom of his files, and this study benefits from some material to which his references have led. Mr. Morison himself says that he did not undertake to cover the economic aspects of the College's history, though obviously he frequently touches upon them. I have differed in minor ways with some of his findings, but anyone who reads this book will recognize my heavy debt in the frequency of the footnotes "*FHC*," "*HCSC*."

I appreciate the help of Secretary to the Corporation David W.

Bailey, Assistant Librarian Robert H. Haynes and his staff, Custodian of the University Archives Clifford K. Shipton, and especially the cordial hospitality of Mr. Kimball Elkins and the staff in the Archives, without whose cooperation this study would not have been possible or nearly so pleasant.

The Mount Holyoke College Williston Library has proven extremely convenient. It has in its own collection, or has promptly borrowed from its Hampshire Inter-Library Center affiliates, copies of practically all the materials I have needed for final checking

Mrs. Theodore Carlin and Mrs. David Canney have given very able assistance and support in the production of a difficult manuscript. Finally, the kindly editors of the Harvard University Press could not have been more understanding and efficient. I hope they will be pleased with our book. Of course, I take the responsibility for any errors or omissions which may become evident.

The quotation "out of smalle beginings . . ." has been used many times in connection with Harvard history, notably on the tercentenary medal and by Mr. Morison in the epigraph of *Harvard College in the Seventeenth Century*. It seems to fit the period and the situation so much better than any other that I am using it once more. The phrase was a part of Governor William Bradford's eloquent comment in his *Of Plimmoth Plantation*,

> Thus out of smalle beginings greater things have been produced by his hand that made all things of nothing, and gives being to all things that are; and as one small candle may light a thousand, so the light here kindled hath shone unto many, yea in some sorte to our whole nation; let the glorious name of Jehova have all the praise.

MARGERY SOMERS FOSTER

South Hadley, Massachusetts
May 1962

## *CONTENTS*

## *TABLES*

*TABLES*

# *FIGURES*

## *ILLUSTRATIONS*

*All facsimiles made from documents in the Harvard University Archives follow page 74*

## *ABBREVIATIONS USED IN NOTES*

| | |
|---|---|
| AAAS | American Academy of Arts and Sciences |
| AAS | American Antiquarian Society |
| *Am. Hist. Rev.* | *American Historical Review* |
| *A&R* | *Acts and Resolves of the Province of Massachusetts Bay* |
| *ASA* | *Collections of the American Statistical Association* |
| *CSM* | *Publications of the Colonial Society of Massachusetts* |
| *DAB* | *Dictionary of American Biography* |
| *FHC* | *The Founding of Harvard College*, by Samuel Eliot Morison |
| *HCSC* | *Harvard College in the Seventeenth Century*, by Samuel Eliot Morison |
| HUA | The Harvard University Archives, Widener Library |
| *Mass. Bay Recs.* | *Records of the Governor and Company of the Massachusetts Bay in New England* |
| MHS | Massachusetts Historical Society |
| *NEHGR* | *New England and Historical and Genealogical Register* |
| QBB | The Stewards' Quarter-Bill Book, in Harvard University Archives |
| *Plym. Col. Recs.* | *Records of Plymouth Colony* |

*"OUT OF SMALLE BEGININGS . . ."*

# I

# *THE GENERAL SETTING*

## IN THE BEGINNING
## 1636–1654

ON the twenty-eighth of October, 1636, the Great and General Court of the Massachusetts Bay Colony "agreed to give £400 towards a schoale or colledge. . . ."* This is the first recorded notice of the institution which was to become Harvard University, and significantly it is a notice concerned with finance. We shall find that from 1636 to now the history of Harvard as an educational institution has been entwined with its history as a financial institution, and no doubt it will continue so throughout the future: somewhat adequate finance is, if not sufficient, at least a necessary condition for somewhat adequate education.

In this founding vote we may detect two important influences which were to act strongly upon the infant college. No doubt the idea of a college had been brewing in the minds of some of the more imaginative and foresighted of the Massachusetts Bay Colonists, but it was not until the Court "agreed" that the foundation could go forward. The Court itself was the governing body of a colony only lately developed from the Massachusetts Bay Company, a joint-stock company chartered by King Charles in 1629. Though the Company had ceased to function, the Company's charter continued in use as the plantation charter.[1] But what authority had even a properly chartered colony itself to charter another

* *Records of the Governor and Company of the Massachusetts Bay in New England,* ed. Nathaniel B. Shurtleff, M.D. (Boston, 1854), I, 183.

The "Great and General Court" is still the official name of the legislature of the Commonwealth of Massachusetts.

Most references, and additional notes, will appear in the chapter notes at the end of the book. Abbreviations used in footnotes follow the list of illustrations.

body? Straightening out the legal status of the College occupied an unbelievable amount of the time and energy of the College's friends and enemies until it was settled, we hope once and for all, in 1708; throughout the Puritan Period the fortunes of the College swung to a large extent with the political fortunes of the Colony.

The vote of October 1636 "agreed to give" the £400, and went on "whereof £200 to be paid the next yeare, and £200 when the worke is finished, and the next Court to appoint wheare and what building." The Court here made no provision for a source of the £400, and it was some years before this amount was extracted from the "Country's" Treasurer or his suppliers. So the new college was largely dependent on an infant colony whose own financial matters were worked out only with a considerable amount of difficulty.

The vote goes on: "The next Court to appoint. . . ." We shall see that the College not infrequently waited for "the next Court to appoint," and if the Court was distracted by an Indian War or if the Court's temper had changed, the waiting no doubt seemed interminable to the College's administrators.

Thus in reading this first report we find dependence on dubious and slow-working legal authority and reliance on a very unsubstantial colonial economy.

To its seventeenth-century officers, to their enthusiasm and their invincible determination, we owe the survival despite its weaknesses, of English America's only institution of higher learning. We can imagine that it was the "Master" of the College and possibly members of the first Board of Overseers who in 1638 inspired John Harvard, a young minister in neighboring Charlestown, to leave half his considerable estate to the College. We can picture the President making difficult decisions when ends would not meet because "corne was deare" or the important income from the Charlestown ferry came to him in "bad [wampum] peague."

If the odds against the new "Universitie" in a primitive land were heavy, there were powerful forces in its favor: (1) the leading men of the Colony were themselves graduates of, or connected with, British universities;[2] (2) these men and many of the lesser citizens believed that it was essential to have a source of trained civil service and an educated ministry; (3) all sought understanding of the Bible, and for that, education in the classics and even Hebrew was desirable; (4) influential and wealthy persons in England felt that this college in the Puritan colony was perhaps the only place in the world where the truth was taught; (5) one of the objectives of the supporters of the Colony was "propagating the Gospel to the Indians," and to accomplish this objective both Indians and teachers of Indians must be educated. Such factors as these caused the men and women of Colonial New England to work and to sacrifice that the future of their children might not be limited by lack of educational opportunity, that "learning may not be buried in the graves of our forefathers."[3]

Since the purposes, as well as the details of operation, of an institution determine to a large extent the financial resources it attracts, the objectives in the establishment of the College are relevant to our investigation.

There is disagreement among authorities as to the *primary* purpose of the founding of this College.* The question is whether the object was primarily to train ministers or to provide general education. At Harvard College, as in Cambridge, England, prospective ministers received training identical with that of gentlemen's sons who had no intention of becoming ministers, though often the ministers-to-be continued their education for a longer period. Moreover, ministers and teachers were to some extent interchangeable — a man tended to teach a while until a desirable parish opened up.

As to whether Harvard was educating ministers or civic leaders we may say that in seventeenth-century New England, though the ministers were by law not allowed to be "magistrates," they certainly were civic leaders; and just under half the graduates from 1642 to 1700 went into the ministry. Mr. Morison gives the distribution shown in Table 1 for occupations of Harvard alumni of the classes of 1642 to 1700; he shows also that the distribution did not change materially over this period.[4]

Another moot point is whether or not Massachusetts Bay Colony

* Professor Morison feels that the College was founded to give a general education as well as to educate ministers. Mr. Hudson states that the idea of founding for general education is a "myth." See Morison, *FHC*, pp. 54, 248–250, 432, 434; *The Puritan Pronaos* (New York, 1936), p. 29; *Three Centuries of Harvard* (Cambridge, 1946), pp. 22–25. Also Winthrop S. Hudson in *Church History* (June, 1939), pp. 148–157.

*Table 1. Occupations of Harvard Alumni of the Classes of 1642 to 1700*

| Occupation | Number |
|---|---|
| Clergymen | 266 |
| Physicians | 35 |
| Public Officials (not local) | 67 |
| Teachers | 17 |
| Merchants | 20 |
| Planters, Gentlemen | 18 |
| Soldiers, Mariners | 10 |
| Miscellaneous | 6 |
| Died Young | 31 |
| Occupation Unknown | 73 |
| Total | 543 |

*Source: HCSC*, p. 562; information based upon Sibley and Shipton.

was a theocracy. This problem need not concern us at length here, but we must recognize that a prevailing influence throughout the Colony for at least the major part of the seventeenth century was that of the clergy. Winthrop gives a good example of the way this worked when he tells how the General Court called in the church elders "to reconcile the differences between the magistrates and deputies";[5] and how in a dispute over division of land, "at the motion of Mr. Cotton [a minister of Boston], who showed them, that it was the Lord's order among the Israelites to have all such businesses committed to the elders, . . . they all agreed to go to a new election . . ." presumably to replace and improve upon the former election when "their choice left out . . . the chief men."[6] The magistrates, who were the Governor and his Council, were almost invariably classmates or personal friends of the church elders, and the latter seemed pretty consistently, though not invariably, to sustain the former's decisions.

The essential fact for early New England seems to me to be the general agreement among the leading people of the time that the Puritan religion should be the basis of life in Massachusetts Bay and that for a Puritan life, the only good life, it was necessary to have a thorough grounding in the scriptures, as well as in rhetoric, logic, and other related subjects — all of which, more or less incidentally, as you choose, were useful in pursuits other than the ministry proper.

Among the passengers on "two great ships" which arrived in Massachusetts in October 1635 was a minister of the English Church of Rotterdam, one Mr. Hugh Peter, whom Winthrop aptly characterizes as "a man of a very public spirit and singular activity for all occasions."[7] Peter became the minister of the Salem church, but his activities covered all New England. He had hoped to found a Puritan college at Rotterdam, and he had not lost the hope when he crossed the ocean to New England.[8]

Early, Peter shopped around for a site. Then in 1636 the General Court "agreed to give £400. . . ." In November 1637 the Court chose Newtown, as Cambridge was then called, as the site, and appointed twelve men "to take order for a colledge" there. Newtown was a logical place: it was located near Boston, had a very dependable minister in Thomas Shepard, and had just lost some colonists who had gone with Thomas Hooker to Hartford. Because of the College, the General Court in May 1638 changed the name of the town to Cambridge. Because of the legacy of John Harvard, the General Court later in that same year named the new institution Harvard College.

But before that time the "twelve men" had been active.

## THE FIRST MASTER
## 1637–1639

In June 1637 Nathaniel Eaton, a young man of about twenty-seven years, arrived in Boston with his wife, in the company of his brother Theophilus, an organizer of the Massachusetts Bay Company. Though Nathaniel had left Trinity College before receiving his degree, he was a recognized scholar and the writer, under William Ames, of a religious tract of some significance.[9] Sometime in the fall of 1637 Master Eaton (he apparently never was called "President") was engaged to attend to the College. He was "the Professor," and, as we shall see later, he received and expended College monies, but the twelve Overseers, or such of them as lived and remained in the area, supervised his activities. Exactly when "the Professor" actually moved to Cambridge is uncertain. The proprietors of the Town of Cambridge made grants of land to

Eaton on May 3, 1638, for himself and for the College,[10] and about then he or the Overseers acquired the Peyntree House and land in Cow Yard Row on Braintree Street (Massachusetts Avenue).

Meanwhile, in the summer of 1637 another young man, John Harvard, who had received an A.M. from Emmanuel College in 1635 and had been at Cambridge at the same time as Nathaniel Eaton, had come to Boston and shortly settled in Charlestown.[11] Harvard had not been here much more than a year, and was not yet established as pastor of a church, when on September 14, 1638,[12] he died "at *Charlestown* of a Consumption," leaving to the College his library and "the one Moiety or halfe parte of his estate, the said Moiety amounting to the sum of seven hundred seventy-nine pound seventeene shillings and two pence."[13] This sum was almost twice the original "Country" grant and about equal to the average total annual tax rate of the Colony. It was sufficient to encourage the construction of the first building built specifically for Harvard College — a building which was shortly and for many years to be known as "the Old College."*

Under Eaton the first classes were held in the Peyntree House in the summer or early fall of 1638. Winthrop says the schoolmaster "had many scholars, the sons of gentlemen and others of best note in the country."[14] But by September of 1639 Eaton, convicted by the General Court of

> sundry abuses and inhumane severityes by him acted towards the schollars under his charge, was openly sentenced and removed from his abovesaid Trust.
>
> The care of carrying on the building begun by mr. Eaton was then committed to the mannagement of mr. Samuel Shepard and the College Stock putt into his hand.**

* Since occasional question arises whether John Harvard left the College £400 or £800, we quote from Thomas Shepard's autobiography, *CSM* XXVII, 389: "The Lord put it into the Hart of on mr. Harvard who dyed woorth £1600 to give halfe his estate to the erecting of the Schoole. . . ." See also *New Englands First Fruits*, 1643, reprinted in *FHC*, pp. 420–446; the following is on page 432: "It pleased God to stir up the heart of one Mr. Harvard . . . to give the one halfe of his Estate (it being in all about £1700) towards the erecting of a Colledge. . . ."

President Quincy goes to some trouble to prove that Harvard's legacy was approximately £400 rather than £800, but his proof is not convincing to me, for it directly contradicts Danforth in the College records. Cf. Josiah Quincy, *The History of Harvard University* (Cambridge, 1840), I, Appendix I, 460–462.

** Treasurer Thomas Danforth in *CSM* XV, *Harvard College Records*, 173. The

## DUNSTER'S ADMINISTRATION

## 1640–1654

Thus in September 1639 the College was without a "Professor," and men qualified and willing to head the infant institution were not easily found. Though the religious and economic difficulties which harassed England under Charles I had carried a steady influx of immigrants to the Massachusetts Bay Colony during the 1630's, the decline in the power of Archbishop Laud and the imminent Civil War put an end to the arrival of new ship-loads of colonists with their supplies of new goods and funds. In the early 1640's New England entered upon a severe depression and some colonists even returned permanently to England. Nevertheless the men who "took order" for the College, who were later to be called the Overseers, fortunately managed in August 1640 after an hiatus of operation of almost a year to hire Henry Dunster, who was, as he says,

> to undertake the instructing of the youth of riper years and literature after they came from the grammer schools. . . . No further care or distraction was imposed on mee or expected from mee but to instruct. For the building was committed to Mr. Hugh Peeter, Mr. Samuel Shepheard, and Mr. Joseph Cook, who prudently declined the troble and left it to the two first. They also when they had finished the Hall . . . went for England leaving the work in the Carpenters and masons hands without Guide or further director, no floar besides in and above the hall layd, no inside separating wall made nor any one study erected throughout the house. Thus the work fell upon mee, 3d October 1641: . . . the students . . . came into commons into one house September 1642, and with them a 3rd burthen upon my shoulders, to bee their steward, and to Direct their brewer, baker, buttler, Cook, how to proportion their commons. . . .[15]

"Nine bachelors commenced at Cambridge" at the first commencement in 1642, "and it gave good content to all."[16] In that year the General Court established the College government more explicitly in the hands of the "Company of Overseers."[17] By this

"College Books I, III, and IV" are printed in *CSM* XV and XVI; when we refer in the future to Corporation votes giving the date, it may be assumed they come from these two volumes.

Samuel Shepard was the brother of the Reverend Thomas. For more detail see Winthrop I, 310–315.

time one of the twelve men named in 1637 was dead, one had moved to New Haven, one was on the way to England, and three, including Humphrey, Weld, and Peter, were in England on a mission for the Colony and the College, to pacify creditors, explain the New England cause, and raise some needed funds.[18]

The next year at a meeting of the Governors of Harvard College in the College Hall December 27, 1643 (Plate I), "Herbert Pelham Esquire was Elected Treasurer of the said Society. . . ."[19] Pelham was the first Treasurer officially appointed and apparently he never did really function in that capacity. In 1644 he "seems to have been in England"; he returned by 1645 and served the Colony in various high official capacities, but by 1647 he "seems to have returned to England for good."[20] President Dunster throughout this period managed the business of the College without much assistance or interference from anyone, and by dint of persistent hard work and devotion he established the new institution, if not on a firm basis, at least as a respected contributor to New England's well-being.

On May 30th, 1650, the General Court on petition of Dunster took upon itself a sovereign right and "made and granted under the Seal of the Colony"[21] a charter for the corporation named the "President & Fellowes of Harvard Colledge," with Henry Dunster the "first President, . . . Thomas Danford to be the present Treasurer," and five Fellows to complete the Corporation. The larger group of "Overseers" was retained and their consent was required to elect members of the Corporation, to make orders and by-laws, and "in great and difficult cases, and in cases of non-agreement."[22] It is under this charter and an appendix to it passed in October 1657 that the College has been governed since that date with short intermissions, and continuously since 1707. As a corporation it is given the right of perpetual succession, the right to receive and own property, to sue and be sued, and other perquisites of such bodies.*

* The use of the word "Fellow" is confusing. In the College records there are no less than seventeen variations on the word with modifying adjectives or phrases. Until 1692 all Tutors were Fellows, but Fellows were not necessarily Tutors. In this study up to 1692 we shall use the words "Fellow" and "Tutor" almost interchangeably, with a distinction made where necessary by calling teaching Fellows "Resident Fellows" and non-teaching Fellows "Fellows of the Corporation." This is a distinction

Though Thomas Danforth was legally the Treasurer from the time of the Charter of 1650, the President appears to have kept tight hold of the reins and Danforth actually took over only on the resignation of Dunster. Danforth's excellent though abbreviated Treasurer's accounts start in October 1654 and cover the period until February 1669.*

In the community, President Dunster persistently spoke out against the validity of the prevailing infant baptism, and though he was given every possible chance to recant, he refused to so do. He was therefore forced to resign in June 1654, the General Court on the third of May having said:

> Forasmuch as it greatly concernes the welfare of this country that the youth thereof be educated not only in good literature but sound doctrine, this Court doth therefore commend it to the serious consideration and speciall care of the overseers of the colledge, and the selectmen in the severall townes, not to admitt or suffer any such to be continued in office or place of teaching . . . in the colledge or schooles that have manifested themselves unsound in the fayth. . . .[23]

Dunster was shortly replaced by the scholarly sixty-two-year-old minister Charles Chauncy, whose belief in baptism by immersion was displeasing to the church fathers, but whose conscience, after many years of difficulty on the subject, permitted him to agree to keep these ideas to himself.

### CHAUNCY'S PRESIDENCY

### 1654–1672

Chauncy was the first president who on his appointment took over an actual college. Eaton and then Dunster had come into office as the heads of nonexistent student bodies, at a time when the economic state of the Colony was very sad indeed. In contrast, Chauncy found around fifty students and three considerable buildings (the rather handsome "Old College," Goffe College, con-

---

we make for clarity and it must not be thought that any such neat differentiation was actually used. After 1692 a Tutor was not necessarily a Fellow of the Corporation, though up until 1780, except in the years 1697 to 1700, at least one Tutor was also a Fellow of the Corporation. *CSM* XV, cxxxii–cxxxv.

* *CSM* XV, 212–217. Danforth was also clerk of the Corporation, and it is to him that we owe much of our knowledge of Harvard up to 1683.

verted from Mr. Goffe's house, and the President's Lodge), plus an unfinished house "intended for a print house."[24] There was a library and a moderate amount (very moderate by any modern standards) of equipment, and gifts and grants had resulted in the ownership of several parcels of land. Assets exceeded liabilities by a very slight margin. Not only was the College itself in somewhat more comfortable condition, but the trade of the Colony had recovered from the worst of the depression of the forties, and the general financial situation, though hardly a flourishing one, was certainly more cheerful than it had been in 1638 or 1640.

During the last years of Dunster's administration the economic condition of the Colony had begun to pick up. The Puritan government in England sympathized with the Puritan colony, and the British were too busy at home to interfere very much with Colony affairs. Trade was encouraged; it was at this time that the three-cornered traffic between New England, the West Indies, and the British Isles was worked out and began to supply the colonies with currency with which to conduct their business.

After the Restoration of the Stuarts in 1660, religious toleration was presumably guaranteed, but the Episcopal Church was re-established in England, the Presbyterian in Scotland. "Dissenters" lost many of their personal rights, and their interest in New England again quickened.[25]

The Massachusetts Puritans, operating under the old Massachusetts Bay Charter, managed by various delaying tactics in a time of very slow communications to confound any Royal Commissioners appointed and to avoid compliance with most orders aimed at (1) modifying their rigid Puritanism, (2) diminishing their independence, or (3) controlling their trade. In 1664 Massachusetts did comply with instructions to the extent of passing a law allowing non-churchmen to be freemen — if they had enough money and were "certified" by a minister; actually this made little change.

The college at Cambridge was especially suspect as a breeding ground of disloyalty to the King, and there was validity in this accusation.[26] In 1665 the Commissioners wrote, "It may be feared that this colledge may afford as many schismaticks to the Church, and the Corporation as many rebells to the King, as formerly they have done if not timely prevented."[27] Deputy Governor Willoughby of Massachusetts justified their lack of cooperation by saying, "We must as well consider God's displeasure as the King's. . . ."[28] There was some trouble from 1660 to 1666, but after the fall of Lord Clarendon in 1666, nearly ten years passed before England again made serious efforts to govern New England or the members of the College there.

Though President Chauncy was a notable scholar and a much admired teacher, Harvard during the sixties seems to have suffered from a rather general lack of interest in education. There was a falling-off in the number of students in the grammar schools and a consequent lack of young men who came to Cambridge.[29] It is hard to say whether this might have been a reflection of the lengthening time since the founding fathers had come from England, or the result of some religious dissension from the early Puritanism such as that shown by the Half-way Covenant; perhaps the difficulty was largely with the local college administration, for in 1666 some especially effective tutors were secured and the size of the entering college classes again picked up for three years.

In 1668, because there were "obstructions in the Colledge touching providing for the Schollars in poynt of dyett" and the Steward had resigned, Treasurer Danforth was persuaded, he says in College Book III,[30] "to take the care and charge of that affaire for one yeare," and the Overseers and Corporation "do declare . . . that all meet Encouragement shall be allowed unto him." Danforth resigned his Treasurership and was replaced by Captain John Richards, a prominent merchant of Boston, who held the office, except for a visit to England, until 1693. (Danforth kept the Steward's position until 1682!)

## HOAR, OAKES, ROGERS — PRESIDENTS
## 1672–1684

In 1672 President Chauncy died. His successor was Leonard Hoar, who is listed as receiving an A.B. at Harvard in 1650, the A.M. in 1653. Hoar had preached for several years in England and there had received the Cambridge A.M. and "Doctor of Physick" (M.D.).[31]

The General Court gave every encouragement to the new President: they raised the President's salary, spent a considerable amount of money fixing up his Lodge, and somewhat revised the Charter of 1650 making the Corporation's powers more explicit. Hoar's educational plans and ideas were very promising, but he ran into trouble governing the students. Despite the continuing support of most of the older members of the community, the President had no choice but to resign when by 1675 the student body had practically disappeared.

Shortly the Corporation and the Overseers, confirmed by the General Court, chose Urian Oakes (A.B. 1649) to head their college. Oakes had resigned his fellowship at Harvard two years before in displeasure at the way things were being run. Perhaps his most distinguishing characteristic, when viewed from this distance, is his great ability as a humorous orator in the Latin tongue; however, he was apparently well qualified in other respects for the work he was called to do, and he agreed to be "Acting President" until the Corporation could locate a suitable candidate for the permanent position.[32]

Oakes continued his care of the College from year to year while the Corporation searched and persuaded, but finally Oakes himself accepted the full appointment, only to die a year and a half later in 1681. Lasting memorials to his administration included a new President's Lodge on the site of the present Massachusetts Hall, and the New, shortly to be called "Old," Harvard Hall, built where the present Harvard Hall now stands. Both buildings were ordered and largely paid for by direction of the General Court, which in 1671 had sponsored a subscription from the towns toward replacing the first Harvard Hall with the new one. Throughout this period, despite the fact that few students were enrolled, the endowment funds were gradually building up from bequests and gifts, some of which came from patrons whose interest in the College had been aroused a good many years before.

In 1682 the Corporation, confirmed by the Overseers and so far as was necessary by the Court, elected John Rogers President of the College. In July 1684 Rogers died suddenly, and once more the search began.

It is really not surprising that at this time there should have been difficulty in finding a scholar who would give up his parish and take over the running of the College. The educational institution was greatly affected by the fortunes of the Colony, and the fortunes of the Colony were in a rather ambiguous state. In 1664 the British had captured New Amsterdam, but in 1673 the Dutch recaptured it. In 1674 the British took the city again, and it remained in their hands from then on. Secondly, Indians from the forces of Massasoit's son, King Philip, penetrated to Sudbury, Massachusetts, right at the back door of Harvard, and during 1675 to 1676 all the New England colonies were thoroughly upset and their resources drained by King Philip's War.

Massachusetts had recently been fairly free of British interference, but when in 1676 Edward Randolph was sent to New England as a messenger and spy of sorts, we begin to see the end of the Bay Colony's cherished independence.

### INCREASE MATHER, ACTING PRESIDENT 1685, RECTOR 1686–1692, PRESIDENT 1692–1701

In England, on the death of Charles II in 1685, the Tories, Anglican and more moderate than the Puritans toward the Catholics, had established Charles's brother, the Catholic James II, on the throne. Shortly Whigs and Tories alike combined against James's arbitrary rule and in 1688 invited his elder daughter Mary and her husband, William of Orange, Anglicans, both grandchildren of Charles I, to be the King and Queen. The Toleration Act of 1689 maintained the established churches but provided freedom of conscience and the legal right for dissenters, not including Catholics, to worship in public. Parliament was now secure in the power it has held ever since that date, and the government of England was in the hands of the aristocracy, the country gentry, and persons with commercial and financial interests.[33]

Practically continuously from 1689 to the Treaty of Utrecht in 1713 England was at war with France, with only a slight partial respite after the Peace of Ryswick in 1697. Queen Anne replaced King William in 1702. She died on August 1, 1714.

The rights of Englishmen in England were secured by the Revolution, but the rights of Englishmen were not so secure for

English colonists. Moreover, despite Parliament's clear supremacy in England, the Colonies were still to be governed by a combination of Royal decree and the mercantile policy of the growing Whig oligarchy.

Under this regime, Edward Randolph's persistence and his reports home, especially after he became King's Collector in 1681, led finally in 1684 to the English courts' declaring the Massachusetts charter forfeited, and to the consolidation of the northern colonies into the Council for New England under Deputy President Joseph Dudley (Harvard 1665 and a son of the original old Governor Thomas Dudley). Upon Dudley's inauguration in Boston in May 1686 and the end of the Colony's charter, "the calf died in the cow's belly," as Governor Dudley purportedly said later,[34] and it was assumed by many persons that the College, chartered — and that none too legally — by the Colony, was itself now lacking in legal status.

In December 1686 Royal Governor Sir Edmund Andros replaced Dudley at the head of what was to become the Territory and Dominion of New England. Andros' governorship was extended in 1688 to cover New York and New Jersey. In April 1689, however, the Bostonians heard of the Glorious Revolution in England and they lost no time in imprisoning the Governor and some of his supporters, including Joseph Dudley. A temporary government constituted itself under the old charter as the Council for Safety of the People and Conservation of the Peace; it served until the arrival of Governor Sir William Phips and the new Provincial Charter in May 1692. Phips's Lieutenant Governor was William Stoughton, Harvard 1650, who in 1692 presided over the notorious witchcraft trials.

Governor Phips died in 1694 and was temporarily succeeded by Lieutenant Governor Stoughton. In 1698 the new governor, Lord Bellomont, arrived in New York, of which also he was governor. He came to Boston only in 1699. On Bellomont's death, the next to be appointed was Joseph Dudley, who was the Royal Governor from June 1702 until November 1715.[35]

One of the most vocal and influential of the Puritan ministers during all this troubled period was Increase Mather (Harvard 1656). Mather, who had been a Fellow of the Corporation at

Harvard from 1675 and was an obvious choice to be periodically offered the Presidency, was persuaded to become the Acting President, succeeding Rogers in 1685. When the Council for New England was established in 1686, President Mather automatically gave up his office. Council President Dudley held a Council meeting in Boston, where of the seven men present four were Harvard men, three of them graduates. "The Colledg of Cambridge being in an unsetled posture," the Council decided to reconvene in Cambridge the next Friday "to consider of some form of settlement thereof."[36] At that second meeting the Reverend Increase Mather was "desired to accept of the Rectorship of the Colledge," John Leverett and William Brattle were asked to "be the Tutors and enter upon the Government of the Colledge" under the old rules.[37] And the College went right along as before.

Increase Mather had more important business than "only to expound," as he said some years later, to a college of "40 or 50 Children."[38] He was happy to keep the oversight of the College and to be known as its head, but he did not intend it should interfere with his duties in his large Boston parish or prevent any trips he might wish to make to England. He did visit Cambridge, preach, moderate exercises, and preside at some Corporation meetings, but the day-to-day government of the College and the conduct of its affairs were left to the Tutors and the Treasurer.

Under the new Provincial Charter of 1691 a new College Charter, that of 1692, was adopted. For the preceding three years Mather had been in England as one — and the most effective — of the representatives of the Colony in negotiations for the new Massachusetts charter. When the document was finally sealed it provided a governor and council the first major members of which had been nominated by Mather, so Mather's relationships with the new Provincial government were of the most cordial. The new College Charter was soon forthcoming. The old Corporation and Board of Overseers were combined into a new Corporation consisting of the President, Treasurer, and eight Fellows. Increase Mather was to be President, John Richards, Treasurer. Of the Fellows, six were ministers of neighboring churches and the other two were the Resident Fellows, John Leverett and William Brattle.[39]

It would seem that this might have settled the controversies over the legal status of the College for as long as the Province Charter was effective, but Harvard's administration was disturbed for the next fifteen years by intrigues and political maneuverings in regard to Provincial or much-desired Royal charters for the College, and appointments to be made under various temporary or suggested charters.

In July 1693, after twenty-four years of service, Treasurer John Richards asked to be relieved of his duties for the College and was replaced by Thomas Brattle, brother of Resident Fellow William Brattle. The new Treasurer was a Boston merchant, one of the wealthiest men in New England.* Thomas Brattle is known as a founder in 1699 of Boston's Brattle Street Congregational Church, which issued a "manifesto" modifying some of the strictest tenets of the Puritan creed.

The government of the Province had settled down somewhat by 1693. For the next twenty years there were wars with the French and their Indian allies, but by the end of the Brattle period there was peace, and Massachusetts was entering on a time of growth and prosperity. From 1700 on the finances of the Province were beset with inflation and increasing prices. The College during these years was pulled back and forth between the British and the Colonials, the Church of England supporters and the Puritans. With the continual controversy about the College charter, College officers were frequently appointed and deposed. Brattle, however, continued to handle College finances under such votes as that of the Corporation on August 5, 1700: "Voted that Mr. Thomas Brattle be desired to Continue to act as Treasurer of the Colledg until his Majesty's Pleasure be known referring to the settlement of the Colledg, or that the General Court shal take further Order."

Tutors Leverett and William Brattle gave up their Resident Fellowships in 1697, Leverett to study law and give more time to the Legislature, and Brattle to become the minister of the Cambridge church. Their successors carried on the devoted pair's management of College affairs, but the peripatetic nature of President Mather's life was given by the writers of a new Charter in

* When his father died in 1683, "his estate was nearly £8000, generally considered the largest of the time." William B. Weeden, *Economic and Social History of New England, 1620–1789* (Boston, 1894), p. 292. Thomas was his father's executor.

1700 as a reason for requiring that the President of the College be resident in Cambridge. Mather refused to move there. A Vice-President had been nominated and there was no requirement of residence for him, so when Mather finally resigned in 1701, the Reverend Samuel Willard was, as Vice-President, "desired to take the care and Over Sight of the Colledge and Students there. . . ."[40]

## SAMUEL WILLARD, VICE-PRESIDENT AND ACTING PRESIDENT 1701–1707

Samuel Willard, Harvard 1659, the brother-in-law of Joseph Dudley, performed his "temporary" duties creditably for six years, during each of which charter maneuverings were going on. The College coasted along under Willard's part-time supervision and the direct charge of the Tutors until the Vice-President's death in 1707. During his incumbency the policies of Leverett and Brattle had continued in force as before, but the rigidly Puritan Mathers had begun to feel that there was too much liberalism creeping into this nursery of the Prophets. Accordingly the Mathers were not in favor of the vote of the large majority of the Corporation that Mr. Leverett be asked to be the new President.

The Corporation's recommendation of Leverett was submitted to the Legislature. At this time the majority of the lower house was composed of conservatives from rural areas, who tended to agree with the Mathers; Governor Dudley and his Councillors were more friendly to Leverett and the Brattles. Approval of both houses and the Governor was necessary for any successful candidate. It was at this juncture that the Governor made a proposal that if the lower house would approve Leverett's nomination, he and the Council would concede that the College Charter of 1650 was still in force, a concession from the Royal governor which much pleased the House by its admission of the right of the General Court to charter the institution. The General Court then resolved, and the Governor approved:

> Inasmuch as the first Foundation and Establishment of that House and the Government thereof had its Originall from an Act of the Generall

Court, made and passed in the Year One thousand Six hundred and fifty, which has not been Repealed or Nulled,

The President and Fellows of the said Colledge are Directed from time to time to Regulate themselves according to the Rules of the Constitution by the Act prescribed. . . .[41]

The Charter of 1650 is still in force in 1962.

## JOHN LEVERETT, PRESIDENT 1708

The Matherian suspicions were probably correct that Tutors Leverett and Brattle and some of their successors had departed from the strict faith of the founding fathers. Now, with Leverett's election to the Presidency, the thoroughly Puritan era of the College had come to an end. Yet, if Leverett had leanings toward the Church of England, he managed throughout his term of office to conduct himself and the institution in such a way as to be reasonably satisfactory to both the "liberal" Puritans (only slightly more liberal than their forebears) and the official party in power.

As soon as the Leverett administration begins we notice a marked increase in the formality of the records which have come down to us. As a teacher and administrator under President Mather, Leverett had had great respect for the contribution the College and its graduates would make, but his experience in the Legislature and as a judge had apparently impressed upon him even more strongly the need for systematic management if the institution was to maintain its place in the increasingly complicated Provincial world. We find lawyer Leverett, in addition to doing some teaching and "admonishing" of students, carrying on extended correspondence and negotiation with donors and executors of donors in England and elsewhere to assure that any possible resource of moral or financial support would be utilized.*

On April 7, 1713, the Corporation voted "that in Consideracion of the faithful service of Thomas Brattle Esquire as Treasurer of the Colledge for now Twenty years, [he] be allowed £60, to be paid out of the College Treasury." The minutes go on,

Mr. Treasurer Brattle at this Meeting presented to the Corporation sundry papers to be registered, Vizt The Account of the College Stock

* He, with William Brattle, was made a Fellow of the Royal Society in 1713 (*HCSC*, p. 505).

Anno 1696, with a Breviate of receipts and payments from July 4th 1693 to the 11th of July 1696, And an Inventory of the Estate belonging to Harvard College, as it was in his hands July 1st Anno 1712. And they are here Entered in their Order.

Only a month later, May 18, 1713, Thomas Brattle died.[42] William Brattle was his brother's executor and was appointed Acting Treasurer.

The new Treasurer shortly appointed was Mr. John White; the Brattle accounts were turned over to him as of August 16, 1715.

In the summer of 1715 the College was securely chartered under the Provincial government, was well embarked with President Leverett, and the era of the successful financial management of the Brattles had come to an end. It seems suitable to leave the economic history of Harvard in the Puritan Period at this fairly well-documented point.

This sketchy outline gives us the framework on which to build an analysis of Harvard's economic situation during the first period of its history. Figure 1 gives an idea of its "production," though by no means an index of its influence.

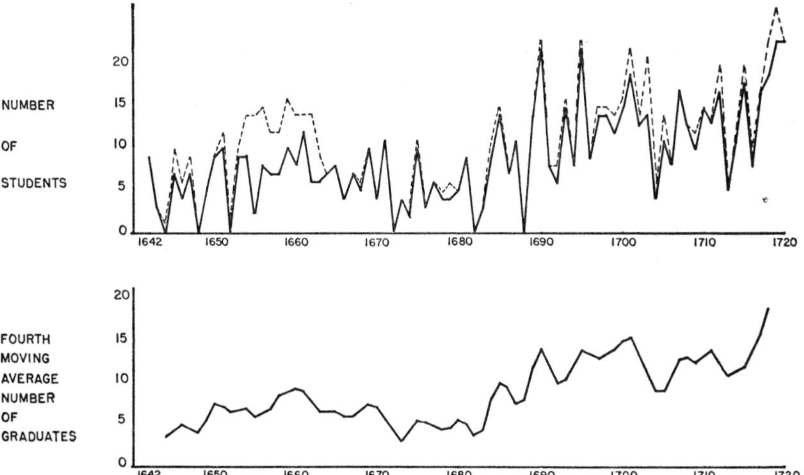


Figure 1. *Recipients of A.B. degrees at Harvard College to 1720, plus known nongraduates, by class. Two classes graduated in 1653, to make the transition to a four-year course; the second class is here added to 1654. Numbers are approximate because of variations in assigning students to classes. Nongraduates are incomplete.* Sources: CSM *XV, 82–93; XXXI; XVII, 271–285; QBB; Shipton, IV, V, VI; Proc.* AAS *n.s., XLII, 420–424.*

# II

# HARVARD FINANCIAL RECORDS IN THE SEVENTEENTH CENTURY

In any study of the workings of an institution three hundred years ago, our first question will be, "What records are available?" And then, "How effectively were the records kept? How complete and how accurate is the knowledge we are now able to deduce from the records we have? What was the general magnitude of the figures involved? What do these figures mean in real values?"

## THE EXTANT RECORDS[1]

In addition to the records of meetings of the Corporation and the Board of Overseers, to the votes of the General Court, and to the miscellaneous manuscript papers in the Harvard Archives and elsewhere in collections in greater Boston, we are extremely fortunate to have several formal manuscript financial record books from this period: Chesholme's Steward's Ledger of 1650–1659;[2] Treasurer Richards' Journal and Ledger, 1669–1693; Quarter-Bill Books of 1687–1720; the Journal of Thomas Brattle, 1693–1713; Steward Andrew Bordman's Ledger of 1703–1731 and the Steward's Audited Accounts 1713–31.

Unfortunately for the ease with which we may interpret these findings, the business administration of the College in the seventeenth century did not record its transactions with the methods used by their descendants three centuries later. Harvard was then a very small institution, despite its wide influence, and its accounting methods were no doubt fairly adequate to the purposes of the day. Were we to examine the books of an institution of similar size today we should probably find some simple system, serving the purposes of the persons concerned, with all sorts of little inner systems and items carried in the heads of the administrators. Moreover, accounting practice in the seventeenth century, though the lineal ancestor of the present methods, was understandably not developed to the point of present-day trust accounting; in some ways it is *more* comprehensible to the uninitiated than the twentieth-century formalized and technical practice.

But probably the factor which most forcibly strikes the student of any seventeenth-century American records is that the primitive nature of the economy of this country necessitated a psychology of record-keeping more nearly like that used in Europe some centuries earlier: there would have been little point, had our ancestors known how to do it, in establishing a modern-type day-by-day bookkeeping record of receipts and disbursements to describe receiving "4 cowes, 3 oxon, and 1 steer, valued att £35, in lieu of Sheep . . . Paid the driver from Cambridge money," four shillings. The three oxen were sent back as "poor, not fit for butcher," so £7 10*s*. was deducted from the account, leaving £27 10*s*.; when the remaining were sold for £21, Treasurer Richards did not get the money but set up accounts for the buyers. The £21, as well as £3 forbearance (interest), were paid in boards (£22 10*s*.) and money (£1 10*s*.) two years later. Then of course the boards had to be used or sold. £6 10*s*. was lost, including the four shillings for the driver.[3]

| | £ | | £ | *s*. | |
|---|---|---|---|---|---|
| Cattle | 35 | Sent back | 7 | 10 | |
| | | Sold | 21 | | |
| | | Loss | 6 | 10 | |
| | 35 | | 35 | | (plus £3 interest) |

| | £ | | £ | *s*. |
|---|---|---|---|---|
| For cattle | 21 | Received boards | 22 | 10 |
| For interest | 3 | Received money | 1 | 10 |
| | 24 | | 24 | |

And at that, Richards was fortunate to get the pound and a half of money so that the transaction could be closed; more frequently the odd amount would string along for some time and be added in on a new transaction. Keeping books was certainly necessary as an aid to memory, but an impatient bookkeeper would have been out of place.

Richards and Brattle entered items in a one-column journal, and they used a system of cross-reference from the journal to the ledger, as well as between the equal and opposite entries in the ledger accounts.

These two treasurers kept ledgers with a "College Stock" account and other accounts for individuals. Richards used the College Stock account to record all transactions of both cash and investment accounts;* Brattle kept an account for Cash and another for Stock. Both Richards and Brattle made payments out of the Stock accounts (Brattle, through Cash) for current operations, and they entered both capital and income there indistinguishably. All the Treasurers made occasional lists of assets, but none figured from receipts and disbursements what the operating surplus or deficit was, or reconciled it with the change in assets.**

Plate 3 shows a page of Richards' Harvard College Stock account, Plate 4 a page of Brattle's journal.

## HARVARD BALANCE SHEETS

When we speak of "double-entry," opinions vary as to just how "double" the entry need be. The Harvard men kept their debit and credit ledgers and they balanced the accounts periodically, not at the end of any regular periods but usually when a President or a Treasurer left office. The sum of the balances of these individual accounts was listed as the outstanding "Harvard College Stock" at the end of the period. There was therefore a check of

* "All" is an exaggeration; he kept several supplementary accounts entirely independent of the main books.

** Danforth was apparently the only one who approached such a reconciliation at all. If the others did, we have no record of it. We do not know the form of Danforth's basic records, for we have only his "Abbreviate," made up in the charge and discharge pattern; the information for it might have been taken from double-entry books. The books kept in Dunster's period were probably not in double-entry form, for the references to them in the Corporation Papers quote page and column, with successive columns in some instances containing figures for succeeding years.

sorts — income including capital equaled expense including money invested — and a type of very incomplete double-entry resembling charge and discharge; however, the change in the "Harvard College Stock" so listed was not reconciled with the difference between Income and Disbursements, as we said in the paragraph above.

But a person familiar with modern educational finance misses also in the Harvard accounts a second "degree" of double-entry, a balance sheet giving the breakdown of the capital account into equities. This comes from maintaining a separate set of capital accounts with equal and opposite running entries of changes in assets and equities, including their income, and with the new balance of assets and equities clearly shown at the end of each.

The Harvard College accounts also lacked any differentiation between capital and (endowment) income, as intimated above. Actually the distinction between capital and income was not always clear in British accounting until the permanent capital principle was used in the "non-terminable" stock companies of the sixteenth, and, more commonly, the seventeenth, centuries.[4] Although the Italians well knew how to carry this all the way through, the seventeenth-century English transactions seldom went beyond what we call the "trial balance."

Double-entry made possible keeping capital and income separate; but despite the broad experience with charitable endowments, full balance sheets were seldom used in English trust accounts for many years.[5] It was not until Victorian times that English laws actually prohibited commercial companies from reducing permanent capital to pay dividends.[6] And in very recent years in this country we have seen educational institutions which were far from clear in making the distinction between permanent endowment and expendable income. Is it any wonder, then, that our seventeenth-century educational administrators were not one hundred per cent clear about recording this distinction? We shall discuss the use of funds in more detail in later chapters.

### COMPLICATIONS, CAUSED LARGELY BY THE SPECIE SHORTAGE

Many of the details of the manuscripts which have come down to us add interest as well as complication to this study. When one first glances quickly at Harvard records he has no idea that business was conducted in any medium of exchange other than pounds (£ or ł or łł), shillings (/ or *s.* or *sh.* or 6), pence (*d.*, for denarius), and farthings (one quarter of a penny, and occasionally in Harvard records called a "cue"). There are of course fractions of these denominations, such as the hapenny-farthing, which is three farthings and is designated "ob. q.," or just "ob." We find that the accounts were kept in this Massachusetts money as a measure of value, but since Massachusetts money was practically nonexistent, it was *only* a measure of value and not a unit of exchange. After 1652 there were a few pine-tree shillings, half-shillings, and farthings produced at the Massachusetts mint, but these soon emigrated, and the coins actually used in transactions were those brought in by foreign trade. Spanish silver dollars, called pieces of eight and designated 8/8, were the most common;[7] they were occasionally supplemented by British, French, Portuguese, and especially Dutch coins.* Often these coins were "clipped," so the only safe thing to do was to weigh them. And all these pieces had to be translated into Massachusetts money before they could be received.

On May 14, 1690, Treasurer Richards totaled up his losses on money he had taken in since he became Treasurer — £3 17*s.* 6*d.*[8] He entered on the next page (to paraphrase)**

I sold to Mr. Conry, the goldsmith, a parcell of 108 pieces of eight which I had received. Some of them I knew lacked in weight perhaps 2 dwt. or 3 dwt. or 4 dwt. of the standard 17 dwt. per piece but I forgave the short weight. Others were taken in at their New England money value by actual weight. I had received the total on my books at £32 8*s.* 6*d.* Mr. Conry now weighed the lot and found it weighed $87\frac{7}{8}$ oz. [an average of about $16\frac{1}{4}$ dwt. each], which at $6\frac{1}{2}$*s.* per ounce of silver amounted to about £28 11*s.* [$87\frac{7}{8}$ oz. × $6\frac{1}{2}$*s.* per oz. = $569\frac{3}{16}$*s.* or £28 $9\frac{3}{16}$*s.*] which he paid me in New England money immediately.

If I had passed them as coin I should have had to allow at least an average of 6*d.* on each piece; since they are legally worth 6*s.* each this would have been at a rate of less than $5\frac{1}{2}$*s.* The 108 pieces would then have brought less than £29 14*s.* 6*d.* [$594\frac{1}{2}$*s.*] or about what I got from Mr. Conry

* According to Weeden, an Old English shilling "picked up in the highway at Flushing, Long Island, in 1647" was "so great a curiosity that [it] drew public attention, many never having seen a similar coin. . . ." William B. Weeden, *Economic and Social History of New England* (Boston, 1894), p. 41.

** "Dwt." in the following quotation is "pennyweight."

and it saved me the time and trouble of an argument every time I spent one of these coins.

Thus we see how he calculated the £3 17*s.* 6*d.* loss he had recorded (£32 8*s.* 6*d.* less £28 11*s.*).

At the time Harvard was founded a good proportion of the economic dealings of New England were conducted with beaver pelts and wampumpeage as media of exchange. I have not come upon any reference in the records to Harvard's dealing in beaver, but there were many occasions when the College received wampum in payment. In Danforth's "Abbreviate of the Colledge Accounts" for 1654 to 1663[9] we find, "to loss in peage received at 8 a penny . . . £55 6*s.* 11*d.*" Wampumpeage (strings of shell beads) was usually valued at from four to six pieces a penny, so receiving it at eight a penny sounds like a bargain, but the College often was paid in "bad peage" worth perhaps nine or ten to a penny. The amount lost, over fifty pounds, was a large sum even spread over ten years. The lost £55 was equivalent to the average annual salary paid President Dunster, or to one half the annual amount allotted Mr. Chauncy. The ferry seems to have been a particularly troublesome source of income in this respect, for the small charge was often paid, in the absence of small coins, in wampumpeage, and President Dunster complained it was often "bad peage" at that.* As late as 1676 we find Richards recording the receipt of seventeen bushels of peage, which with some corn and malt was all worth £5 15*s.* 6*d.*[10] Wampum was not a very convenient medium for transactions.

"Commodity money," "country pay," was somewhat more convenient, but it had grave disadvantages. Samuel Shepard's account of receipts for 1639 to 1641 includes "Lost by paying out the Corne received at 4*s.* the bushel and payd out at two shillings eight pence, little at 3*s.*, and some at 2*s.* 6*d.* In the whole my ould account is but lost £9 8*s.* 9*d.* I doubt it was more."[11] Commodity payments were very frequently used, and various goods like corn

* The Court early turned over Charlestown ferry rents to the College.

In 1641 the Court permitted certain persons to trade for furs with the Indians and stipulated "that they shall take of all the wampam from the college, provided it exceed not £25, and to make payment for it." *Mass. Bay Recs.* I, 323.

See Weeden, pp. 32–41, for an excellent description of wampum. Wampum was used longer in New York than in New England, but it was still used in New England as late as 1704, in the class with silver, not "country pay."

or wheat were from time to time made legal tender. Of course the College did not always lose money on these transactions, but gains were rare, largely because the Treasurers or the Stewards were glad enough to get something on their accounts and could not argue long with those willing to pay. This was true in dealing in any commodity, but especially in produce, where the value fluctuates with the harvest as well as with the general economy, it must be stored, and there is danger of spoilage. Then there is the well-known Harvard account, "Received a goat 30*s.*, of payment of Watertown rate, which died."[12]

Conversely, when an annuity gift stipulated payment of five pounds in country pay, the College regularly and gladly settled for four pounds in money. As Brattle later expressed it, "Cash received. . . . Should be £5 per annum, but, being paid in money, £4 accepted."[13]

An item which can amount to quite a sum is the cost of transportation, and for this reason agreements tended to specify where payment was to be made. Dunster's accounts of May 3, 1654, report his expenditure over ten years, "By so much paid for fraught and cariadge of the townes Contributions," £12 6*s.* 6*d.* This was the "Colledge corne" coming in; the gross value received was £266 18*s.* 7*d.*, so transportation had cut the revenue by almost five percent.[14] This was a mild case. Sometimes the College recorded net payments as receipts on the books and sometimes gross; the bookkeepers seldom specified.

Another possible result of the use of commodity money was that frequently payments to Harvard College, particularly interest and rents in the first years of the College, were made in odd amounts different from those due, even when payment was made in money. This may indicate that the source of the money had been the sale of some goods, and that the ready cash to round out the payment was not at the time available. We have a picture of how this worked in a letter written by Brattle to Mr. Pelham, one of the leading citizens. The Treasurer had heard that Mr. Pelham had been in town and collected some money due him but then had ignored his debt to the College. Brattle remarks, "It seems you went away with it. . . ."[15]

Dates were seldom exactly kept, payments were very often

made in arrears and very occasionally a month or two (or more) in advance.[16] Harvest time was a period for paying bills.

Commodities were used as a medium of exchange well into the eighteenth century. In fact, when Middlebury College was founded in 1800, many of the first tuition payments were made in "country pay."[17] At Harvard it was usually the Steward who accepted the bulk of the commodity money when he received the tuition payments. The Treasurer was saved much of this trouble by taking on his books only the net results of the Steward's operations.

For *barter* of commodities to take place, rather than the use of commodities directly as money, each "must want what the other has"; this gives rise to "bookkeeping barter." For example, a cow is exchanged for tuition. If one party to the transaction does not want what the other has, they may bring into the transaction either one or more additional persons, or time plus accounts. The College does not want the cow, but the College is in debt to someone who can use the cow; or perhaps the College will take the cow in six months. Such transactions are called bookkeeping barter.

The College's acting as banker is illustrated by an excerpt from Brattle's journal of May 20, 1696, which we show below and follow by an interpretation.

> Thomas Pollard, Joseph Foster, and Thomas Ross, all of Billerica, are Dr. to Cash £20 lent and delivered the said Pollard at Interest, to pay £21 4*s*. on the 20th May next, as per their bond. . . .
>
> Cash is Dr. to Simon Crosby of Billerica £20 received of him that the abovesaid Pollard, etc., have given their bond for in payment of the £60 due by his and Joseph Crosby's bond, as per receipt Sent him by said Pollard.
>
> Memorandum. The abovementioned £20 was paid to Pollard and received of Crosby by discount, the said Pollard being indebted to Mr. Crosby about that Summe, and Mr. Crosby telling me if I sent him up a receipt for So much, he would discompt said Summe with said Pollard.

"Discount with" in early New England usually meant "pay to" or "credit to."

What happened in this piece of finance was this: The two Crosbys in Billerica owed the College £60 on their bond. Pollard *et al*. in Billerica wanted (or owed) £20. Crosby gave (or credited)

Pollard £20. Pollard went to Cambridge and signed a note *to the College* for £20 plus interest. Pollard carried back to Crosby in Billerica a receipt sent by the College for a £20 reduction in Crosby's £60 bond — paid by Pollard's note. And all that was necessary was two entries in the College books (plus payment in Billerica of £20 or its equivalent): the first, Pollard received £20 and gave bond to the College for it; and, second, Crosby paid £20 to the College, via Pollard. Such a transfer was particularly useful when Pollard received in Billerica, as may have been the case, not £20 in cash, but "about that Summe" in a good cow or two; it then saved the transport of the cow to Cambridge, and saved the College from having to dispose of the cow, which was wanted in Billerica.

Cotton Mather, who "lived in a period when pounds, shillings, and pence served only as a money of account," claimed, in fact, that money was necessary only because of "a general ignorance of Writing and Arithmetick." If accounting were known, he thought, there would be no need of money.[18]

F. G. James feels that it is "far from certain that the relative importance of credit is today greater than it was in the medieval period, or during the intervening centuries."[19] As we shall see below, Harvard was, on a small scale, a source of local credit.

It was of course extremely convenient, even necessary, for the College to have as its Treasurers men who were leading merchants of Boston. Then, as now, the personal connections of the Treasurer greatly facilitated transfers and the disposal of goods; and, conversely, being a College officer did no harm to the standing of the merchant. We find in the College books references to transfers from "my account," "my booke," "carried to my owne bookes misentered here," "intended for college account" and put in his by mistake,[20] "out of my own Cash to make it agree."[21] Moreover, Richards and Brattle maintained their own accounts in London, so a gift made in England could be credited to Brattle's account in London and then paid by him to the College in Cambridge, with the appropriate markup for change from English sterling to New England money.[22]

The bookkeeping records were based on a formal system and

were in many ways very carefully kept, but occasionally we are startled by what seems a rather casual attitude. When a complicated series of transactions came to a money conclusion, sometimes the Treasurer would write over a figure such as £22 9*s*. 6*d*. to make it £22 10*s*. so that the account would balance out. Understandably he was not going to quibble further.[23]

We do find in the records occasional minor errors of arithmetic. Sometimes the figures have been written over later; sometimes (checking back to the manuscripts in the case of printed records) they are difficult to decipher now, and they may have been equally so even when they were first written down.[24] Auditors had good reason to guard against this possibility and usually signed after their inspections, "Errors excepted," or "Vera Comput: Error: Exceptis."[25]

Time was not important, as we have mentioned above in connection with commodity payments. People did not worry about interest for a few months; the risk factor was larger. Moreover, entries in the books were not always made immediately, and occasionally the same item in two accounts has different dates or details.

In the Middle Ages, sometimes "the written, as contrasted with the verbal, contract was looked on with suspicion. . . ."[26] There was far more literacy in the seventeenth century, yet a large number of people still signed by mark. The necessity for *written* instructions did not seem so imperative then as now, and we find numerous instances of verbal transactions of which a memorandum was made some time later.

The chattiness in some of the records adds a certain charm to working with them. The casualness may have been necessitated by the shortage of currency, but it also reflects an attitude which sometimes makes interpretation difficult. In August 1680 Richards says in the journal, "I suppose I gave a note to one of the fellowes for £10 rent of ferry. . . ." Again, on June 13, 1686, between the date of Governor Andros' appointment and his arrival in Boston, Richards writes, "Mr. Mather now enformes me that he received of Stevens in Aprill last, £3 17*s*."[27] Treasurer Richards was not infrequently (and quite justifiably) impatient with President Mather's easy treatment of money matters.

Brattle himself seems to appreciate this point, for it was he who inserted "so expressed" in the following entry in his journal for March 6, 1695:

> Cash received also of Richard Hood £3 7*s*. in full of Some little matter behind of his share of payment as partner with Robert Burges and Robert Ingalls in Colledg marsh, which little matter (so expressed) he covenanted to pay when the said Burgess and Ingolls paid theirs according to their bill, the said little matter Hood said was as he remembered about £40.

As well as casualness, the records show also certain inconsistencies of practice. Sometimes gifts in kind are valued and listed, and sometimes they are not. Assets not actually in hand are, like the Mowlson money, sometimes included in Stock and at other times not. The Mowlson fund was taken on the books, so far as the summary shows, between 1663 and 1669, though it had been received by the Colony and had paid income in the forties.* In some instances amounts due are included, but not always.

The items that are listed by income are variously handled. At one time they are ignored, at another listed by income only. They are never valued. Sundry non-income-producing assets are sometimes listed without value, sometimes not listed. Such properties as land grants from the Country were in many cases allowed to lapse, it seems, for lack of attention; had some value or mention of them been carefully included in the accounts, they might not have been so long neglected.

But for every one of these entries or practices — to us entertaining or odd — there are of course hundreds which are, if not in modern form, at least meticulously conventional in treatment.

## CHECKS ON THE SYSTEM

We do not really know who actually kept many of the books, but the officers themselves did much of the work. Richards and Thomas Brattle kept their own Treasurers' accounts, and the handwriting in their books is consistent over the years. Richards' method seems to have been to make little notes which he collected and in due time entered in the account book. Several of these notes were found in his book when around 1860 it was returned

* *HCSC*, p. 388, says "Stock" included only undesignated gifts. I do not find that this distinction holds: the Mowlson scholarship capital is in Stock.

to the College. Also, he would of course eventually get back some of his orders, endorsed as paid; we still have many of these. The Steward, and very possibly some of the other financial officers, had occasional student assistance.[28] Frequently we find small credits to students' accounts "alowed" for "writing" for the various College officers. Fellows Leverett and Brattle received £10 between them in 1691 "for making up the Colledge Accounts etc., to be paid by the Steward."[29]

Whoever actually made up the accounts, they were in such form that they could easily be checked. By means of cross-references and indices it was relatively simple to refer from one account to another. However, as we said above, balances of the Treasurers' books were infrequently taken, at least so far as any written record shows, and there was little periodic checking by balancing. Stewards' books on the other hand were balanced often so that they could collect any amount due them from the College, and the College Orders were very specific in requiring periodic accounts of the books of the Steward, Cook, Butler, Brewer, and Baker.[30] The Quarter-Bill Book of 1687 to 1720 was closed at periods varying from two years to two months. The books contain the standard little hieroglyphics to be used in reading accounts to sources and to each other.

Not only did the Fellows themselves receive occasional reimbursement for making up the accounts of other officers, but the Corporation, as a whole or in part, frequently read back the records and performed various sorts of audits of differing degrees of formality. We have the record that several times inventories were taken of the College properties, going down in great detail even into kitchen equipment. Steward Bordman also kept a "shop book" which, too, was audited and the items purchased "all viewed" by auditors.[31] The Corporation apparently went around and read these back. When the officers did change and balances were taken, the resulting reports were always formally perused and accepted at Corporation meetings.

The entries of payments by the Treasurer very often include some authorization by the Corporation, the President, or the governing Fellows. During Governor Andros' regime some payments were made by his order or by order of two of the Governor's

Council, William Stoughton and Joseph Dudley. Probably as much care as possible was taken in this respect, though it did seem to the annoyed and annoying King's officer Edward Randolph that there was a bit too much autonomy in the College.[32] Certainly if there had been any wish on the part of the Corporation to defraud in the use of the College's money and two or three of the members had agreed about it, such dishonesty could easily have taken place. The Corporation was continually ordering payments to its own members — how else could the payments be authorized? — but approval of appointments to the Corporation was by the charter wisely reserved to the Overseers.

From time to time, again usually when there was some crisis, further and quite detailed checks were made by committees of the General Court. Dunster even indicates that an annual report was made to the Court.[33] I find no such reports that were not fully sympathetic with the officers, and usually the investigators recommended more help to the College than the General Court was willing to grant.*

The Colonists had knowledge of much precedent in England for very careful regular audits. At least as early as the thirteenth century government fiscal officers' accounts were frequently audited. Receivers-general and stewards of manors regularly submitted their accounts to careful scrutiny in the sixteenth century, as did the financial officers of the colleges. The auditor was an important officer in the economy with powers to fine and imprison. It was "the hearing of the accounts" which took place, for few could read and fewer could write. A public hearing was sometimes held to test the books against public knowledge of what had taken place. Occasionally in England very distinguished committees made detailed audits and reports of the condition of the universities.[34] Auditing of this type was largely for "accountability," not control.[35]

It would seem then that despite this precedent there was

* We can be thankful that the occasional Court audits did not involve the complications attendant upon many of the dealings with the government in England. Trinity College accounts were kept in Roman numerals in the 1620's (*FHC*, p. 85), and in 1745 to 1760 the British Treasury practice forced the House of Hancock to maintain some accounts in that same somewhat awkward medium. (Baxter, *House of Hancock*, p. 160.)

something left to be desired in at least the frequency of audits at Harvard even by the standards of the day; but, again, it was one thing to go through the necessary procedures for a large institution which worked with specie as currency, as in England, and a quite different matter to go to all the necessary bother for a small operation with which all concerned were quite familiar and which did business with the awkward media of exchange in use by the Puritans in this country. Moreover, as the financial resources of Harvard increased and with the growing influence of John Leverett, the procedures became more formal.

### SUMMARY OF RECORDS

We can give tentative answers to three of the questions we asked about the records. We have seen that there are many original financial records extant, but we do not by any means have all of them. We must make our study on the basis of partial records, filling in and interpreting from other sources as best we can. Certainly we have enough material to get an excellent idea of methods used at certain periods, though not continuously, during the eighty years we are investigating. And we have in most cases, if not the detailed records, at least some statements and summaries based on those records.

We have seen that there were sundry checks on the work at the time it was done, and we have in general no reason to question the accuracy of the figures presented. There may be two very slight exceptions to this statement. The records available for the first eighteen years of the College are sketchy, and apparently they were sketchy in 1654. Surely the various estimates based on those figures are reasonably sound, but they cannot be relied upon as much as those of the later periods. Then during the Andros regime the College was in a sense marking time in the hope that things would change. There may be reason to suspect that less than full information was given the King's Governor during those two and a half years. But, though Andros and Randolph *may* not have had the whole story, we, looking back from here, perhaps can fill in some of it.

In speaking of the effectiveness of records for the purposes of their time, we must not be too critical of lacks by modern standards.

After all, the classic second principle of accounting was that common sense should act as a drag on inventiveness,[36] and to complicate administration by too elaborate bookkeeping would not have been common sense then, any more than now. The primary objective for Danforth, Richards, and Brattle was "accountability," and that, in a small enterprise, was taken care of by the method Harvard used. More frequent statements and a better distinction on the books between permanent endowment and income would have made the true picture clearer. Some sort of valuation would have been a requisite for a full balance sheet, though not for a partial capital account; and even the European textbooks, which were in advance of American practice, were vague about valuation at that time and for many years thereafter.[37] Further, the English custom, still used for tax and other purposes, of valuing property by the income it produces, worked against any impractical attempt to list assets in the modern manner.

In the twentieth century, when "control" as well as "accountability" is an object of institutional accounting, the situation is not the same as when in the seventeenth century the control was exercised largely by outside factors. Moreover, accounting for the services of trustees even today is very different from a commercial audit which prepares figures for taxes and analyzes the sales and production of a business.

Any lacks which we may find in seventeenth-century Harvard would have taken more than a bookkeeping system to correct. But we hope that a more complete method was instituted shortly after the end of the Brattle era, for otherwise the increasing size and complexity would have been difficult to understand, let alone to control.

It is obvious that a study of Harvard's finances over the years involves much more than a perusal of the records of the Treasurers. After 1655 and until 1712 tuitions went directly to teachers as part of their salaries. Receipts from the ferry and the Piscataqua donation were more often than not handled in the same way, for salaries. Students' charges for board and room and other fees were paid to the Steward, whose balance from operations, paid to or by the Treasurer, was not great. The President was usually paid directly by "the Cuntry." The "Cuntry" or special subscriptions

*Table 2. Harvard College in the Puritan Period; Preliminary Figures*

| Year | Approximate[a] number of undergraduate students | Approximate[b] Massachusetts population (thousands) | [c]Assets: Capital assets NE £ | [c]Assets: Additional annual income incl. ferry NE £ |
|---|---|---|---|---|
| 1636 | 0 | | 0 | 0 |
| 1640 | | 15 | 0 | 28 |
| 1652 | 50 | 20 | 263 | 45 |
| 1669 | 25 | 32 | 711 | 61 |
| 1682 | 25 | | 2142 | 91 |
| 1683 | | | 2358 | 95 |
| 1686 | 45 | | 1353 | 93 |
| 1693 | 53 | 50 | 1896 | 98 |
| 1712 | 54 | | 3283 | 143 |
| 1715 | | | 4085 | 115 |

| Period | [d]Financial Officer | Average annual known[e] — Receipts, including gain in stock (excluding return of principal) NE £ | Average annual known[e] — Expense, excluding investments NE £ |
|---|---|---|---|
| 1637–1640 | Eaton, Shepard | — | —[f] |
| 1641–1652 | Dunster | 168[e] | 174[e] |
| 1654–1669 | Danforth | 318[e] | 268[e] |
| 1669–1682 | Richards | 444 | 260 |
| 1682–1683 | Danforth | — | —[f] |
| 1683–1684 | Nowell | — | —[f] |
| 1686–1693 | Richards | 295 | 300 |
| 1693–1712 | T. Brattle | 529 | 443 |
| 1713–1715 | W. Brattle | — | —[f] |

*Note:* This table is for preliminary discussion only. It does not ordinarily include the capital expenditures for major buildings, though some of the charges of finishing the original Harvard College were in Dunster's accounts: the Indian College was constructed in 1655 by the "Commissioners for Massachusetts," and some of its cost may be included in Danforth's expenditures for 1654 to 1663; the second Harvard College was built 1674 to 1682 at a cost of about £2000 by a subscription from towns and individuals; Mr. Stoughton spent over £1000 on Stoughton College in 1699. For more complete figures, see below, Tables 32 and 35.

[a] From *CSM* XV, 82–91, and Stewards' Books. See also Figure 1.

[b] See below, pp. 37 and 38.

[c] Under "Assets — additional income," the table shows income from capital not held or not listed by the College. The capital value of this income has not been included here in receipts. Treatment of the Keayne house has been made consistent over the years.

[d] The years shown beside the officers' names are those for which average annual receipts have been calculated and are not necessarily the total years of service of the officers.

[e] Stewards' gross food accounts are not included. Some of the Stewards' receipts and the expenses from them *contra* are included to 1660; they are not on either side after that — only the net balance of the Steward is there. To make the content of the figures more consistent before and after 1669, some adjustment has been made: we know that there is about £10 in fees and £5 in study rents included in Dunster's period, and about £14 in study rents in Danforth's, so I have taken these amounts out of the annual receipts and expenses.

[f] Complete figures are not available for these periods.

outside the Treasurer's accounts ordinarily paid for new buildings. The Treasurer, then, used investment income and gifts which came to him to pay for the balance of the Fellows' salaries, his own salary, some scholarships, and odd small expenses and repairs.

In order to give some idea of the scale of Harvard activities, and with the caution that interpretation or use of these figures should be strictly subject to limitations set forth in the text of this and succeeding chapters, we can show as Table 2 a very rough picture of the change in Harvard's total financial picture over the years. These figures are made from the basic accounts, using such supplementary records as we can find. They *have weaknesses* listed in the notes to the table. In subsequent chapters (see pages 148 and 160 below) we shall try to eliminate these and other weaknesses and present revised figures, as well as to indicate what the figures meant in real terms.

# III

# *ECONOMIC VALUES IN PURITAN NEW ENGLAND**

IN 1693 Harvard College had invested assets of £1285. In 1652 the tuition rate was 6*s.* 8*d.* a quarter. The Charlestown ferry paid £40 a year in 1675. The second "Harvard College," completed in the late 1670's, cost £2000. A tutor in 1695 received a total compensation of £50 a year. What do these figures mean?

It behooves us not only to describe what our forebears at Harvard spent or received in *their* currency, but also to indicate how their currency changed in value over the century and what these money values meant to them in real values. The figures must be fixed in an economic setting.

## INTRODUCTION — CONTEMPORARY LIFE

By 1642, with Puritan fortunes in England definitely improving, and with risk capital unavailable because it was otherwise employed or had been lost by the King's supporters, migration to New England had virtually stopped; the population of Massachusetts at that time has been variously estimated, but it must have been somewhere in the neighborhood of 16,000.[1] Not only were prospects in England better than before, but what migrants there were tended to go to the West Indies where commercial possibilities were interesting and the climate more beneficent than in the northern colonies. Indeed, the migration went definitely into reverse, and in June 1641, Winthrop was saying:

> The parliament of England setting upon a general reformation both of church and state, the Earl of Strafford being beheaded, and the archbishop (our great enemy) and many others of the great officers and

* Trade and other investment opportunities will be treated in Chapter VIII below, in connection with investments and endowment. See pp. 156–159 and 183.

judges, bishops, and others, imprisoned and called to account, this caused all men to stay in England in expectation of a new world.[2]

By July 1642 a bad depression was at its depth in New England.

But the depression ended, and a trickle of new settlers again started to come in. Few came over during Cromwell's time, and around the year 1660 women and children were not infrequently being stolen and forcibly transported to New England.[3] There was a wave of Huguenots from 1686 on, especially to 1689, and from 1708 on there was "an influx of Irish, English, and Huguenots of low social orders."[4] The population of Massachusetts, including Maine and Plymouth but not New Hampshire, may have risen from about 28,000 in 1665 to 49,000 in 1689. In 1700 there were approximately 7,000 people in Boston, 80,000 in New England, and 250,000 in English colonies on the mainland.[5]

Cambridge in New England was a long way from Old England. Ships were known to make the eastward passage in as little as 23 days, but it could take ten weeks for the westward journey.[6] Time of passage varied widely with the ship, the season, the weather. Over the seventeenth century there was little change in average time required, though often hazards other than weather interfered, such as capture by an enemy, or, later in the century, by pirates.

Cambridge was also a long way from other towns. If there was to be a special meeting of the Overseers of the College, it took a messenger some time to take the word, as the Laws of the Colony required, to "all the magistrates of this jurisdiction" and to the ministers involved, even though the latter usually lived in the "sixe next adjoyning townes." In 1639 the General Court passed an act directing that highways be laid out. "Each town was to appoint two or more men to connect the roads with the next town."[7] Taverns were established in the towns in the 1640's. It was an especially momentous event in Harvard's affairs when in 1663 the bridge over the Charles River at Cambridge was completed. Fortunately for Harvard's revenue from the ferry, the Charlestown Bridge to West Boston was not opened to traffic until 1793.[8] In 1672 a post route was set up "to goe monthly" from New York to Boston,[9] connecting Massachusetts by land with the colony recently taken over from the Dutch.

So throughout the Puritan Period our College was functioning in a world with few people compared with Europe at that time or with Cambridge in 1962; and in this world distances were long, and transactions involved expenditure of — to us — inordinate amounts of time.

Though there were periods of hard times, according to Weeden[10] "we hear no more of any general want in the country" after 1631. The Massachusetts Bay Colony had been able to meet its citizens' basic needs very quickly, for it had been settled originally on a larger scale (though hardly a munificent one) than other early English colonies on the mainland and had had the advantages of a continued flow of new recruits through the thirties, as well as the benefit of other colonies' experience and relative proximity. Though their economic level may not seem high to us, " 'a poor servant that is to possesse but fifty acres of land' can have wood and timber in abundance, and can keep a better fire than many noblemen in England can afford."[11] In addition to enjoying the abundance of land, he profited from local products such as corn, plus hunting, wild berries and nuts, and maple sugar.[12]

The paternalistic government here took no chances that any such improvements in his condition should go to the head of the "poor servant." The Colony elders carefully controlled the inhabitants' dress and pleasure trips from town to town; the degree of freedom varied with economic status.[13]

Compared with some periods we might study, prices seem to have been remarkably steady throughout the century. Events in both Old England and New England contributed to the fluctuations we do observe. It is well known that throughout our period England was trying to follow a mercantilist policy of economics — to build up its home economy, especially manufacturing, to assure itself a favorable balance of foreign trade, and, except during the Protectorate, to sponsor colonies only insofar as they contributed to her own prosperity. But at least until 1686 England was unable because of distance, disputes at home, and wars, to exercise any effective control over Massachusetts, and the Colony felt it should follow its own local mercantilist policy, keeping its specie on this side of the Atlantic and building up independent trade and manufacturing here as far as possible. Though as the century progressed the colonists were more and more successful, at no time were they able or did they all wish to ignore their semidependent state; but they were dependent on a parent country which because of wars and economic cycles was not at this time in a very stable financial condition herself and therefore little likely to contribute to stability over here.

Harvard's own financial affairs were affected by England in three major ways: (1) The English economic condition acted upon New England's economy by (a) influencing the number and type of immigrants, (b) affecting New England's trade, a large part of which was with the mother country, and (c) controlling investment of English funds in the Colonies. (2) Despite repeated failure to bring Massachusetts Bay to rein, the King's government did, especially toward the end of the century, determine the form of government in the Colony and thereby materially affect the government of the College and the financial support the College received from the "Country." (3) Gifts to the College by Englishmen were influenced not only by their personal economic resources but also by conflicting needs for money at home, and on the other hand by their wish to support a way of life which was *not* available at home.

## MONEY IN NEW ENGLAND

Notwithstanding the very real influence of the mother country on the College in New England, the economics of Massachusetts were regulated largely by New England interests, since this colony because of its charter was more independent than the southern colonies.[14] For this reason the College's most immediate economic problems had their origin here.

As we have said, the decade of Harvard's founding was the time of "the Great Migration," and New England received a steady stream of immigrants with cash and manufactured goods to exchange for the provisions grown here. When the migration stopped in 1639 and 1640,

> the merchants were caught with outstanding orders arriving on incoming ships, which brought none of the expected purchasers with money in their pockets. When these same vessels sailed back for London, they took with them many of the more energetic and younger settlers, eager to return to the homeland to share in the excitement of the struggle, . . .

[and] these departing settlers called on the merchant-bankers for the return of funds that had been placed in their hands for safe-keeping.[15]

Money became very scarce, and prices fell in some cases to a fourth their previous level.[16]

But, as Winthrop recorded in February 1641,

> The general fear of want of foreign commodities, now our money was gone, and that things were like to go well in England, set us on work to provide shipping of our own, for which end Mr. Peter, being a man of a very public spirit and singular activity for all occasions, procured some to join for building a ship at Salem of 300 tons, and the inhabitants of Boston, stirred up by his example, set upon the building another at Boston of 150 tons. The work was hard to accomplish for want of money, etc., but our shipwrights were content to take such pay as the country could make.[17]

Then on June 2, 1641, Winthrop reported:

> No man could pay his debts, nor the merchants make return into England for their commodities, which occasioned many there to speak evil of us. These straits set our people on work to provide fish, clapboards, plank, etc., and to sow hemp and flax (which prospered very well) and to look out to the West Indies for a trade for cotton. The general Court also made orders about payment of debts, setting corn at the wonted price, and payable for all debts which should arise after a time prefixed.[18]

A neat economic microcosm began to be worked out, and in the working we find the origin of the three-cornered trade which was to make New England prosper.

To alleviate currency troubles the General Court was forced to make corn legal tender for many years to come. They also attempted to set prices and wages during the 1640's and off and on in later years, but they had little success. If it was necessary to get in a harvest, and if a laborer was available and willing to work, it was impossible to keep even a God-fearing Puritan from hiring the laborer whatever the price. All the government could do in this regard was to specify at what price grains would be received in payment of taxes and adjudicate suits over fixing a just price. Nonetheless, though after the 1640's the Puritan leaders largely gave up their efforts toward price-fixing, "Preacher, planter, historian, diarist and law-maker insisted that the government must regulate economic activity." This was partly a heritage from medieval times, partly mercantilist dogma, and partly a necessary response to immediate circumstances.[19] "The function of government," said Jonathan Mitchell, "is to increase the welfare of the people." And there are two phases of welfare: spiritual (the more important) and temporal.[20]

Writers from Winthrop to the present day emphasize the money shortage as the cause of most early Massachusetts financial troubles. In speaking of the economic thinkers of the sixteenth and seventeenth centuries, Keynes says,

> There was wisdom in their intense preoccupation with keeping down the rate of interest with usury laws . . . , by maintaining the domestic stock of money and by discouraging rises in the wage-unit; and in their readiness in the last resort to restore the stock of money by devaluation, if it had become plainly deficient through an unavoidable foreign drain. . . .[21]

Other writers point out that the shortage of bullion was a symptom, not a cause, or that in 1640 demand was down, or that despite the cumbersome shortage, a very prosperous community grew up over the next hundred years; or they quote Adam Smith to the effect that "money, like wine, must always be scarce with those who have neither wherewithal to buy it, nor credit to borrow it."[22]

Whatever the merits of this perennial discussion — there is probably some truth in all the arguments — the supply of money may have increased, but it did not seem to increase fast enough, and the early colonists felt quite certain that their troubles stemmed in large part from the shortage of coin; there is no question but that this shortage necessitated a good many awkward expedients which increased the complexity of managing an institution such as Harvard College.

As a device to unify and retain what hard currency there was, the General Court took upon itself in 1652 the sovereign right of establishing a mint, and it was there that the famed "pine-tree shilling" was produced.* This was "New England money" and was the unit of account in this neighborhood even long after it had disappeared from actual circulation. In the hope that these

* Table 3 will give a comparison of the values of coins.

*Table 3. Possible Equivalent Values in Sterling and New England Pounds and in Spanish Dollars*

| Year | Remarks (1) | London exchange: NE £ per £ Stg. (2) | London exchange: £ Stg. per NE £ (3) | Exchange of dollar by weight: Dwt.[a] per $1 (4) | Exchange of dollar by weight: Value of $1 in NE £ (5) | Exchange of dollar by weight: Value of $1 in £ Stg. (6) | Exchange of dollar by weight: Value of £1 NE in $ (7) | Price of silver per ounce: in NE £ (8) | Price of silver per ounce: in £ Stg. (9) |
|---|---|---|---|---|---|---|---|---|---|
| | | | | | s. d. | s. d. | | s. d. | s. d. |
| 1641 | | 1. | 1. | 17½ | 4 6 | 4 6 | 4.44 | 5 2 | 5 2 |
| 1652 | The Mint Act | 1.20 | 0.833 | | | | | | |
| 1654 | Rate actually minted | 1.33 | .75 | 17½ | 6 | 4 6 | 3.33 | 6 10 2/7 | 5 2 |
| 1654–1704 | Rate often used | 1.35 | | 17½ | 6 2 | 4 6 | 3.24 | 7 | 5 2 |
| | | or | | 17 | 6 | | 3.33 | | |
| | | 1.37 | | 16 | 5 7½ | | | | |
| | | | | 15 | 5 3½ | | | | |
| | | | | 13 | 4 8 | | | | |
| 1682 | Law | | | | | | | 6 8 | |
| 1704 | Proclamation of Queen Anne (not followed) | 1.33 | .75 | 17½ | 6 | 4 6 | 3.33 | 6 10 2/7 | 5 2 |
| 1705–1710 | There were no 17½ dwt.[a] coins around, and 15 or 13 dwt. passed for 6*s*. | 1.55 | .645 | 17½ | 7 | 4 6 | 2.86 | 8 | 5 2 |
| | | | | 17 | 6 9½ | | | | |
| | | | | 16 | 6 4½ | | | | |
| | | | | 15 | 6 | | 3.33 | | |
| | | | | 13 | 4 2½ | | | | |
| 1711 | Silver used to here | | | | | 4 6 | | 8 4 | 5 2 |
| 1712–1713 | | | | | | | | 8 6 | 5 2 |
| 1714–1715 | | | | | | 4 6 | | 9 | 5 2 |
| 1716–1717 | | | | | | | | 10 | 5 2 |
| 1718 | Silver disappeared from N.E. | | | | | 4 6 | | 11 | 5 2 |
| 1719 | | 2.25 | | | | 4 6 | | 12 | 5 2 |
| 1728 | | 3.40 | | | | 4 6 | | 18 | 5 2 |
| 1741 | | 5.50 | | | | 4 6 | | 28 | 5 2 |
| 1749 | | 11.00 | | | | 4 6 | | 60 | 5 2 |

*Source:* Composed and extended from Davis, *Proc. AAAS*, pp. 196–197; Davis, *Currency*, pp. 31, 37–38, 45, 367, 370, 388–390; Nettels, pp. 232, 237, 243n, 256.

[a] An ounce Troy weight is 20 pennyweight — 20 dwt.

shillings and the corresponding fractional coins would stay in this country, the New England shilling was made about $22\frac{1}{2}$ per cent lighter than the British standard sterling shilling. The light American shilling would then obviously buy less abroad than the British, and if the prices had remained the same here, the New England coins might have stayed at home and other money have come in to the mint to be reissued; but of course prices very soon adjusted. Whereas the pound sterling was worth in purchasing power approximately 4.444 "heavy" Spanish dollars (or the dollar was worth 4*s*. 6*d*. English money), the New England pound was at a discount of about 25 per cent under the British and became the equivalent of only 3.333 dollars. (The converse was that sterling exchange sold for 1.33 or 1.35 New England pounds, and the dollar rose until it was equal to five and then six New England shillings.) That is, average prices of goods in Boston, expressed in New England money, rose 25 per cent.*

New England shillings did *not* stay at home, though their export was prohibited; the majority of the coins used here were the Spanish dollars (pieces of eight) brought in by the West Indies trade or by the pirates, and the colonists saw little point in paying the seigniorage to have these dollars stamped at the mint, "A Spanish Cross in all other places being as well esteemed as a New England Pine."[23] Then the New England mint was closed when the Colony lost its charter in 1684. Toward the end of the century we find pieces of eight practically the only coin specifically mentioned as being received by Harvard.

The weakness of all these coins, aside from the question of assay, was that they were "clipped, filed, and rounded" so they contained less silver than when minted. Not only did different Spanish territories *mint* pieces of eight of different weights, but the heavy or "broad" 8/8 of $17\frac{1}{2}$ dwt. per piece did not *stay* heavy. It therefore became customary to accept all coin by the ounce. From the 1680's on we find much discussion in terms of the price in New England money of silver per ounce, and anyone who dealt in money kept a small weighing scale handy.** Table 3 gives a

* More work should be done to trace, if possible, the effect of this light-weight shilling. See also pp. 48, 65, and 82 below.

** An ounce Troy weight is 20 pennyweight — 20 dwt.

summary of various exchange values; in practice these columns were not always equivalent.

New England money was tied to the English pound sterling, which was itself being clipped, filed, and rounded in England. The better coins were exported to the Continent, and British foreign exchange sold at an especially high discount in Amsterdam whenever (which was frequently) the King of England was having difficulty financing his wars.[24]

One effect of the difference between the British and the New England pounds was that Harvard appeared to gain a bookkeeping, though seldom a real, advantage when gifts were made in England in sterling. Sir Matthew Holworthy died in 1679 and bequeathed the munificent sum of £1000 to the College, the largest single gift made to the College during the seventeenth century. Treasurer Richards was "empowred, to take care of the donation of Sir Matthew Holworthy, and to gett it over into the country by exchange or otherwaies, as he shall see meet, as soone as may bee."[25] Richards lists the personal bills of exchange of individuals in England on merchants and others in Boston as bringing £1234 2*s.* 6*d.* money (NE) to the College Treasury.

In August 1671 William Pennoyer in England left an annuity to Harvard, to be paid out of the revenues of a farm in Norfolk (in England). The "advance" (premium for New England money over sterling) on these bills of exchange was 25 per cent in 1685 and 1686;[26] in 1697 and 1700 Brattle was allowing 36 per cent advance, though in January 1702 he allowed 30 per cent, in July 1703 40 per cent.[27] (In March 1703, Mr. Mico was authorized to "gett over" the Pennoyer money; by investing the £15 in "stuffs" [cloth] which Brattle sold in Boston, the £15 was "advanced" to £27 15*s.* 4*d.*, an increase of 85 per cent by this method, but with some trouble entailed for the gentlemen involved.)[28] To end this series — in 1715 William Brattle allowed 50 per cent on the Pennoyer money.[29] So from 1685 to 1715 the premium on sterling exchange went from 25 per cent to 50 per cent.*

We have seen that New England transactions were affected by (1) the money shortage and consequent 1654 debasing of New

* The difference between New England and English money involves not only different value in London, but the risk of transport and collection across the ocean.

England coin by 25 per cent, (2) use of Spanish dollars of varying weights; (3) exchange of New England money for British. Nevertheless, Table 3 shows that after the devaluation in 1654 and until 1704, except for variations in weight, the purchasing power of the "New England money" remained quite constant. To understand what went on after 1704, we must go back a few years to 1690.

Throughout the discussion of shortage of specie in Massachusetts there had been suggestions that banks be established, but such schemes had never worked out successfully.* When the Province's perennial shortage of funds made it appear that Massachusetts would not be able to pay the troops which had come back from the disastrous 1690 expedition to capture Quebec, the General Court adopted the temporary expedient of issuing Colony bills of public credit in anticipation of the next tax levy, and the bills were in a form which could be used as currency for the Colony.[30] These were very short-term bills and were redeemed promptly. But over the years, more and more bills were issued and they were redeemed after longer and longer periods. Practically speaking, for purposes of business transactions these bills of credit, also, were "New England money," in addition to various kinds of coin, and local prices of goods were quoted both in the bills and in silver by the ounce. Their purchasing power held up almost to 1704, but from that time on they gradually lost value and any remaining silver coins gained correspondingly in terms of bills. In 1704 Queen Anne issued a proclamation (see Table 3) with the object of unifying currency in her various dominions. She reiterated the New England rate of exchange with Britain at 133 and also stipulated that the full weight ($17\frac{1}{2}$ dwt.) piece of eight should pass at six shillings New England. This was not realistic, for by this time New England money had gone down a bit and practically all heavy pieces of eight had disappeared; pieces of 15 and even 13 dwt. were being accepted at six shillings (the $17\frac{1}{2}$ dwt. official rate). This meant that the value of silver had gone up to eight or more New England shillings an ounce. From 1707 to 1714 *light* dollars and bills continued almost at par with each other, but this made the sterling exchange for New England money 155. By 1718 silver had disappeared entirely.[31]

* The Bank of England was not founded until 1694.

The result of this process was that in addition to having to worry about the weight of foreign coins, as had been the case to some extent since the Colony was founded, Thomas Brattle and his successor, William, now had to try and assure that the money returned to them was at least as good as the money "lett out." This was possible if the terms of written obligations were properly expressed. There is every evidence that the Treasurers had the necessary foresight; Harvard was well protected in this respect during the first fifteen years of the seventeenth century, and Brattle usually received payment in good coin.* In 1670 the Massachusetts General Court had passed a law that corn and other produce were no longer to be accepted as money, and that contracts made thereafter payable in specie should be paid in the same specie as contracted.[32] This helped when clipping of coin and inflation of paper money occurred.

The increased amounts which the Treasurer received because the New England money had been devalued added up in some cases to sizable sums. Edward Pelham owed the College on a mortgage loan given him by Richards, and Brattle had had a very difficult time pinning Pelham down to making any payments. (Mr. Pelham is the gentleman to whom we referred above[33] who came to town, collected some money owed him, and "went away with it" without paying Brattle.) Yet, when in November 1711 the Pelham account was finally settled in full, the College received not only the basic £341 4*s*. of the mortgage, but accumulated interest of £123 10*s*. 6*d*., plus £61 18*s*. 6*d*. for the difference between 15 and 17 dwt. on both principal and interest.[34] The New England money in which the contract had been made was equivalent to heavy silver coin, and that is what Brattle was to receive back, not paper money; and since he was paid in light coins (pieces of only 15 dwt.), he had to have enough more of them to equal the original weight. But when he got this weight it was worth £61 18*s*. 6*d*. more of the now devalued New England money of account he recorded in his book; the additional £61 covered the inflation in

* We get the impression that Richards did only fairly well in the one case we quote on page 24 above, for he received light coin which he sold in 1690 at 6½*s*. per ounce. However, the paper money problem faced by the Brattles had not arisen in the time of Richards, nor was the problem of underweight coin so serious in his time. Underweight coin was long a serious problem in other parts of the world.

(New England money) prices of goods he might buy. Would there were such a solid base for contracts made in 1962!*

PRICES

There was a fairly constant rate of exchange and real value for New England money to 1704, but there were some temporary fluctuations in the general price level as well as changes in the relative demand for specific goods because of special scarcities or surpluses.

After Puritan New England recovered from the chaotic shortages incident to its founding and from the worst of the depression of the early forties, its growing trade prospered under the usually benign regime of the Puritans in Old England, and, as we have said, there was no effective outside control even during the Restoration until about 1686. But the Dutch War and then King Philip's War in the seventies, with its attendant very heavy taxes, were certainly major influences in a decline of real estate values.[35] Then when the Massachusetts charter was annulled, tenure of property and all legal status in the Colony became uncertain and remained so at least until the Provincial Charter of 1691 provided some basis for confidence. From 1691 on we enter the long period of inflation of values, slow at first, in terms of Massachusetts currency.

*Commodities*

Meaningful economic series of any length are remarkably hard to find for the American colonies in the seventeenth century. We can pick up only occasional pieces of information which give a feeling of the way commodity values were running.[36] Thanks largely to Winthrop there is a fairly good picture available for the days when the College was founded. At that time, a good cow was worth £25 to £30, a pair of bulls or oxen £40. Corn was bringing 5*s*. a bushel. A suit of clothes or a coat cost £1, a pair of shoes 3½*s*., a pair of stockings 1½*s*., 4 yards of homemade cloth 6*s*. A day's food for a laborer then cost 10*d*. (£16 a year). In the 1641 crash the price

* The progression of this change as it shows in Brattle's journal is interesting also to anyone concerned with the question of just *when* the change took place, for evidence on this subject seems to be meager. (Cf. Davis, *Currency*, p. 388, and Nettels, writing later, relies heavily on Davis.) Notes at the end of this chapter give some examples taken from Brattle's book.

*Table 4. Prices per Bushel of Grains Paid in Lieu of Money for Taxes, as Set by the General Court of Massachusetts Bay for the Years 1635 to 1694 (New England Shillings)*

| Year | Month & day | Wheat | | [a]Barley | | Rye | | Peas | | Corn | | Oats | |
|---|---|---|---|---|---|---|---|---|---|---|---|---|---|
| | | *s.* | *d.* | *s.* | *d.* | *s.* | *d.* | *s.* | *d.* | *s.* | *d.* | *s.* | *d.* |
| 1635 | 3/4 | – | | – | | – | | – | | 5 | | | |
| 1636 | – | – | | – | | – | | – | | 5 | | | |
| 1637 | 11/2 | – | | – | | – | | – | | 3 | 8 | | |
| 1642 | 9/8 | 4 | | 4 | | 3 | 4 | 3 | 4 | 2 | 6 | | |
| 1643 | 5/10 | 4 | 6 | – | | – | | – | | – | | | |
| 1645 | 5/14 | 4 | | 4 | | 3 | 6 | 3 | 6 | 2 | 8 | | |
| 1647 | 10/27 | 4 | 6 | 4 | | 3 | 6 | 3 | 6 | 2 | 6 | | |
| 1648 | 10/18 | 5 | | 5 | | 4 | | 4 | | 3 | | | |
| 1649 | 10/17 | 5 | | 5 | 6 | 4 | | 4 | | 3 | | | |
| 1650 | 10/15 | 5 | | 5 | | 4 | | 4 | | 3 | | | |
| 1651 | 10/14 | 5 | | 5 | | 4 | | 3 | 8 | 3 | | | |
| 1652 | 10/19 | 5 | | 5 | | 4 | | 4 | | 3 | | | |
| 1654 | 10/18 | 5 | | 5 | | 4 | | 4 | | 3 | | | |
| 1655 | 11/13 | 4 | 6 | 4 | 6 | 3 | 6 | 4 | | 2 | 6 | | |
| 1656 | 10/14 | 4 | 6 | 4 | 6 | 3 | | 4 | | 2 | 4 | | |
| 1657 | 10/14 | 4 | | 4 | | 3 | | 3 | | 2 | 6 | | |
| 1658 | 10/9 | 5 | | 4 | | 4 | | 4 | | 2 | 8 | | |
| 1660 | 10/16 | 5 | | 4 | 6 | 4 | | 4 | | 3 | | | |
| 1662 | 10/8 | 5 | 6 | 5 | 6 | 4 | 6 | 4 | 6 | 3 | | | |
| 1663 | 10/20 | 5 | 6 | 5 | | 4 | | 4 | | 3 | | | |
| 1664 | 10/19 | 5 | | 4 | 6 | 4 | | 4 | | 3 | | | |
| 1665 | 8/1 | 5 | | 4 | 6 | 4 | | 4 | | 3 | | | |
| 1667 | 10/9 | 5 | | 4 | | 4 | | 3 | 6 | 2 | 8 | | |
| 1668 | 10/14 | 5 | | 4 | | 4 | | 3 | 6 | 2 | 8 | | |
| 1670 | 10/11 | 5 | | 4 | | 4 | | 4 | | 3 | | | |
| 1671 | 9/12 | 5 | 6 | 5 | 6 | 5 | | 5 | | 2 | 8 | | |
| 1673 | 10/– | 5 | | 4 | | 4 | | 3 | | 3 | | | |
| 1674 | 10/7 | 5 | | 4 | | 4 | | 4 | | 3 | | | |
| 1675 | 10/13 | 6 | | 4 | | 4 | 6 | 4 | | 3 | 6 | 2 | |
| 1676 | 10/11 | 5 | | 4 | | 4 | | 4 | | 3 | | 2 | |
| 1678 | 10/2 | 5 | | 4 | | 4 | 6 | 4 | | 3 | | 2 | 6 |
| 1680 | 10/13 | 5 | | 4 | | 4 | | 4 | | 3 | | 2 | |
| 1680 | 11/5 | 5 | | 3 | 6 | 3 | | 4 | | 3 | 6 | 1 | 8 |
| 1681 | 10/12 | 6 | | 4 | | 4 | 6 | 4 | | 3 | | 2 | |
| 1682 | 10/19 | 5 | 6 | 3 | 6 | 4 | | 4 | 6 | 3 | | 2 | |
| 1683 | 10/10 | 5 | | 4 | | 3 | 6 | – | | 3 | | 2 | |
| 1685 | 10/14 | 5 | 6 | 4 | 6 | 4 | | 4 | | 3 | | 2 | |
| 1686 | 12/8 | 5 | | – | | 4 | | 4 | | 2 | 9 | 2 | |
| 1687 | 9/28 | 4 | | 3 | | 2 | 8 | 3 | 6 | 1 | 8 | 1 | 4 |
| 1688 | 7/1 | 2 | 9 | 2 | 6 | 2 | | 3 | | 1 | 2 | | 10 |
| 1689 | 11/9 | 5 | 6 | 3 | 6 | 3 | | 4 | | 3 | | – | |
| 1690 | 3/14 | 5 | | 4 | | 4 | | 4 | | 3 | 6 | 1 | 6 |
| 1690 | 11/21 | 4 | 6 | 4 | | – | | 4 | | 3 | | 1 | 6 |
| 1694 | 3/27 | 5 | | 2 | 3 | 2 | 9 | 3 | 6 | 2 | 3 | 1 | 4 |

*Source:* This table was made by Miss Ruth Crandall from Joseph B. Felt, "Statistics of Taxation in Massachusetts," *Coll. Am. Stat. Assn.*, I, iii (1847), 232, 257–258, 276, 310.
[a] And barley malt after 1656.

of a cow fell in one month from £20 to £5, that of a goat from £3 to 10*s*. Indian corn was costing 5 to 6*s*. a bushel before 1640, 4*s*. in 1640, 2*s*. 6*d*. in 1642, 3*s*. in 1650. After that time until the end of the century, the price of corn remained about the same, and seldom went above 3*s*.[37] It did fluctuate, of course, within the year according to the season, and from year to year according to whether the harvest was a good one or not — these are the perils of commodity money. This general consistency is shown in Table 4, which gives the amounts allowed for grain paid in lieu of taxes. We note that prices of grains were low in 1655 to 1658, high at the time of King Philip's War (1675), high about 1681, very low in the late eighties (Andros period), but over the long run remarkably steady.

Material based also on the allowance against Massachusetts taxes shows that approximately the same statement can be made for livestock prices after the opening of the mint in 1652, though there seems to be a definite, though slight, tendency toward a decline at least to 1688.[38]

Occasional figures taken from Richards' book are consistent with those from other sources, but his entries confirm the hazards of using grain for money: in 1676 he accepted Indian at 3*s*. 6*d*. but sold it at 2*s*. 6*d*., received peas at 4*s*. and sold them for 3*s*. This was in payment of the Finch legacy of 20*s*.; of the 20*s*. he ended with 14*s*. 6*d*. in money and a loss of 5*s*. 6*d*.[39] In March 1679 Richards received eight bushels of wheat at 4*s*., sold them 3*s*. 6*d*., accepted rye at 3*s*. 6*d*. and sold it for 3*s*. This was a fairly consistent picture when the College was paid in country pay.[40]

When we want to put some of these commodity prices together and find the cost of meals, we read that in September 1643 there was an assembly of about fifty elders in Cambridge, and "They sat in the college, and had their diet there after the manner of the scholars' commons, but somewhat better, yet so ordered as it came not to above sixpence the meal for a person."[41]

The expense allowance stipulated for county officers in 1679 was 1*s*. for noon dinner for marshalls and constables, 1*s*. 3*d*. for jurymen, and 2*s*. each for magistrates. The allowance was to include "wine and bear, etc."[42]

From time to time, and every year during the last years covered by this study, we have the details of the food served at commencement banquets, with its cost. Let us sigh for the days of 1688:[43]

4 Barrels of Beer (at 10*s*. per barrel)
11 Gallons of Madiera wine (at 2*s*. 6*d*. per gal.) & clarett & cyder
10 Bushels of Wheat
Fowls (at 4*s*. 7½*d*. a doz.), chickens (at 4*s*. a doz.), 1 lamb and 16 fowls (total cost 1*s*. 6*d*.), pork (1*s*. 3*d*. a pigge), bacon, tongue and udder, beef, veal, mutton (5*s*. a lamb), geese (1*s*. 6*d*. each), 1 salmon (5*s*.)
Apples, cucumers, oranges & pineapples, capers and anchovies,
Pepper, nutmegs, mace, cloves, white salt, Bay salt
Gooseberryes, cherryes
Squashes & salad herbs, carrots, turnips, onion & parsley, boiling herbs

The cooke's work for three days at 6*s*. a day, 2 men 4 and 5 days each and 3 men one day each at 1*s*. to 2½*s*. a day, the help of the Steward himself, his wife, and "Beck's", all for £2, two turnspitt Indians at 9*d*. a day.

[Plus other odds and ends, including brown paper for 2½*s*. — for the roasts?]

In 1692 and again in 1707 the Harvard Steward complained about the high prices. The Corporation sympathized and raised the amount he was permitted to charge per "part," that is per meal for one person. The major changes in charges are shown in Table 5.

*Table 5.*[a] *The Price per Part, 1693 to 1714*

| | *d.* | *f.* |
|---|---|---|
| April 1693 | 2 | 3 |
| August 1694–August 1699 | 3 | |
| November 1699 | 2 | 1[b] |
| August 1700 | 2 | 2 |
| May 1704 | 2 | 1 |
| March 1707 | 2 | 2 |
| August 1708 | 2 | 2 |
| June 1709 | 2 | 3 |
| April 1710 | 3 | |
| April 1713 | 3 | 1 |
| October 1713 | 3 | 2 |
| December 1714 | 3 | 3 |

*Source: CSM* XV & XVI, 344, 346, 349, 350, 352, 353, 359, 363, 364, 365, 372, 377, 383, 387, 388, 391, 397, 407, 421, 425.
[a] A farthing (*f.*) was a quarter of a penny (*d.*). For more about a "part" see Chapter IV below.
[b] "because of The Present Plenty,"

The Steward's Ledger of 1703–1731 shows that by then most of the students paid their college bills in cash. However, some did pay in food or other commodities. The amounts allowed indicate that on some articles prices are up since the earlier century, but on others they have fallen. For wheat the Steward allowed:

| | |
|---|---|
| 1705 (winter wheat) | 4*s.* |
| 1705, October | 4*s.* 3*d.* |
| 1706, July | 7*s.* |
| December | 5*s.* |
| 1707, December | 6*s.* |
| 1709, February | 6½*s.* |
| 1711, April | 6*s.* |
| 1712, April | 5½*s.* |
| 1713, December | 8*s.* |
| 1716, October | 5*s.* |

A cow in July 1706 credited a student only £1 11*s.* 8*d.*; had prices fallen so much, or was she a very ancient cow? In November 1706 Indian meal brings 2*s.* 6*d.*, in September and December 1708 3*s.*, 4*s.* in January 1715, but still 3*s.* in February 1716. Meat seems to be down: beef in January 1706 brings 2½*d.* a pound, and pork in January 1718 3½*d.* (Beef was 3½*d.* in 1650 to 1660, pork 4*d.*, as quoted by Steward Chesholme.) Of course all these prices vary according to whether delivery is in Cambridge, at the mill, or "at his father's warehouse," and vary considerably with the month of the receipt.

This roster of prices is not significant in any exact sense, but it does show us that so far as money values go, food prices have not fluctuated wildly over the century. Such fluctuations as there have been were no doubt important to the Steward who was working on a narrow margin of profit, but for our purposes in trying to establish comparative costs we can only consider that prices were relatively stable with the possible exception of the last ten years from 1705 to 1715.

*Wages and Salaries*

The scarcity of labor in the Colonies was a factor in promoting immigration, for in early Massachusetts Bay wages in equivalent money were 25 per cent to 50 per cent higher than they were in England.[44] A man could get his passage to New England for from £6 to £10 and then shortly earn enough to work for himself here; or, lacking the passage-money, many an Englishman of good stock had his fare paid in exchange for working as an indentured servant for from three to seven years.[45]

A continuous picture of wages is given by quotations brought together in Table 6 by Miss Ruth Crandall from various town histories and records.

*Table 6. Wages for One Day's Work*

| Year | Wage s. | Wage d. | Type of work | | Place |
|---|---|---|---|---|---|
| 1641 | 1 | 8 | summer | highways | Ipswich |
| | 1 | 3 | winter | | |
| | 6 | 8 | summer | a team | Ipswich |
| | 5 | | winter | | |
| | 6 | 8 | summer | a cart, | Hampton |
| | 5 | | winter | 4 oxen, 1 man | |
| 1650 | 2 | 3 | one day going to Salem | | Rowley |
| 1655 | 3 | | penalty (that is, 2 × the regular wage?) failing to work on fort | | Salem |
| 1663 | 6 | 10 | | carting | Boston |
| | 7 | | | | |
| 1670 | 1 | 6 | | | Dorchester |
| 1678 | 2 | | January | raising town house | Springfield |
| 1679 | 5 | | January | 1 team | Springfield |
| | 2 | 6 | | to build fence | Topsfield |
| 1681 | 2 | 6 | | | Springfield |
| | 2 | | | | |
| 1682 | 2 | 6 | | man | |
| | 6 | | | man and team | Topsfield |
| 1684 | 2 | 6 | one day getting copy of will | | Salem |
| 1684 | 2 to | | | | |
| | 2 | 6 | | | Hadley |
| 1683–1686 | 2 | | | highway labor | Salem |
| 1688–1694 | 2 | | | highway labor | Salem |

*Source:* Made by Miss Ruth Crandall from various town histories.

There are few quotations of salaries available for the seventeenth century, largely because there were few salaried positions. Doctors and lawyers were not ranked very high in New England, and teaching "was not exactly a profession."[46] College teachers were usually clerically trained, but the grammar school masters often had less education. The schoolmaster of Dedham received £20 a year in the 1640's; his salary was raised in 1695 to £25. Cambridge in 1648 paid £10, probably plus fees, and Watertown in 1651 paid £30, raising it in 1715 to £36. The Latin School master of Boston received £20 in 1684; he had nine pupils.[47]

The Boston Town Records sometimes give schoolmasters' pay: for example, Mr. Woodmansey received £50 in 1650 to 1651, and Mr. Hincheman had £40 to assist Mr. Woodmansey in 1666 to 1667. In 1684, for a year's work, John Cole was paid £10 in money and £20 in country pay. In 1700 to 1701 Mr. Henchman had £40.[48] The trouble with these figures, as with any salary figures for this period, is that we do not know how many extras there may have been, such as fees from students, food and lodging, and country pay. Moreover, some of these were part-time jobs, and even the ministers and teachers were almost always part-time farmers as well.

By about 1643 ministers' salaries ranged apparently from £30 to £90, with Mr. Symmes of Charlestown and Mr. Cotton of Boston getting the most, the three next £80, five others £70, six others £60, and so on down, the pastor at Reading receiving the least — £30.[49]

Winthrop comments upon the employment situation: "The scarcity of good ministers in England, and want of employment for our new graduates here, occasioned some of them to look abroad. Three honest young men, good scholars, and very hopeful . . ." had gone, Higginson to England and then the East Indies, Buckley to England, George Downing to the West Indies.[50] The Reverend Mr. Mitchell said, "Most men, even of the Richer sort doe chuse to put their children to more advantageous Imployments."[51] An interest in going into trade, plus a lessening fervor for the strict Puritan faith, showed up also in the common and grammar schools, where numbers of pupils fell off.[52]

A class of salary which was subject to more than ordinary variation, particularly in the later years of the century, was the compensation allowed the governor, which often changed with the temper of a not always friendly legislature. Winthrop was to get £100 to £150 a year,[53] but in 1641, when Bellingham was elected governor, the former order for £100 a year was repealed, Savage thinks, because "the court was less friendly than the people to Bellingham,"[54] but it may well have been that the Treasurer lacked the £100. The governor's allowance (sometimes they were careful not to call it salary) became a subject of great controversy when after 1686 this position was filled by royal appointees. Governor Phips received £500 a year for 1692 to 1694; Lieutenant-Governor Stoughton had amounts of £200, £300, £250, £300 from 1695 to 1698. In 1699 Bellomont was paid £1000, and again in 1700. Stoughton as the substitute once more in 1701 was paid £200. Dudley averaged £500 over his several years in office.[55]

Earning power in England was not very different: In 1688, "of shopkeepers, artisans, farmers, freeholders, clergymen, army and naval officers, . . . all fall below £100" a year. The annual income of laborers in London was £25 in 1700.[56]

### *Cost of Living*[57]

We wonder, "What would salaries buy?"

It is obvious that both faculty and students at Harvard lived on a scale above that of the ordinary man, who used few manufactured goods, wore homespun or leather, and in good weather often went barefoot (as did his wife). For purposes of illustration in Table 7 we shall assume that the Harvard President had an earned cash income of about £150, as was the case for most full-time Presidents after 1672; the College provided his house, a good one, worth perhaps £300 and usually large enough to rent a few rooms to students; he had little land — not even enough to keep a cow, according to President Chauncy[58] — and had to buy most things used by his often large family. The President's sons fortunately had scholarships for their college fees, and they lived at home.

We shall assume further that the Resident Fellows earned around £75 a year. Each Fellow was provided with a chamber and a study (and a wine cellar), but sometimes students slept in the room with him. He had to pay for his meals at the College Commons. Fellows were required to live at the College and to be unmarried.

A skilled laborer of this period may have earned 2*s*. 6*d*. a day (perhaps £37 a year if he worked six days a week, which was unlikely), and an ordinary laborer 1*s*. 9*d*. a day (£25 a year for full time work by the day).

Table 7 shows some things which might have been bought with these incomes.

Clearly the man with a large family had a hard time. Servants, if they could be found, were fairly cheap to hire, but expensive

*Table 7. The Purchasing Power of Salaries*

| President: £150 a year | | | Fellow: £75 a year | | | Laborer: £25 a year | | |
|---|---|---|---|---|---|---|---|---|
| | £ | *s.* | | £ | *s.* | | £ | *s.* |
| | | | *Regular Items* | | | | | |
| Feed family of 6[a] @ £9 | 54 | | Food | 12 | | Feed family of 6[a,b] | 13 | |
| 2 maid servants @ £4 | 8 | | Wine ¼ butt | 4 | | | | |
| 1 man servant @ £10 | 10 | | Cord of wood | | 1½ | | | |
| Feed 4 servants @ £9 | 36 | | 5 pounds tobacco | 1 | 5 | | | |
| Maintenance of horse | 12 | | | | | | | |
| | | | *Occasional Items* | | | | | |
| Horse | 9 | | 10 dinners in town | | 15 | A house[c] — value | 40 | |
| Saddle | 3 | 12 | | | | Cow | 5 | |
| 2 pigs | 2 | | | | | Ox | 6 | |
| | | | | | | 2 sheep | 3 | |
| | | | | | | 2 pigs | 2 | |
| Clothing: | | | | | | | | |
| Dress | 1 | 10 | | | | Man's shoes | | 4 |
| Suit | 3 | | Suit (one in 10 years) | 3 | | Child's shoes | | 2½ |
| Coat | 2 | | | | | | | |
| Pair boots | | 16 | Pair boots | | 16 | | | |
| Hat | | 5 | Hat | | 5 | | | |
| Furniture: | | | | | | | | |
| Bedstead | | 5 | | | | Ropes & mattress | 1 | |
| Featherbed and bolster | 3 | | | | | | | |
| Trundle bed, ropes and mattress | 1 | 10 | | | | | | |
| Chest drawers | 2 | | | | | | | |
| A good table | 2 | | Plank table | | 10 | Plank table | | 10 |
| 2 chairs | | 15 | 2 chairs | | 10 | | | |
| Clock | 1 | | | | | | | |
| Equipment: | | | | | | | | |
| Musket | 1 | 10 | Razor | 1 | | Musket | 1 | |
| ½ barrel powder | 2 | | | | | Barrel powder | 4 | |
| Axe | | 2½ | | | | Plough | | 6 |
| Scythe | | 2 | | | | Scythe (old) | | 1 |
| Spinning wheel | | 2 | | | | Spinning wheel | | 2 |
| Pair sheets | | 9 | | | | | | |
| 12 napkins | | 10 | | | | | | |
| Quilt | 1 | 6 | | | | | | |
| 10 books | 5 | | 10 books | 5 | | | | |
| 100 sheets paper | | 2 | 100 sheets paper | | 2 | | | |

*Source:* A composite from various sources including Weeden; Shannon, pp. 81–87; Winthrop II Appendix, 1826 ed., 376–379; the Steward's books. For Harvard salaries, see Chapter VII below.

[a] Families were usually larger than this.

[b] Grows ¾ of food.

[c] Partly built by self.

to feed; however, since most things used were made or grown at home, extra hands were necessary. The resident Fellow was not so badly off financially — since he had no family* — but if he wanted to buy books he could soon use up his money, and perhaps he had in mind getting a few household articles to use when he left the College and was ordained in a church. The laboring man could progress if he worked hard both for pay and at home; it was extremely difficult for him to find £10 or so a year to send a son to College, though this amount assumed that the son helped himself with jobs and scholarships.

In an attempt to evaluate all such figures, economic statisticians today construct a cost of living index which tries to show how our prices vary from one year to the next. A basic concept of such an index is the "market-basket": the statistician chooses a representative basket of goods, including, in 1962, an automobile, some food, clothing, a washing-machine, and so on. He then determines how the prices of this market-basket change from year to year. This is a satisfactory device over short periods, when there is some consistency in the content of the basket and the quality of the goods. But how do we compare the twentieth-century with the seventeenth-century market-basket of the Harvard parent? Our ancestor needed, among other things, clothing (most of which he grew, and his family spun and sewed), food (almost entirely grown in the back yard or on the farm), a horse, and a good musket for hunting and protection. Obviously we are in trouble.

Thus if we try to find a figure by which to multiply seventeenth-century pounds to get 1962 dollars, or vice-versa, we must vary the multiplier with the products being purchased, for the relative demand has changed. Table 8 gives some examples.

Relative real value may be compared by comparing the "Historic Multipliers" in Table 8. This avoids evaluating currencies or quoting price changes. For example, 100 bushels of wheat in the seventeenth century bought 5/12 of a small house; in 1962 that much wheat is worth 1/36 of a small house. Thus 100 bushels of wheat bought 15 times as much house then as now. Similarly, 100 bushels of wheat then bought 5 times as much food at college,

* It might seem that present low faculty salaries are a holdover from the days of semiclerical university teachers.

*Table 8. Relative Approximate Costs, Seventeenth Century and 1962*

| | 17th century | 1962[a] | Historic multiplier[b] |
|---|---|---|---|
| 100 bushels wheat | £ 25 | $ 250 | × 10 |
| Small house | 60 | 9 000 | × 150 |
| Medium-sized house | 300 | 45 000 | × 150 |
| 4 pairs shoes | 1 | 64 | × 64 |
| 2 average books | 1 | 10 | × 10 |
| Horse (second-hand car) | 10 | 1 000 | × 100 |
| Annual charge for food at college | 10 | 500 | × 50 |
| Annual tuition fee | 2 | 1 250 | × 625 |
| Presidents' salary (gross of taxes) | 150 | 20 000 | × 133 |
| Faculty salary (gross of taxes), lower ranks | 75 | 7 500 | × 100 |
| Laborer's wages (gross of taxes) | 25 | 5 000 | × 200 |

[a] I make no attempt to justify the costs chosen here. Any criticism of 1962 prices could also be applied to those of the seventeenth century. Seventeenth century *descriptions* and prices were the starting point, and I attempted to choose 1962 prices at a comparable point in the scale of size and value.

[b] NOTICE that this is *not* the amount by which prices have risen. Making such a figure would require converting the money, which involves more complications. Clearly one cannot compare pounds and dollars; the object of this table, as the text amplifies, is to show the *relative proportions* of changes in prices.

62½ times as much college tuition, as now. In other words, the purchasing power of wheat as money (and it was often used as money) was then 15 times what it is now in housing, 5 times now in food, and 62½ times now in tuition (the ratios of the "Historic Multipliers"). So we see that in those days the relative value of food was high, housing was next, tuition least. Tuition was cheap; food, books, shoes were expensive in the seventeenth century compared with the twentieth century.

*Real Estate Values*

We also need a concept of the value of Harvard buildings. In 1638 a house and lot and six acres of arable land and five acres of meadow was sold to a "gentleman" for £10, and a dwelling-house and garden of a cooper in Boston for £28 sterling. In the same year "a mansion and parts of an old house" brought £200 sterling. In 1639 a leading citizen sold the house next to the governor's, with garden, orchard, sundry lands, including 500 acres at Mt. Wollaston, all for £1300 sterling, a very large sum.[59] In 1641 there was built in Boston for £21 a house "16 foot long and 14 foot wide, with a chamber floare finished summer and joists, a cellar floare with joists finished, the roofe and walles

Clapboarded on the outsyde, the Chimney framed without dawbing, to be done with hewan timber." In 1656 a house in Essex County, "38 x 17 and 11 foot stud," clapboarded, with three chimneys, was valued at £45 in corn and cattle.[60]

Weeden says that in the 1650's in country areas there still were log huts and sunken pits lined with boards and roofed over, but in the towns wealthy people were building some larger houses with four or more rooms on the first floor and the second floor finished. Many homes now had carpets and curtains.[61]

In the Suffolk Deeds and in some lists made by Miss Crandall, real estate transactions of from £200 to £400 were common by 1685, and they go up to £1000 or £1500 occasionally. A few transfers are shown which involve friends of the College: one for £2000 by Sewall in 1685, and in 1689 a £3000 sale by Francis Foxcroft. In 1685 William Brown, Jr. of Salem bought a house for £500. When later we see that he and members of his family gave £100 to Harvard on several occasions, we realize that such a gift from them was a notable amount. We find that in 1688 the Newdigate farm at Rumney Marsh, which was subject to an annuity of £5 forever to Harvard College, was sold for £350 to Mr. Shrimpton, who thereafter paid the £5 to the College. In 1693, the year he became Treasurer, Thomas Brattle sold a house and land for £550 (see note 35 to this chapter).

Some concept of the consequence of the first Harvard College building may be had from the following from Winthrop in 1632: "The congregation of Boston and Charlestown began the meeting-house at Boston, for which, and Mr. Wilson's house, they had made a voluntary contribution of about one hundred and twenty pounds."[62] Then in 1641 the new meeting-house in Boston cost about £1000, which despite the depression was "raised out of the weekly voluntary contribution without any noise or complaint, when in some other churches which did it by way of rates, there was much difficulty and compulsion by levies to raise a far less sum."[63]

## SCALES OF OPERATION

We may then ask, "What was large money?" When we say that the original Court grant of £400 to the College was equal to about half the total annual budget of the Colony government, it appears that the College started off with a large sum of money. This impression is dissipated when we realize that considerably more than the £400 was spent for the first building built expressly for the College, and it probably cost less than the £1000 spent on the 1641 Boston meeting-house.

For comparison — another project which required capital was the Iron Works, granted in 1643 at first to John Winthrop, Jr., and his partners. The Colony records of May 1645 reported that these men had "already disbursed between 1200 and 1500 pounds," and that "there will be need of some 1500 [additional] pounds to finish the forge, etc., which will be accepted in money, beaver, wheat, coal, or any such commodities as will satisfy the workmen."*

By the end of the century individuals were putting through transactions involving £1000 or £2000, not commonly, but occasionally. Thus, consideration of other outlays tends to confirm that £1000 for a Harvard building or, later in the century, £2000 in assets were considerable though not extraordinary sums for the Colony. Compared with items of the British economy, however, they were exceedingly small.

A few representative figures from England show that men of the seventeenth century there did sometimes think in terms of millions, if not the 1962 billions. Scott gives several miscellaneous pieces of information: Up to the year 1624 the First Virginia Plantation Company had laid out £200,000, the New England Council, the New Plymouth Adventurers, and the other plantation companies a total of £25,000. "In 1634 the capital employed in the Newfoundland fishing was close on £300,000." Scott says Sir William Petty estimated the national wealth of Great Britain at £250 million and the national income at £40 million about 1664, and that King gave figures not far from this (£320 million and £43.4 million) for 1688. The foreign trade of the City of London in 1663 was £2,022,812 4*s*. in exports and £4,016,019 18*s*. in imports. This was about 28 per cent of the foreign trade for all of England. In 1663 a water system put into the City of London required a capital outlay of £300,000. "For 1654 the actual cost of the Navy was

* The Court recommended that people subscribe to this useful venture. *Mass. Bay Recs.* II, 103–104.

£1,159,382 18*s.* 9*d.*" The Navy during the Dutch War and other operations in 1664–1666 cost £3,200,000.[64] We may add that the Bank of England was first incorporated in 1694 with £1,200,000,[65] and that in ten counties of England, including London, there was by 1660 over £2,500,000 in capital assets under trusteeship for charitable purposes.[66]

We can only wish that more of the English money had come the way of the Colonies and perhaps of the infant Harvard College.

### NOTE TO CHAPTER III — CHANGE IN MONEY

### 1699–1711

See Table 3, Columns (4) and (5)

*17 dwt. taken for granted, 6s. per piece.**

Richards' regular procedure and Brattle's during the first years of his Treasurership was to record transactions with no mention of the kind of money involved except to differentiate sometimes between country pay and "money." In January 1699 Brattle records a transaction of 12*s.* involving two pieces of eight, with no mention of the weight of the coins. (Brattle, page 55.)

*Gain by trade of heavy for light.*

In 1703 he tells of the receipt of pieces of eight for Captain Richard Sprague's bequest of £400. In January 1704 he records receiving lighter pieces of 8/8 for 372 pieces of Capt. Sprague's, with a resulting gain of £12 10*s.* (page 80). Seven months later (page 82) he does the same with some more of them: "Received for the Exchange of 461$\frac{1}{3}$ pieces of 8/8, 393 ounces of Capt. Sprague's, for so many light [pieces], 347 ounces, £14 8*s.*" His 1703 books had already listed receipt of the £400; this additional entry is paper profit which was credited to Stock.

* Topics at the side give a reason for including the quotations that follow, but there are other characteristics worth noticing.

*Contract by weight and value per piece.*

In February 1704 we find (page 81), "£36 lent to Robins on mortgage to pay in 1 year in good pieces of 8/8 weighing full 17 dwt., each piece at 6*s.* per piece, as every piece of the 120 now paid him by me did, or rather better."

*7½s. per ounce, contract by total weight, 16 dwt.*

On March 20, 1704, a Mr. Angier promises to pay Brattle (page 81) "£51, that is to say 170 pieces of 8/8 weighing in the whole full 136 ounces."

*Receipt at 8s. per ounce; gain.*

October 1705 pieces of 8/8 are accepted from Mr. Green "at 8*s.* per ounce." (page 86). On the same page, "8½ ounces pieces of 8/8 is £3 8*s.*," and is in payment of only £3 due.*

*Bills and coin. 17 dwt. still around. Gain on heavy coin.*

On June 27, 1705, the Treasurer received £58 13*s.* 6*d.*, "whereof £50 was paid in 17 dwt. and Bills, and the rest in 15 dwt." Shortly there is another entry concerning this transaction: "Memorandum: 110½ ounces mony at 8*s.* per ounce with £19 13*s.* in Bills comes to £63 17*s.*, the difference betwixt which and £58 13*s.* 6*d.* is £5 3*s.* 6*d.*," which is again paper profit and taken to Stock (page 85).

*Penalty for underweight. "Profit" 1/15.*

May 13, 1706 (page 88): "Received 4 months Interest of £50 should be 16 dwt. 20*s.*, is at 15 dwt. £1 1*s.* 4*d.*," means that 20*s.* was due for four months interest of £50, but it was paid in 15 dwt. when it was supposed to have been in 16 dwt., so £1 1*s.* 4*d.* is received instead of £1. This amount of £1 1*s.* 4*d.* and multiples of it become so common an entry that Brattle soon ceases to explain it.**

* See Table 3 (1705 to 1710). 8½oz. × 8*s.* per oz. = 68*s.* = £3 8*s.*

** The calculation is a simple proportion:

$$\frac{1}{x} = \frac{15}{16} \qquad 15x = 16 \qquad x = £1\tfrac{1}{15} \qquad \text{or} \qquad £1\ 1s.\ 4d.$$

Brattle, 90, September 1706, shows £1 1*s.* 4*d.* taken in for £1 (15 dwt. for 16 dwt.) without explanation.

*Penalty for underweight, but no profit noted as such.*

In August 1706 (page 89) £113 1*s.* 4*d.* is received in 15 dwt. instead of £100 plus its interest of £6 which were due in 16 dwt. — paper profit again. This time he just receives the £113 1*s.* 4*d.* on the books without the entry showing the "profit." Should he have entered just the £106 in his Cash account and put the extra in Stock, or is it more realistic to let the money increase in amount in the working account as it goes down in value?

*Penalty 2/15.*

December 2, 1706 (page 91), there is an entry of the receipt from Colonel Josiah Quinsy of "£24 7*s.* 4*d.* 15 dwt. received of him in full of his bond, vizt of £20 principall and 30*s.* for 1¼ year's Interest to the 1st instant, at 17 dwt." This represents an increase of 2/15 of £21 10*s.* for the difference between 15 and 17 dwt.

*Contract at 8s. per ounce.*

The next entry shows that immediately there was £40 15 dwt. lent Quinsey for which he agreed to pay "£42 8*s.* in pieces of 8/8 at the rate of 8*s.* per ounce" at the end of one year — 6 per cent interest. This defines one shilling as ⅛ ounce and really protects the lender.

*8s. per ounce total weight N.E. money.*

On October 4, 1708, Brattle received 165 ounces N.E. money at 8*s.* per ounce, for a value of £66: 165 times 8 gives 1320*s.*, which divided by 20 is £66, however many coins are involved.

*2/15 on old bond.*

October 26, 1708 (page 97), the difference between £15 at 17 dwt. and at 15 dwt., that is £2, is charged Matthew Bridge when he pays his old bond in "cash," no doubt in the light coin. Bridge's bond showed already on the books as taken over from Richards in April 1693.[67] One is pleased at Brattle's being able to extract this difference on old bonds; new ones were written to provide for the difference, but some of the old bonds go back to days before the worst of this complication had arisen. Perhaps it was worded, as was the William Smith deed now in the Archives dated 1687, "in like currant money of N.E."

*Alternate: Bills or coin.*

January or February 1709 (page 99) sees 15 dwt. still coming in for 17 dwt. April 28, 1709 (page 101), however, shows Brattle taking a "bond to pay £63 12*s*. in silver mony at 8*s*. per ounce, or in Bills which of the two I shall choose," which is cautious on his part, but two pages later he lends £36 to be repaid "in Province Bills" in one year — with no alternate. The one-year contract may make this safe enough, but it would be risky if the bond strung along from year to year, as was often the case; very likely Brattle would not have allowed the renewal if the terms no longer pleased him.

*Bills only.*

*Bills.*

From February 1711 (page 109) on we find more received "in bills" than previously.

Our heart warms to Mr. Brattle when we read on page 111 that when the Widow Jackson arranged for final payment on the 17 dwt. mortgage she and her husband John had given as security for a loan originally made by Treasurer Richards, Brattle sent back to her 57*s*. representing her payment of the difference between 15 and 17 dwt., "which if I had received of her I should have accepted at 15 dwt., she being very poor and low."[68]

# IV

## INCOME FROM STUDENTS

THE work which "fell upon" Dunster when he accepted the Presidency of Harvard College included setting up all the regulations and financial arrangements for the students, of whom there were from 10 to 40 in College at any one time.* These arrangements he based in general upon the organization of the English colleges.

The amount of the College's expenditures in the seventeenth century, as now, were to a large extent determined by the amount of current receipts. And receipts, even more in the beginning than now, came in large part from students. Students now face a fairly simple system of charges, but then each Harvard man found a long list of items on his "quarter bill."[1] Table 9 gives an outline of the various costs involved in acquiring an education at Harvard in the Puritan Period. We shall discuss in detail the material summarized in the table. Many of these charges appear on the Quarter Bill shown in Plate 5.

### QUARTERLY CHARGES TO THE STUDENT

*Tuition.* The most obvious regular quarterly charge, though not by any means the largest, is tuition, which the records tell us was 6*s.* 8*d.* a quarter (£1 6*s.* 8*d.* a year) in 1650. When in 1652 the Massachusetts mint was authorized to turn out pine-tree shillings with silver content below that of the current English shilling, there appears to have been an inflation in prices which just about offset the debasement of the coinage. The subject of exactly what happened to prices at that time needs much more study, but we know that in the period from June to December 1653 the Harvard tuition was raised to 8*s.* a quarter. This was an increase by almost

* In this book we shall touch only briefly on the life at College. For more details, see Samuel Eliot Morison, *The Founding of Harvard College* (Cambridge, 1935) and *Harvard College in the Seventeenth Century* (Cambridge, 1936).

*Table 9. Cost per Person of an Undergraduate Education at Harvard in the Puritan Period (New England Pounds)*

| | Approximate quarterly fees and charges* | | | Average *annual* payment per student enrolled* 1687–1712 |
|---|---|---|---|---|
| | 1650–1652[a] | 1655–1659 (probably 1655–1686) | 1687–1712 | |
| *Regular fees each quarter* | | | | |
| Tuition | 6s. 8d. | 8s. | 10s. | £1 14s. |
| Detriments — if nonresident | [5s.] | [5s.] | [5s.] | [6s.] |
| Study rent — all residents | (£2 3s. cost)[b] plus 1s. 5d. | av. 4½s. | flat 5s. | 16s. |
| Cellar rent — all residents | 0 | 0 | 9d. to 18d. | 1s. |
| Sweeper — all residents | 1s. | 1½s. | 2 to 2½s. | 6s. |
| *Charges per quarter* (vary with individual) | | | | |
| Commons & Sizings — all students[c] | £2 | £2 10s. | £2 15s. | £6 5s. |
| Punishments — all students | 5s. to 2d. | 5s. to 2d. | 5s. to 2d. | 2s. |
| Glass-mending — residents | 1s. | 1s. | 0 to 7s. | 2s. |
| Monitor | — | — | 4d. to 7d. | 2s. |
| *Charges other than quarterly-per quarter*[d] | | | | |
| Wood & candles — all students | 6d. | 6d. | 3d. | 5d. |
| Gallery money — freshmen | (15s. cost)[b] plus 3d. | 2½d. | 2½d.[e] | 1s. |
| Commencement Fee — A.B.'s at £3[f] | 5s. | 3s. 9d. | 3s. 9d. | 15s. |
| *Quarterly total*[d] — residents | £2 16s. 10d. | £3 10s. 9d. | £4 10d. | |
| *Annual total*[d] — residents (quarterly × 4) | £11 7s. | £14 3s. | £16 3s. | £10 4s. |
| *A.B. total* — residents (annual × 3 or 4) | £34[a] | £57 | £65 | £40 16s. |

*Source:* Quarter-Bill Books, Harvard University Archives.

* *NOTE:* "Fees and charges" are the amount the College charged a student who was fully active (or, in case of detriments, entirely absent) during a quarter. "Average annual payment," in the last column, is the average of actual payments of all registered students; it is a smaller amount than four times the fees because not all students were fully active all quarters. Detriments are of course not paid if the other fees are.

[a] Three-year course.

[b] Money in parentheses was returned on graduation.

[c] Price of parts was 1½d. (bevers ½d.), 2¼d., and 2¼d. to 3d., respectively.

[d] Irregularly imposed fees are split into quarters or years.

[e] Raised to 4½d. in 1708.

[f] In addition there were tips of from 5s. to 15s.

the same percentage as the silver content of the New England shilling had gone down.

In 1686 the President of the Province of New England and his Council, who were temporarily in charge of the College, raised the tuition rate from 8*s.* to 10*s.* a quarter, which continued to be the rate through at least 1715. There were thus two periods of thirty years each without a tuition change.

Not all students paid the same amount of tuition, for some of the more wealthy students enrolled as "fellow-commoners." We know of thirteen of these before 1715. Each fellow-commoner was expected to present the College with a piece of silver plate and probably to pay double tuition.

Another variation on the standard tuition charge occurred when a student "discontinued," that is, left town and did not attend classes but wished to maintain his place in his class. In this case he was charged "half-tuition."

*Commons and Sizings.* For his food a student paid perhaps five times his tuition, and this was the largest charge to which students were subjected. The Steward's department provided dinner and supper, when food was called "commons," and, in the morning and at tea time, two other meals called bevers, when "sizings" were served (mainly bread and beer, and later cider). The standard charge for the beer and bread for sizings was in 1650 to 1660 about a halfpenny each serving; the "price of parts," that is the cost of one meal in commons for one person, was in Dunster's time apparently a penny and a half. The price of parts was raised in 1654 to twopence farthing (2¼*d.*). This was the usual rate until the 1690's when the rate went up as high as 3*d.* a part, then returned to 2*d.* 1*f.* in 1699, only to start up again in 1707 as the inflation got under way.*

Thus the student paid according to what he ate. The Butler (a student) kept track of those present at each meal, and totaled his accounts periodically. The Butler reported to the Steward, who in turn made up each student's quarter bill, and from this the whole College's Quarter Bill. Then the Steward turned over the net gain or loss to the Treasurer. The average individual's quarter bill for commons and sizings and food "extras" for 1650 to 1660

* See Table 5, page 51.

was in the neighborhood of two to two and a half pounds, making the annual charge for a student in full-time residence around ten pounds a year. Some students managed on less than two pounds a quarter, and a few had appetite and means to dispose of over four pounds' worth of the Steward's wares each quarter.

In 1687 the student's quarter bill for commons and sizings was just about the same as it had been in the late 1650's; up to 1694 the bills seldom went above three pounds, or four pounds thereafter. A few resident students had board bills of less than a pound a quarter, a fourth of what their richer friends ate. When the price of parts went up, the annual tariff reached, by 1715, the neighborhood of fifteen or sixteen pounds a student. Thus the charge for food might have been between £8 and £16 a year at any time during our period.

A graph of the Steward's receipts from commons and sizings each *quarter* from 1687 on shows that the pattern is irregular, but there was a definite tendency for the scholars to take a vacation the first quarter (at this time July, August, and part of September). No doubt the young men were needed at home. There was for a short time an inclination to take a winter vacation also, during the third quarter. Therefore when we quote the amount of the College quarterly charge it does not show us what the average student actually paid. To get the actual average payment for a year we must include the quarters when the student was not there. That annual figure is the one in the last column of Table 9 and usually is less than four times the quarterly figure. The average annual cost of food actually consumed in 1687 to 1712 was £6 5*s*., not the £11 (£2 15*s*. times 4) we should infer if all four quarters were involved.

*Detriments*. When the student chose not to live in a College house for all or part of a quarter, in addition to the half-tuition he paid if he was not attending classes, he was subject to a charge at the rate of five shillings a quarter, called "detriments." The charge of detriments was made so that the students would share in expenses which went on whether or not they were present, as well as to deter them from boarding out around town. This problem was especially severe in the late fifties and sixties, and many detriments were paid in the eighties; but by the new century most students were in residence again. Only five paid detriments in June 1717. The candidates for the A.M. degree were frequently away for the whole three years of their candidacy, and the detriments for that period, at 5*s*. a quarter, totaled three pounds. (Bachelors who were seriously inclined to go into the ministry usually took the A.M. three years after the A.B., though they seldom stayed in residence all that time.) After 1693 the Corporation relented and gave absent Master's candidates a bargain rate of one pound to cover the three years' detriments.

*Rents.* When Mr. Dunster took over the running of the College he found, as we have seen, a partly finished college building. His method of putting the building into use was to charge each of the first students the cost of finishing his own study. In the pages of the early College records we see, for example, that Mr. Richard Harris (Governor Winthrop's brother-in-law) had a room "sieled with Cedar round about." He paid £1 11*s*. for half the costs of the chimney, 6*s*. 8*d*. for glass and casements, £1 15*s*. for "Boarding round about with all appurtenances of workmanship, nailes, etc." The total charge was £5 19*s*. 11*d*.; his was the most expensive of all the studies, which more often cost only two or three pounds.[2] In addition to this purchase price, there was a small quarterly rent charge.[3]

When a scholar graduated he left his study with his successor, who paid the original owner approximately the cost of construction. The second owner recouped his expense when he in turn left college. This system was gradually changed: In the 1650's the College bought out most of the studies and thereafter charged higher rents.[4] The quarterly rents in effect in 1651 or 1652 averaged 1*s*. 5*d*. (in addition to the original one-time, refundable cost), but when the College bought the studies they raised rents to an average of around 4*s*. 6*d*., with variations depending upon location. Sometime in mid-century a uniform rate seems to have been established, for the Quarter-Bill Book shows that all residents paid 5*s*. a quarter from 1687 to 1720.

Another small expense was first incurred when the newly built Stoughton College in 1700 offered cellars for the storage of the students' wine. The quarterly rental was $1\frac{1}{2}$*s*.

"Bed-making" was an amenity which in 1654 automatically

cost a student a shilling each quarter; when the rates went up in 1655 the charge was 1½*s.* Toward the end of the century, bed-making as a separate charge had disappeared from the accounts, but a "sweep" had turned up there. March 1678 found the Corporation ordering that "Goodman Brown shall have for his service in the Colledge two shillings per quarter from every schollar particularly that holds a study in the Colledge."[5] In 1696 this changed to 2½*s.*

*Monitor.* Every quarter each undergraduate "whose name was in the Buttery" had to pay the College Monitor. This officer was a student "that shall observe them that are fayling eyther by absence from prayers or Sermons, or come tardy to the same . . . ."[6] The Monitor received £3 a year, which was "set upon the heads" of the students concerned, that is, distributed (usually evenly) among those in the Buttery. This cost the students from 3*d.* to 7*d.* quarterly, depending upon the number of students enrolled at the time.

*Fines.* Fines at early Harvard have been well publicized. There was a miscellaneous assortment of possible monetary fines or punishments which added noticeably to the College's income and quite regularly to the student's expense. Financial punishment (somewhat as today) was the first and mildest disciplinary means; more severe misdemeanors were taken care of by admonitions (private, then public), by sentence of sitting alone in commons uncovered, by lowering the rank in the permanent class order of academic seniority, and finally by suspension or expulsion from College.

The tale of a really heinous offense in 1666 was recorded by President Chauncy:

> Mason, Hubbard junior, and Winthrop junior (according to the counsell of the Reverend Elders) were expelled out of the Colledge, and their names cut out of the tables in the buttry by the order of the Praesident in the presence of all the fellowes, for their disorder and injurious cariage towards Andrew Belcher in killing, and having stolne ropes in hanging Goodman Sell's dogge upon the sign post in the night, which fact was deliberately confessed by one of thes delinquents before the corporation, with the reason moving thereunto. . . . Besides two of them afterwards corrupted, and seduced the confessor to unsay his confession;

and many grosse lyes were told by all, and especially and especially [*sic*] by one of them; and ther were many circumstances and probabilityes attesting ther guiltinesse of thes crimes.[7]

The tremendous fine of twenty shillings for having plum cake in their rooms is often cited. Three pence was charged "if any Schollar or Schollars at any time take away or detain any vessel of the Colledges great or smal from the Hal out of the doores from the sight of the Buttery hatch without the Butler's or Servitor's knowledge. . . ." Students were forbidden to go unaccompanied into the butteries or kitchen, "And if any shall praesume to thrust in they shall have three pence on their heads, But if praesumptuously and continually they shall so dare to offend, they shall bee lyable to an admonition and to other proceedings of the Colledge Discipline at the Discretion of the Praesident."[8]

Apparently there was occasional neglect of studies, for the College Orders of 1660 proclaim:

> Whereas uncomfortable experience hath shewed that notwithstanding former Laws and provisions for Colledge Exercises (viz Common places, Disputes and Declamations) [they] have been too much neglected or slightly performed even by senior Schollars who should be exemplary to others. It is therefore ordered, that the President shall have full powr to impose a fine in a way of penalty upon any negligent person according to his discretion, provided it exceed not five shillings for one Offence.[9]

Compared with these serious offenses — punishable by fines, respectively, of 20*s*., 3*d*., "not over 5*s*." — punishment for absence from prayers (on which part of the Puritan reputation is based) amounted to a fine of a mere one penny.[10] Whether or not this form of punishment brought about an improvement in the behavior of the young gentlemen Scholars appears doubtful from the recurrence of fines on their quarter bills quarter after quarter. At the least, however, it made a very pleasant addition to the College's income.

*Glass-mending.* A charge for glass-mending averaged in Dunster's time perhaps a shilling a quarter for each student in residence, later in some cases more than this amount; for some quarters every undergraduate had such a charge. The money was turned over to the College glazier for repairing glass presumably in the students' study windows.*

ANNUAL OR ONE-TIME CHARGES TO THE STUDENT

We have mentioned the usual quarterly charges. There were also charges levied irregularly as incurred, or in some cases annually or before commencement.

Probably Dunster would like to have instituted the English system of "Caution Money," but this measure for the security of the exchequer was not required until the College Laws of 1655. Caution Money was an admission bond or an advance deposit:

> For the removeall of those many distractions and great burthens of Labour Care and Cost that heretofore have pressed the Steward, and the great debts that hitherto sundry have runne into, and unsuitable pay whereby the House hath been disappointed of suitable provision, occasioning offensive Complaints, It is therefore provided
>
> That before the admission of any Scholler, his Parents or Freinds shall both lay downe one quarter expences, and also give the Colledge Steward security for the Future, and without this ingagement noe Scholler shall be admitted into the Colledge.
>
> . . .
>
> That whosoever is indebted to the Colledge at the end of any Quarter . . . in case that the Bill be not payd within a month hee shall not bee Suffered to runne any further into Debt. . . .[11]

The cost of wood and candles was regulated by an order of 1650 that,

> Whereas much inconvenience falleth out by the Schollars bringing Candle in Coarse into the Hall, therefore the Butler henceforth shall receive [20 shillings a year] . . . to provide Candles for the Hall, for

* Mr. Morison assumes, and Mr. Shipton agrees, that this damage was "one outlet for high spirits." (*HCSC*, p. 121. Clifford K. Shipton, *Sibley's Harvard Graduates* [Cambridge, 1933], for example IV, 201, 209, 288, 381, 496, *et passim.*) However, it seems conceivable, judging from my experience with the fragility of old window-glass, as well as from the great regularity of the entry in the books and the fact that Tutors also were so afflicted, that "glasse-mending" may have been just a necessary repair. In February 1693 Brattle has an entry in his Journal showing £31 13*s.* 9*d.* repaid to the Steward because of "omission of the article for Glassemending 5 years and 1 Quarter, the Quarters having severally been viewed." Very frequently the College, also, is charged by the Steward for glass-mending. By 1720 this had become so standard a charge that not only does it show in the previously established column in the Quarter Bill, but there is a *regular* charge of 5*d.* a quarter to *every* student, plus extras to some.

prayer time, and Supper, which, that it may not bee burthensome, it shall be put proportionably upon every scholar who retayneth his head in the Butteryes.[12]

These amounts so "put upon their heads" varied over most of our period from 2*d.* to 7*d.* a year from each student. In addition to the costs of "fyer and candle" for the public rooms, the students were charged with wood for their own fireplaces, if they were so fortunate as to have studies with such a facility.

A combination of the two devices of putting charges "on the heads" and asking the students to make the initial investment was in 1650 used to defray the College's part of the cost of the Second Meeting House of the First Church of Cambridge. This was known as "gallery money." From 1650 on, the East Gallery of the Meeting House was the property of the College. The arrangement was that when he entered or very shortly thereafter each student "lente [15*s.*] towards Buildinge the gallery"; then when he graduated the College usually paid 12*s.* back to him for the "returne of his galleryе" — net cost three shillings. In this case, as with studies, in 1655 the College bought out the students' investments. Thereafter each man paid one charge of 3*s.* 4*d.* on entrance, and received no refund on graduation. In 1708 "gallery money" was raised to 6*s.*, perhaps because in 1706 the College had laid out another £60 toward the Third Meeting House. This was a profitable arrangement for the College which must have paid for the gallery many times over.

Though the individual commencement fee of £3 appears to have been constant throughout the Puritan Period, with £1 going to the President of the College and £2 to the Steward for the commencement feast, this item on the accounts was the cause of more apparent fluctuation from year to year than anything else. Mr. Morison points out that because of the disaffection caused by Dunster's lengthening the A.B. course from three to four years, during the first four years of Chauncy's incumbency — 1655 to 1658 — thirty of the graduates refused their degrees.[13] (President Chauncy's budget suffered by £90 as a result.) Three pounds was twice the annual tuition charge, and as much as a quarter's board. Therefore, when the number of graduates changed (as, for example, it did between 1690 and 1691) from thirty-one to seven, the shift from £62 to £14 on the total Quarter Bill was very noticeable. Whatever this variation did to the College's finances, to the student a £3 fee must have seemed a large tariff to pay, plus the 5 to 15*s*. for a "present unto the officers" who were concerned with running the commencement dinner. The main reason for the fee was the dinner itself, for Harvard Commencement was one of the major annual holidays for many people in the surrounding countryside. The crowds that came were very well treated indeed.

These were all the fees and charges.

### TOTAL CHARGE PER STUDENT

The total charges for a year of education are not clear for the years before 1650, but, as totals on Table 9 show, charges were approximately £11 7*s*. during the years 1650 to 1652, £14 3*s*. from 1655 to 1659, and £16 3*s*. from 1687 to 1712, assuming that the young man was a resident of the College for four quarters. As we have said, the man who was in a Harvard class up to and including that of 1651 normally took three years to earn his A.B. degree, whereas the members of 1653 and later took four. The fees, then, for three years as of 1650 to 1652 might have totaled approximately £34; for four years between 1655 to 1659 — £57; for four years 1687 to 1712 — perhaps £65.

But the assumption that students studied for four full quarters is optimistic; we know there was a tendency to stay out of college for at least the quarter after Commencement. Table 9, in the column of the "average annual payment per student enrolled," indicates that although at the end of this period the total fees for a resident undergraduate added up to £16 3*s*. a year, actual average undergraduate payments came to only £10 4*s*. a year. The difference comes from nonresident students and students who stayed out for one or more quarters and paid half-tuition. For example, the charge for study rent was £1 a year, but an average of only 16*s*. was paid; apparently over these years only about four fifths of the students were in residence: we know about 25 per cent were nonresident in 1687 to 1693, none in 1709 to 1712. Again we have said that the average full-time resident paid £10 or £11 a year for commons and sizings, but we find the average person enrolled paid only £6 5*s*; many students ate out of commons or

C.

At the meeting of the Governours of Harvard Colledge, held in the Colledge-Hall this 27 of 10th – 1643.

It is ordered that,

1. The Accounts of Mr Harvards Gift are to be finished, & Mr Pelham, Mr Nowell, Mr Hibbens, Mr Symes, Mr Wilson are chosen to ~~fini~~ finish it, that an acquittance may be given Mr Allin. And its agreed that if they find things cleared in the fullfilling the will of the dead they are to desire the Governour of the Colledge his hand to it as a full determination & acquittance.

2. Mr Pelham is elected Treasurer of the Colledge by the joynt vote of the Governours of the Colledge.

3. It is ordered that there shall be a Colledge seale in forme following

VE RI
TAS

4. A copy of Mr Adams & Mr Coulsons letter to Mr Eaton.

Mr Eaton,
After our Love remembred to you whereas we understood by your former letter that the money which was appointed heretofore for publique uses was not all then disposed of, we therefore for our parts, desire that what is then remayning, may be expended wholly about the building of the New Colledge at Cambridge, in N. England, which we understand is now erecting. So we Rest your loving friends

Thomas Adams
Christopher Coulson

26 March 1640.

Plate 1. *Extract from the minutes of the meeting of the Governors of Harvard College on December 27, 1643, showing the design of the first "Colledge Seale."*

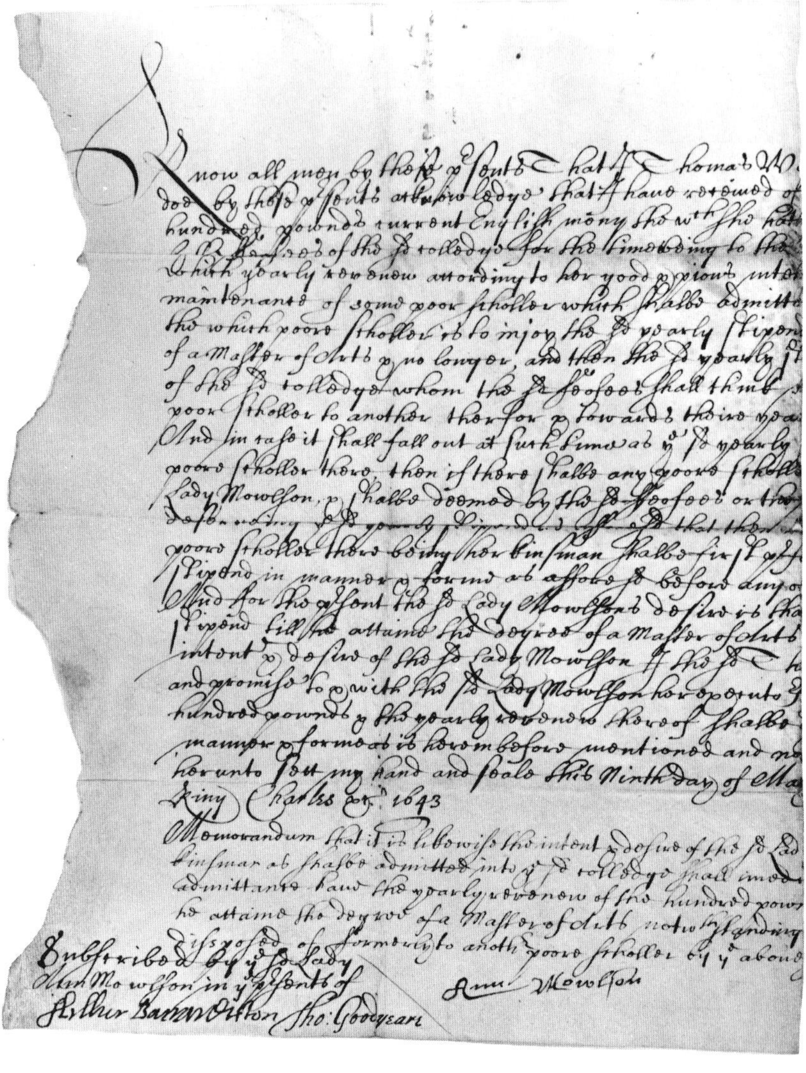

Plate 2. *Lady Ann Radcliffe Mowlson's deed of gift of £100 for Harvard College's first scholarship fund, May 9, 1643.*

...omas Weld Pastor of Roxbury in the Plantation of New Engla...
...the Lady Ann Mowlson of London widdow the full & intire some of ...
...freely given to Harvards Colledge in New England to be imp...
...yearly revenew that may be thought fitt in their wisdome ...
...tion is to be & remaine as a perpetuall stipend for & towards ye yea...
...into the sd colledge by the sd ffeoffees or the major pt of the...
...only till such time as such poore scholler doth attaine to ye degr...
...pend shall by the sd ffeoffees be bestowed upon another poore schol...
...most deserving, and soe the sd stipend to goe in succession from ...
...maintenance in perpetuum in manner & forme as aforesd...
...stipend shalbe appointed by the sd ffeoffees to be bestowed upon anoth...
...admitted into the sd colledge that shalbe a kinsman of the sd...
...major pt of them to be of a good & pious conversation & to be well...
...the reall intention & desire of the sd Lady Mowlson that such a...
...& appointed by the sd ffeoffees to have & injoy the sd yearly...
...other scholler of the sd colledge whatsoever that is not her kinsman
...John Weld now a scholler in the sd colledge shall have the sd...
...To the dew & true performance of which good and pious...
...omas Weld for my selfe my executors & administrators doe coven...
...administrators in and by these presents that the sd some of ...
...disposed of and imployed to the only intent and purpose in ye...
...otherwise In Wittnes whereof I the sd Thomas Weld...
...in the Nineteenth yeare of the raigne of our Soveraigne...

...y Mowlson that such her...
...atly from ye time of his...
...s above mentioned till...
...that it should be otherwise...
...sd ffeoffees./

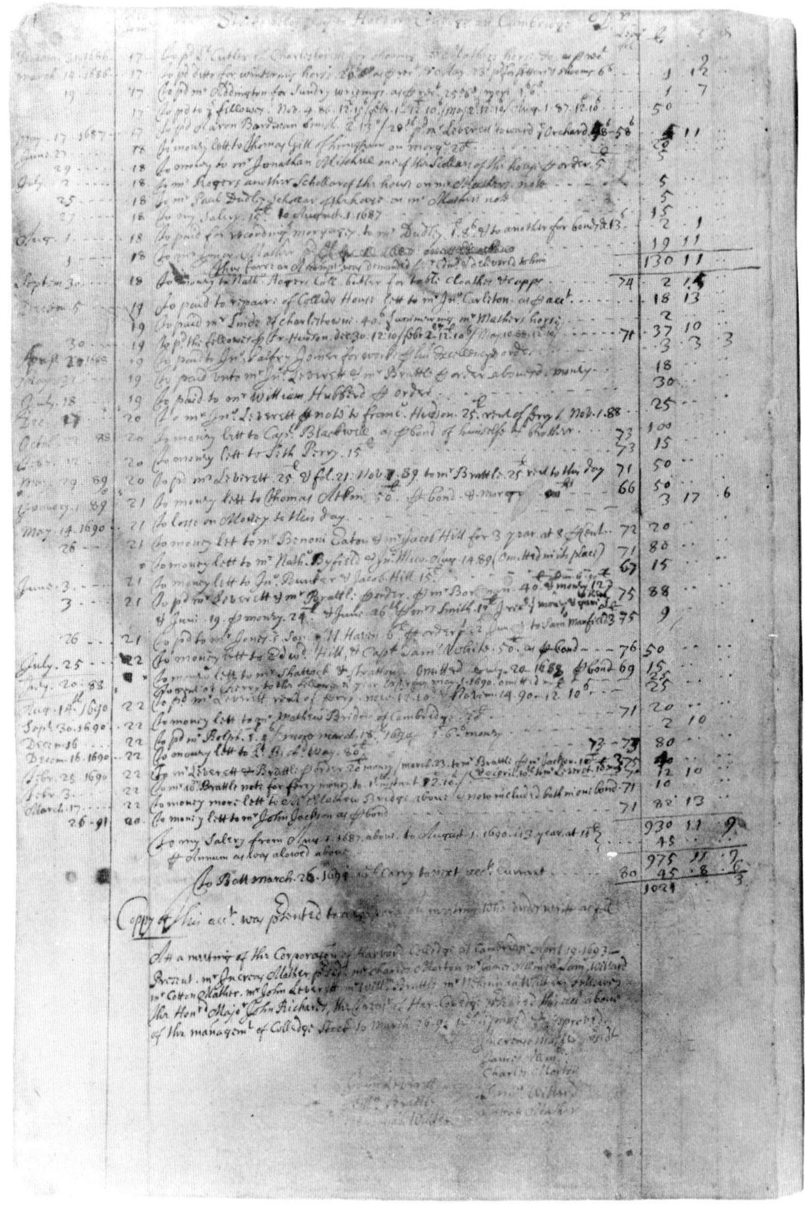

Plate 3. *Treasurer John Richards' ledger account of disbursements from Harvard College Stock, December 31, 1686, to March 26, 1691; page 74 of his book.*

Boston 17. Septemb.r 1711 (112)

64/58 Cash rec.d of Peter Sergeant Esq. 53£ in full of his bond now delivered him up . . . 53

64/39 Cash rec.d of Col. Edmund Goffe by ye hands of mr Elisha Cooke jun.r 99£ 6/ in Bills of Credit allow'd Rate of money at 8/ p oz, whereof 32£ 8/8 is for 3 years Interest to ye 30 7ber last, & the Interest of sd Interest 1 year to ye 30th inst 10£ 4/ is for a years Interest to ye 30th instant, & 56. 13. 4 is in part of ye principal sume of 150£ 17s, so that he now owes just 100£ 17s. his bond for paym.t of 30£ 12/8 36/8 for Interest thereof I deliv'd up to ye sd Cooke, & he should have deliv'd me a rec.t I gave Col. Goffe for sd bond, but he had it not . . . 99.6

Boston 12th Octob.r 1711

61/64 Cash pd mr John Whiting 6£ voted 18. 7ber 1710 to be pd him out of ye Treasurey, over & above his part of ye 100£ ye Ordered among ye Fellows . . . 6

Ditto 15th 1711

61/64 Cash pd mr Andrew Bordman w.t was Ordered Severall of ye Scholars, 18 7ber 1710 — viz. mr Stevens 4£ mr Hale 3£ Williams sen.r 4£, Blake 4£, Berry 4£ being Scholars of ye house last year; mr Walters 2 sons, mr Williams of Deerfield's son & to Walter jun.r to each of ye 3 former 40/ out of mr Hutchinsons gift & to ye latter 6£ being ye Income of mr Hulton's Legacy; to Appleton 4£ out of mr Rogers's Legacy & to Andrews 5£ to Clarke 40/ to Crocker 3£ & to Chipman 40/ out of mr Benj.n Brown's Legacy, in all 47£ as p's rec.t . . . 47

52 & Drawn a Note on ye 2 Fellows to give him Credit 14£ 4/10 when he makes up his Acco.t with ye College, he giving mr Corwin credit 9£ 4/10 & Sr Rogers credit 5£ in their Acco.ts with him

64/61 Cash rec.d of ye President 10£ being mr Eliakim Hutchinson's gift to ye College 1 year till ye Commencem.t 1710 . . . 10

Ditto 31th

64/60 Cash rec.d of Rich.d Thompson 4£ 10/ for Interest of 75£ 1 year to 9th October last . . . 4.10

Boston 22. Novemb.r 1711

64/55 Cash rec.d of Nathaniel Patten 48/ for a years Interest of 40£ due ye 1 of Decemb.r next . . . 2.8

64/18 Cash rec.d of Nathan.l Robbins 20£ principal & 24/ Interest to 8th next Feb.y in full discharge of his Mortgage . . . 21.4

61/64 Cash deliv'd mr Andrew Bordman 41£ 17/ to pay ye Hicks's mr Fessenden &c for work & Materialls upon the Brewhouse in 7ber & 8ber last as p acco.t signed by mr President with mr Bordman's receipt of ye sd sum thereupon (Sam.l Durham & his 2 hands due to be adjusted by my self) . . . 41.17

37 Drawn a Note on Wm Sheafe, Nic Laurence & Oliver Atwood & Nath.l Wilson to pay each party unto Mess.rs Henry Flynt & Jn.o Whiting or either of them 6£ for rent 1 yr of their respective parts in Charlst.n Ferry due ye 1st inst.

61/64 Cash pd mr Whiting in full of their Salary 1 yr to 1 inst. . . . 4.10

Plate 4. *Treasurer Thomas Brattle's journal from September 17, 1711, to November 22, 1711; page 112 of his book.*

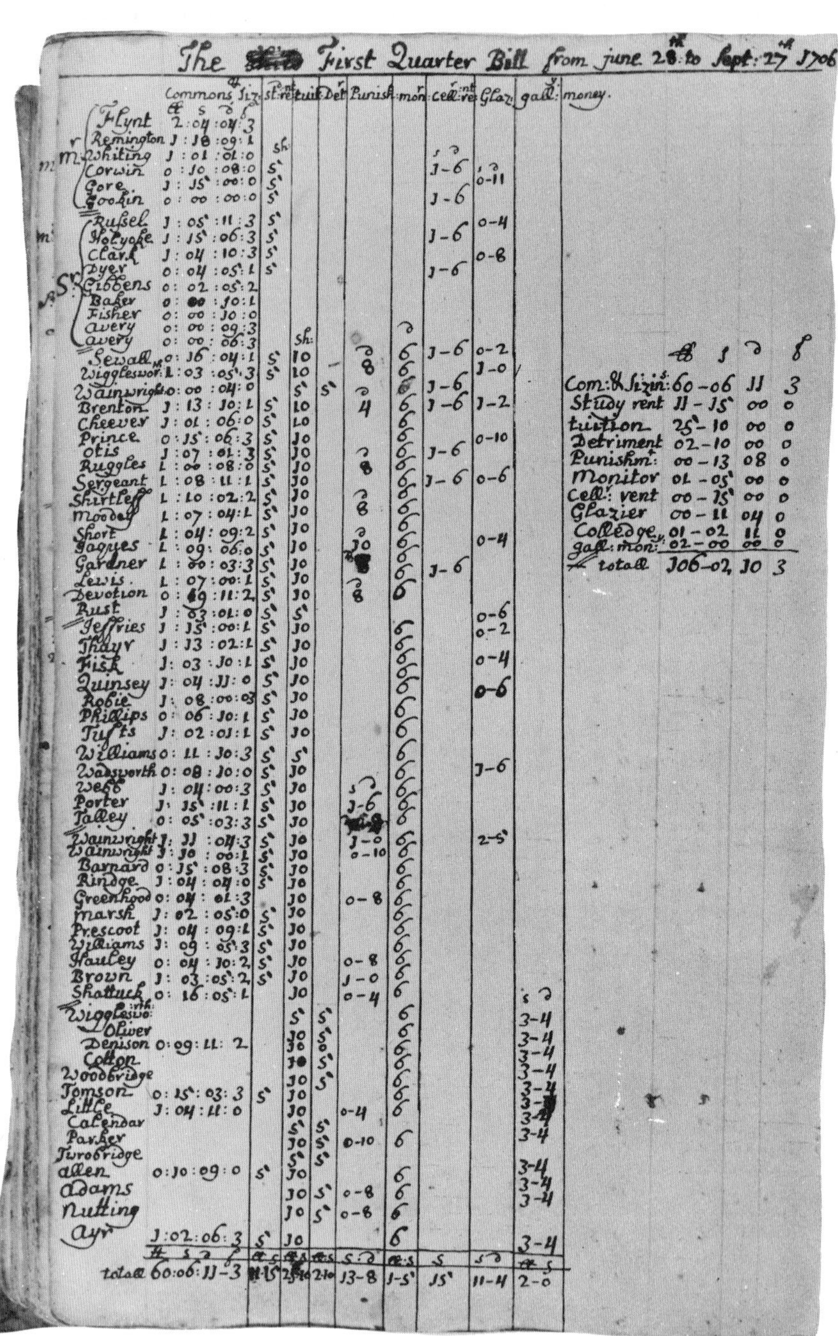

The ~~Secd~~ First Quarter Bill from june 28th to Sept: 27th 1706

| | Commons & Sizings | Study rent | tuition | Detriment | Punishmt | monitor | Cell rent | Glazier | gall: money |
|---|---|---|---|---|---|---|---|---|---|
| | £ s d q | | | | | | | | |
| Flynt | 2:04:04:3 | | | | | | | | |
| Remington | 1:18:09:1 | | | | | | | | |
| Whiting | 1:01:01:0 | sh | | | | | s d | | |
| Corwin | 0:10:08:0 | 5 | | | | | 1-6 | s d | |
| Gore | 1:15:00:0 | 5 | | | | | | 0-11 | |
| Gookin | 0:00:00:0 | 5 | | | | | 1-6 | | |
| Russel | 1:05:11:3 | 5 | | | | | | 0-4 | |
| Holyoke | 1:15:06:3 | 5 | | | | | 1-6 | | |
| Clark | 1:04:10:3 | 5 | | | | | | 0-8 | |
| Dyer | 0:04:05:1 | 5 | | | | | 1-6 | | |
| Gibbens | 0:02:05:2 | | | | | | | | |
| Baker | 0:00:10:1 | | | | | | | | |
| Fisher | 0:00:10:0 | | | | | | | | |
| avery | 0:00:09:3 | | | | | | | | |
| avery | 0:00:06:3 | | sh | | d | d | | | |
| Sewall | 0:16:04:1 | 5 | 10 | | 8 | 6 | 1-6 | 0-2 | |
| Wiggleswort | 1:03:05:3 | 5 | 10 | | | 6 | | 1-0 | |
| Wainwright | 0:00:04:0 | | 5 | 5 | d | 6 | 1-6 | | |
| Brenton | 1:13:10:1 | 5 | 10 | | 4 | 6 | 1-6 | 1-2 | |
| Cheever | 1:01:06:0 | 5 | 10 | | | 6 | | | |
| Prince | 0:15:06:3 | 5 | 10 | | | 6 | | 0-10 | |
| Otis | 1:07:01:3 | 5 | 10 | | d | 6 | 1-6 | | |
| Ruggles | 1:00:08:0 | 5 | 10 | | 8 | 6 | | | |
| Sergeant | 1:08:11:1 | 5 | 10 | | | 6 | 1-6 | 0-6 | |
| Shirtleff | 1:10:02:2 | 5 | 10 | | d | 6 | | | |
| Moodey | 1:07:04:1 | 5 | 10 | | 8 | 6 | | | |
| Short | 1:04:09:2 | 5 | 10 | | d | 6 | | | |
| Jaques | 1:09:06:0 | 5 | 10 | | 10 | 6 | | 0-4 | |
| Gardner | 1:00:03:3 | 5 | 10 | | [illegible] | 6 | 1-6 | | |
| Lewis | 1:07:00:1 | 5 | 10 | | d | 6 | | | |
| Devotion | 0:19:11:2 | 5 | 10 | | 8 | 6 | | | |
| Rust | 1:03:01:0 | 5 | 5 | | | | | 0-6 | |
| Jeffries | 1:15:00:1 | 5 | 10 | | | 6 | | 0-2 | |
| Thayr | 1:13:02:1 | 5 | 10 | | | 6 | | | |
| Fisk | 1:03:10:1 | 5 | 10 | | | 6 | | 0-4 | |
| Quinsey | 1:04:11:0 | 5 | 10 | | | 6 | | | |
| Robie | 1:08:00:0 | 5 | 10 | | | 6 | | 0-6 | |
| Phillips | 0:06:10:1 | 5 | 10 | | | 6 | | | |
| Tufts | 1:02:01:1 | 5 | 10 | | | 6 | | | |
| Williams | 0:11:10:3 | 5 | 5 | | | 6 | | | |
| Wadsworth | 0:08:10:0 | 5 | 10 | | | 6 | | 1-6 | |
| Webb | 1:04:00:3 | 5 | 10 | | s d | 6 | | | |
| Porter | 1:15:11:1 | 5 | 10 | | 1-6 | 6 | | | |
| Talley | 0:05:03:3 | 5 | 10 | | [illegible] | 6 | | | |
| Wainwright | 1:11:04:3 | 5 | 10 | | 1-0 | 6 | | 2-5 | |
| Wainwright | 1:10:00:1 | 5 | 10 | | 0-10 | 6 | | | |
| Barnard | 0:15:08:3 | 5 | 10 | | | 6 | | | |
| Rindge | 1:04:04:0 | 5 | 10 | | | 6 | | | |
| Greenwood | 0:04:01:3 | | 10 | | 0-8 | 6 | | | |
| marsh | 1:02:05:0 | 5 | 10 | | | 6 | | | |
| Prescoot | 1:04:09:1 | 5 | 10 | | | 6 | | | |
| Williams | 1:09:05:3 | 5 | 10 | | | 6 | | | |
| Hauley | 0:04:10:2 | 5 | 10 | | 0-8 | 6 | | | |
| Brown | 1:03:05:2 | 5 | 10 | | 1-0 | 6 | | | |
| Shattuck | 0:16:05:1 | | 10 | | 0-4 | 6 | | | s d |
| Wigglesworth | | | 5 | 5 | | 6 | | | 3-4 |
| Oliver | | | 10 | 5 | | 6 | | | 3-4 |
| Denison | 0:09:11:2 | | 10 | 5 | | 6 | | | 3-4 |
| Cotton | | | 10 | 5 | | 6 | | | 3-4 |
| Woodbridge | | | 10 | 5 | | 6 | | | 3-4 |
| Tomson | 0:15:03:3 | 5 | 10 | | | 6 | | | 3-4 |
| Little | 1:04:11:0 | | 10 | | 0-4 | 6 | | | 3-4 |
| Calendar | | | 5 | 5 | | | | | 3-4 |
| Parker | | | 10 | 5 | 0-10 | 6 | | | 3-4 |
| Trowbridge | | | 5 | 5 | | | | | |
| allen | 0:10:09:0 | 5 | 10 | | | 6 | | | 3-4 |
| adams | | | 10 | 5 | 0-8 | 6 | | | 3-4 |
| Nutting | | | 10 | 5 | 0-8 | 6 | | | 3-4 |
| ayr | 1:02:06:3 | 5 | 10 | | | 6 | | | 3-4 |
| | £ s d | £ s | £ s | £ s | s d | £ s | s | s d | £ s |
| totall | 60:06:11-3 | 11-15 | 25-10 | 2-10 | 13-8 | 1-5 | 15 | 11-4 | 2-0 |

| | £ | s | d | q |
|---|---|---|---|---|
| Com: & Sizin: | 60-06 | 11 | | 3 |
| Study rent | 11-15 | 00 | | 0 |
| tuition | 25-10 | 00 | | 0 |
| Detriment | 02-10 | 00 | | 0 |
| Punishmt: | 00-13 | 08 | | 0 |
| Monitor | 01-05 | 00 | | 0 |
| Cell: rent | 00-15 | 00 | | 0 |
| Glazier | 00-11 | 04 | | 0 |
| Colledge | 01-02 | 11 | | 0 |
| gall: mon: | 02-00 | 00 | | 0 |
| totall | 106-02 | 10 | | 3 |

Plate 5. *The Quarter Bill first and second quarters of 1706 to 1707.*

The Second Quarter Bill from 27 Septbr to 27 Decr 1706.

| | Comons & Sizings | Study Rent | Tuition | Detrimt | Punishmt | Monitr | Cellr | Glaz |
|---|---|---|---|---|---|---|---|---|
| Flint | 4/02/11/0 | | | | | | | |
| Remington | 3/13/01/1 | | | | | | | |
| Whiting | 3/16/10/2 | | | | | | | |
| Brown | 3/02/08/0 | 5 | | | | | | 10 |
| Gore | 3/04/01/2 | 5 | | | | | 1-6 | |
| Gookin | 00/00/00/0 | 5 | | | | | | |
| Russell | 00/19/03/1 | 5 | | | | | 1-6 | |
| Holyoke | 3/02/09/00 | 5 | | | | | 0-0 | [illegible] |
| Clark | 2/09/04/3 | 5 | | | | | 1-6 | 10 |
| Dyer | 1/12/08/3 | 5 | 10 | | | | | 10 |
| Sewall | 2/19/10/0 | 5 | 10 | | | | 1-6 | 1-0 |
| Wigglesworth | 3/01/10/2 | 5 | 10 | | | 0-6 | 1-6 | |
| Wainwright | 0/00/00/0 | 5 | 5 | 5 | | 0-6 | | |
| Brenton | 1/10/00/3 | 5 | 10 | | 2-0 | -6 | 1-6 | 2-9 |
| Cheever | 1/04/09/3 | 5 | 10 | | 1-0 | -6 | | |
| Otis | 0/05/06/1 | 5 | 5 | | | | | -4 |
| Ruggles | 2/11/08/0 | 5 | 10 | | | | 1-6 | |
| Sergeant | 2/17/10/0 | 5 | 10 | | 2-0 | 6 | | -[illegible] |
| Shirtleff | 0/19/09/1 | 5 | 10 | | 1- | 6 | 1-6 | 1-3 |
| Moody | 2/00/00/2 | 5 | 10 | | | 6 | | |
| Short | 0/16/01/1 | 5 | 5 | | | 6 | | -6 |
| Jaques | 2/03/00/2 | 5 | 10 | | | | | 3 |
| Gardner | 2/02/03/1 | 5 | 10 | | 1-0 | 6 | 1-6 | 1-11 |
| Lewis | 0/02/08/1 | 5 | 5 | | 2-0 | 6 | | |
| Devotion | 0/12/09/3 | 5 | 5 | | 0-6 | | | |
| Rust | 0/16/03/3 | 5 | 5 | | 0-0 | 6 | | -4 |
| Jeffries | 3/07/08/0 | 5 | 10 | | | 6 | | |
| Thayer | 3/01/05/1 | 5 | 10 | | | 6 | | -4 |
| Fisk | 2/01/00/3 | 5 | 10 | | | 6 | | -2 |
| Quinsey | 2/01/00/1 | 5 | 10 | | 0-8 | 6 | | 1-0 |
| Rolfe | 2/09/10/2 | 5 | 10 | | 0-8 | 6 | | 1-0 |
| Phillips | 2/13/01/0 | 5 | 10 | | | 6 | | -2 |
| Tuft | 1/19/09/1 | 5 | 10 | | | 6 | | |
| Williams | 0/07/09/3 | 5 | 5 | | | 6 | | |
| Wadsworth | 0/10/08/0 | 5 | 10 | | | | | |
| Webb | 1/12/08/0 | 5 | 10 | | 0-8 | 7 | | -5 |
| Porter | 1/07/00/3 | 5 | 5 | | | | | |
| Talley | 0/08/04/3 | 5 | 10 | | 2-0 | 7 | | |
| Wainwright | 2/02/04/2 | 5 | 10 | | | 7 | | |
| Wainwright | 1/06/10/2 | 5 | 10 | | | 7 | | |
| Barnard | 0/15/11/1 | 5 | 10 | | | 7 | | |
| Rindge | 1/15/03/1 | 5 | 10 | | 1-0 | 7 | | |
| Greenwood | 2/7/02/2 | 5 | 10 | | 0-8 | 7 | | 0-5 |
| Marsh | 1/12/08/3 | 5 | 10 | | 1-0 | 7 | | |
| Hawley | [illegible]/03/04/3 | 5 | 5 | | | | | |
| Williams | 1/10/02/0 | 5 | 10 | | 1-0 | 7 | | |
| Brown | 1/04/03/0 | 5 | 10 | | 1-0 | 7 | | -6 |
| Prescott | 3/00/10/3 | 5 | 10 | | 2-0 | 7 | | |
| Shattuck | 2/11/03/0 | 5 | 10 | | 1-0 | 7 | | |
| Wigglesworth | 00/00/00/0 | 0 | 5 | 5 | | 8 | | |
| Oliver | | | 10 | 5 | 2-0 | 8 | | |
| Denison | 2/17/11/2 | | 10 | | 2-0 | 8 | | |
| Woodbridge | | | 10 | 5 | | 8 | | |
| Cotton | | | 10 | 5 | 1-0 | 8 | | |
| Thomson | 1/17/10/2 | 5 | 10 | | 0-8 | 8 | | |
| Little | 1/18/09/0 | | 10 | | 2-0 | 8 | | -4 |
| Parker | | | 10 | 5 | | 8 | | |
| Adams | | | 10 | 5 | | 8 | | |
| Kalander | | | 5 | 5 | | | | |
| Trowbridge | | | 5 | 5 | | | | |
| Eyre | 2/04/05/0 | 5 | 10 | | | 8 | | |
| Nutting | | | 10 | 5 | 0-11 | 8 | | |
| Allen | 1/17/09/1 | 5 | 10 | | | 8 | | -8 |
| Prince | 1/19/06/3 | 5 | 10 | | 1-0 | 8 | | |
| £ | 101/06/08/1 | 12-5 | 24-0 | 2-10 | 1-10-9 | 1-5 | 13-6 | 16-3 |

| | £ | s | d | q |
|---|---|---|---|---|
| Comns & Siz: | 101 | 06 | 08 | 1 |
| St. Rent | 12 | 05 | 00 | 0 |
| Tuition | 24 | 00 | - | - |
| Punishmt | 1 | 10 | 9 | 0 |
| Monitr | 1 | 05 | - | 0 |
| Cellr | 0 | 13 | 6 | 0 |
| Glaz | 0 | 16 | 3 | 0 |
| Detrmt | 2 | 10 | 0 | 0 |
| Coll: for Glass | 2 | 00 | 5 | 0 |
| £ | 146 | 07 | 7 | 1 |

Errors Excepted

P J. Whiting C } Har Coll Soc

| 1687. | Colledge-Steward Dr. | £ | s | d |
|---|---|---|---|---|
| Octob. 21. | To Allowance out of Commons & Sizings | 1 | 18 | 0-2 |
| | To Study-Rent | 8 | 10 | 0-6 |
| | To Detrimts | 4 | 10 | 0-0 |
| | To Punishmts | 0 | 12 | 0-0 |
| | To Monitor | 0 | 15 | 0-0 |
| | To Glass-mending | 6 | 04 | 9-0 |
| | To Gallery-mony | 1 | 03 | 4-0 |
| Jany. 20 | To Allowc. out of Commons & Sizings | 3 | 16 | 2-0 |
| | To Study-Rent | 7 | 18 | 0-0 |
| | To Detrim: | 4 | 08 | 0-0 |
| | To Monitor | 0 | 15 | 0-0 |
| | To Punishmts | 0 | 16 | 2-0 |
| ffebruy 10. 168 7/8 | Then reckoned wth Aaron Boardman Steward & there is due to the Colledge at this time this just sum of | 41 | 03 | 5-3 |
| | | 30 | 04 | 11-0 |
| | by us Jno. Leverett, Wm Brattle Socii | 10 | 18 | 6-3 |
| Oct: 30. 88 | To Balance his acct when we last Reckoned | 10 | 18 | 6.3 |
| | To Allowance out of Commons & Sizings 3 Quarters to Oct. 19. 88 | 7 | 14 | 5 |
| | To Study Rent 3 Quarters | 26 | 19 | 0 |
| | To Detriments 3 Quarters | 26 | 10 | |
| | To Absent Commons 5 Quarters | 2 | 10 | |
| | To Punishmt 3 Quarters | 4 | 02 | 06 |
| | To Glass mony 3 Quarters | 14 | 04 | 09 |
| | To Monitor for 3 Quarters | 2 | 05 | 00 |
| | To Candles | 1 | 02 | 00 |
| | To Gallery-mony | 1 | 06 | 08 |
| | To Detrimt 1 | | 10 | |
| | | 98 | 2 | 10.3 |
| Octob: 30. 1688. | Then Reckoned with Aaron Bordman Steward & there was due to ye Colledge at yt time ye Summe of | 61 | 8 | 9 |
| | | 36 | 14 | 1 3/3 |
| | By Jno. Leverett, Wm. Brattle Socii H. Col. | | | |
| July 19. 89 | To Study Rent 3 Quarters – ending July 19. 89 | 28 | 10 | |
| | To Detriment 3 Quarters | 9 | 5 | |
| | To Punishmt 3 Quarters | 4 | | |
| | To Monitor 3 Quarters | 2 | 5 | |
| | To Glasse mending 3 Qu: | 3 | 1 | 7 |
| | To Wood & Candles 1-4-6 | 1 | 4 | 6 |
| | To allowance out of Com. & Siz. 3 Quarters to 19. 5. | 14 | 13 | 6 |
| | | 62 | 19 | 7 |
| August 7th 1689. | Then Reckoned wth Aaron Bordman Steward & there was due to ye Colledge ye just Summe of | 36 | 14 | 1.3 |
| | | 99 | 13 | 8.3 |
| | | 63 | 3 | 8 |
| | | 35 | 10 | 3 |
| | Wm Brattle Soc. | | | |

Plate 6. *The Steward's account with Harvard College, October 21, 1687, to August 7, 1689 (from the Quarter-Bill Book of 1687 to 1720).*

| 1687. | Contra Cr. | | | |
|---|---|---|---|---|
| Octob.r 21. | By ~~Good~~ two Quarter Dinners & other Sizings | 4 | 13 | 10 |
| | By a bill to Ephraim Cutter Glasier | 6 | 04 | 09 |
| | By S.r Rogers Buttler | 3 | 00 | 00 |
| | By the Monitor Buckingham | 0 | 15 | 00 |
| | By y.e Lawndresse | 0 | 10 | 00 |
| | By 3 Doz.n of trenchers | 0 | 03 | 00 |
| | By 1. bowl & 1 tray, & 1 pail | 0 | 03 | 06 |
| | By 1444 foot of boards | 2 | 02 | 04 |
| | By 1 Lawn Sive & 5 Doz.n of trenchers | 0 | 08 | 00 |
| | By 2 beer barrells | 0 | 05 | 00 |
| Jan.ry 20. | By S.r Rogers Buttler | 3 | 00 | 00 |
| | By y.e Monitor Buckingham | 0 | 15 | 00 |
| | By y.e Quarter bill | 3 | 03 | 09 |
| | By 1 Colledge Acc.o book | 0 | 03 | 06 |
| | By the Lawndresse | 0 | 10 | 00 |
| ffebru.ry 9. | By Sundrys brought out of y.e Shop-book | 4 | 07 | 03 |
| | £ | 30 | 04 | 11 |
| Oct: 30. 1688 | By Sundryes brought out of y.e shop book ~~each~~ particular having been viewed | 15 | 15 | 11 |
| | By 3 Quarter Dinners & other Sizings to 19.8.88 | 8 | 14 | 8.2 |
| | By Glasse mending 3 Quarters | 1 | 4 | 9 |
| | By y.e Monitor 3 Quarters | 2 | 5 | |
| | By y.e Butler 3 Quarters | 9 | | |
| | By Sundryes ~~diff~~ for fitting up y.e New-Chamber & necessaries for y.e Colledge, Each particular having been viewed | 9 | 17 | 4.2 |
| | By y.e Lawndresse 3 Quarters to Oct. & 1 Barrell 12d 19.88 | 1 | 11 | |
| | | 61 | 8 | 9 |
| Nov. 1688 | By Goodman Shes. 15s. Butler 2d Qu. 3lb Monitor 15s | 4 | 10 | |
| | By y.e Laundresse 10; Wood & Candles 24s. 6d. Qu. Dinner 1-11-3-2 | 3 | 5 | 9 |
| January | By y.e Glasier 15.9d Salt 9d. Skimmer 8d 3d Qu. Din. 1-7-7- Butler 3lb | 5 | 4 | 9 |
| | By y.e Monitor 15s. Glasier. 2-5-10. Laundresse 10s. G. Wyth 6-7-0 | 9 | 17 | 10 |
| May | By a Sieve, Trough, Tubbs, Boards, Posts, Nailes & other particulars | 5 | 10 | 7 |
| | By Lime, Brick, Boards, Nails & many others, all viewed | 4 | 12 | 7 |
| July | By 4th Qu. Din. Butler, Mon. Laund. G. Palfray & others | 9 | 18 | 9 |
| | By [illegible] middle Garrett for work done in fitting up y.e | | | |
| Aug. | By Shop work, & severall particulars, all being viewed | 3 | 3 | 5 |
| | | 56 | 3 | 8 |

Carried to page next

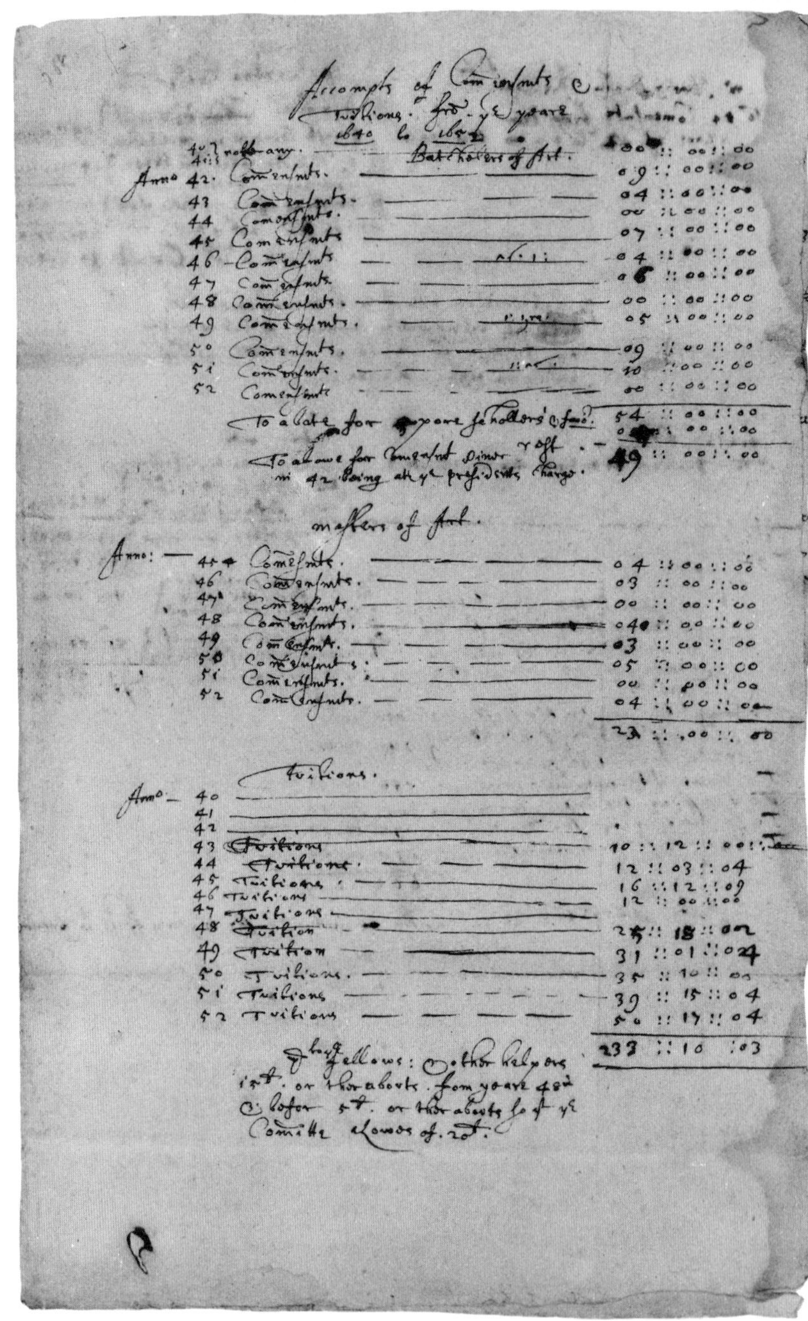

Accompts of Comencments & tuitions from ye yeare 1640 to 1652

Batchelers of Art.

| | | |
|---|---|---|
| 40, 41 | nothing | 00 :: 00 :: 00 |
| Anno 42 | Comencments | 09 :: 00 :: 00 |
| 43 | Comencments | 04 :: 00 :: 00 |
| 44 | Comencments | 00 :: 00 :: 00 |
| 45 | Comencments | 07 :: 00 :: 00 |
| 46 | Comencments | 04 :: 00 :: 00 |
| 47 | Comencments | 06 :: 00 :: 00 |
| 48 | Comencments | 00 :: 00 :: 00 |
| 49 | Comencments | 05 :: 00 :: 00 |
| 50 | Comencments | 09 :: 00 :: 00 |
| 51 | Comencments | 10 :: 00 :: 00 |
| 52 | Comencments | 00 :: 00 :: 00 |
| | | 54 :: 00 :: 00 |
| | To abate for poore schollers [illegible] | 05 :: 00 :: 00 |
| | To allow for [illegible] dinner cost in 42 being at ye presidents charge | 49 :: 00 :: 00 |

masters of Art.

| | | |
|---|---|---|
| Anno 44 | Comencments | 04 :: 00 :: 00 |
| 46 | Comencments | 03 :: 00 :: 00 |
| 47 | Comencments | 00 :: 00 :: 00 |
| 48 | Comencments | 04 :: 00 :: 00 |
| 49 | Comencment | 03 :: 00 :: 00 |
| 50 | Comencments | 05 :: 00 :: 00 |
| 51 | Comencments | 00 :: 00 :: 00 |
| 52 | Comencments | 04 :: 00 :: 00 |
| | | 23 :: 00 :: 00 |

tuitions.

| | | |
|---|---|---|
| Anno 40 | | |
| 41 | | |
| 42 | | |
| 43 | Tuitions | 10 :: 12 :: 00 |
| 44 | Tuitions | 12 :: 03 :: 04 |
| 45 | Tuitions | 16 :: 12 :: 09 |
| 46 | Tuitions | 12 :: 00 :: 00 |
| 47 | Tuitions | |
| 48 | Tuition | 25 :: 18 :: 02 |
| 49 | Tuition | 31 :: 01 :: 04 |
| 50 | Tuitions | 35 :: 10 :: 00 |
| 51 | Tuitions | 39 :: 15 :: 04 |
| 52 | Tuitions | 50 :: 17 :: 04 |
| | | 233 :: 10 :: 03 |

the fellows & other helpers 15li. or thereabouts from yeare 48 & before 5li. or thereabouts so yt ye Comittee allowes of 20li.

Plate 7. *President Dunster's tuition and Commencement receipts, 1640 to 1652.*

Proposalls by Jn^o. Leverett & W^m. Brattle Fellows of Harvard Colledge tendred to y^e Consideration of the Hon: Corporation of Harvard Colledge in meeting at Cambridge June 2^d. 1690.

1. That by the President & Council, the Rev^d. M^r. I. Mather &c. Anno 1686 There was allowed to us, besides the Ferry, the Summe of fifty-eight pounds for that Year, w^{ch} Summe of 58^{lib} we fully rec^d, & were as fully Satisfied with, altho' the s^d Summe was Considerably Less, then had been allowed to y^e Fellows Circumstanced as we were, Since our Remembrance.

2. That for y^e Years 1687, 88 and 89 (Now Expiring) besides y^e Ferry we have not received one Penny.

3. That for these three last Years our Expences have necessarily been as great our Difficulties more Intricate & o^r Services more Burthensome then they were Anno 86. Especially these two last Years, by Reason of y^e Rev^d M^r Mather's Absence, whose pres[illegible] much Mitigated our Difficulties, & Alleviated our trouble & toyle.

4. The Premises being Considered; Viz^t. That 58^{lib} were allowed to us Anno 1686. That y^e said Summe was Considerably less then has been allowed heretofore to y^e Fellows under our Circumstances, & That our Expences, trouble & difficulties have exceeded what before we met w^{th}; (In Consideration hereof) We Conceive; that In desireing y^e s^d Summe of 58^{lib} be Annually allowed & paid us for y^e 3 last Years, Our Desires are but Reasonable just & moderate; and that if desire the Addition of the Odd twenty shillings to make our Annuall Allowance (Severally) thirty pounds we sh^{ld} not be unreasonable or Immoderate; Especially it being Considered, that whereas formerly there was wont Annually to be disbursed upon the Colledge for Reparations, paying Officers and Schollarships more then 40, or 50 pounds Annually; for near these three Years last past y^e Colledge has not drawn one penny out of the Treasury.

We have plainly & fully exprest our Minds, & According to our desires has our Expectation been; Nothing remains but that we Annex our Hearty thanks for this meeting, & Readiness to submitt to yo^r Determinations.

In answer to the Proposalls above the Corporation for the Colledge mett June 16. 1690 at Cambridge (p^rsent m^r Nich^o. Hubbard, m^r Nath^l. Gookin, m^r Cotton Mather, m^r John Leverett and m^r Will^m Brattle, w^{th} my Selfe) agreed that the two Fellowes m^r Leverett & m^r Brattle abovesaid should have 50^{li} p Annum for the yeares. 87. 88. & 89 p^d them out of Colledge money beside the Ferry. So as may not be p^rjudiciall to the Colledge Stock. These 3 yeares Expired the Commencem^t. Viz July. 1690: or August 1. 1690.

Plate 8. *"Proposalls" of John Leverett and William Brattle concerning their salaries, June 2, 1690.*

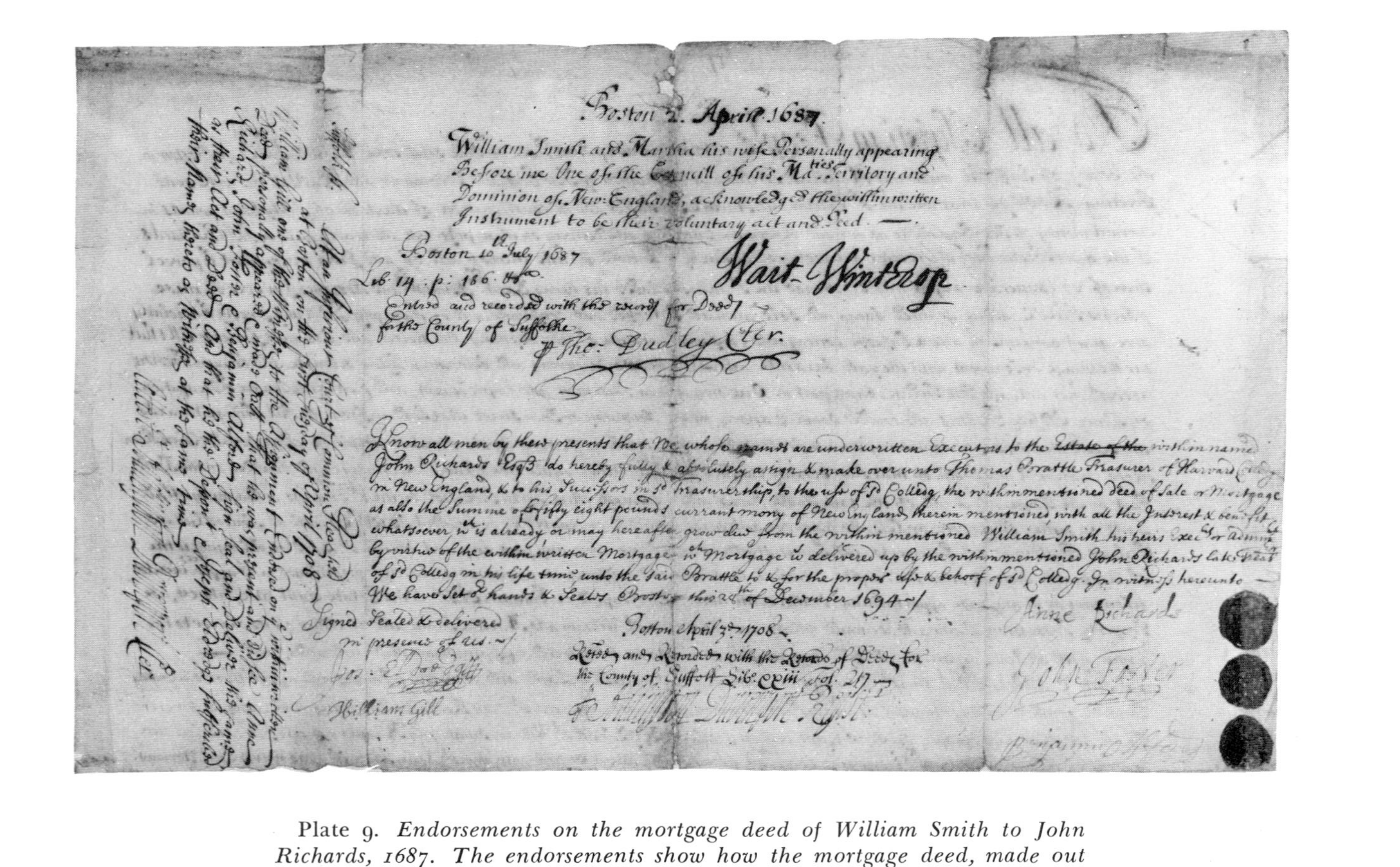

Boston 2. April 1687

William Smith and Martha his wife Personally appearing Before me One of the Councill of his Ma.ties Territory and Dominion of New England, acknowledged the within written Instrument to be their voluntary act and Deed. —

Wait Winthrop

Boston 10th July 1687
Lib 14. p: 186. &c.
Entred and recorded with the records for Deeds for the County of Suffolke
p Tho: Dudley Cler.

Know all men by these presents that We whose names are underwritten Executors to the within named John Richards Esq do hereby fully & absolutely assign & make over unto Thomas Brattle Treasurer of Harvard Colledg in New England, & to his Successors in sd Treasurership, to the use of sd Colledg, the withinmentioned deed of Sale or Mortgage as also the Summe of fifty eight pounds current mony of New England therein mentioned with all the Interest & benefit whatsoever wch is already or may hereafter grow due from the within mentioned William Smith his heirs Exec.rs or Admin.rs by virtue of the within written Mortgage which Mortgage is delivered up by the withinmentioned John Richards late Treas.r of sd Colledg in his life time unto the said Brattle to & for the proper use & behoof of sd Colledg. In witness hereunto We have Set our hands & Seals Boston this 24th of December 1694.

Signed Sealed & delivered in presence of us.
Jos. Eldredge
William Gill

Anne Richards
John Foster
Benjamin Alford

Boston April 3d 1708.
Recd and Recorded with the Records of Deeds for the County of Suffolk Lib. XXIII fol. 217.
Addington Davenport Regr.

Suffolk ss.
At an Inferiour Court of Common Pleas held at Boston on the first Tuesday of April 1708
William Gill one of the Witnesses to the Assignment Endorsed on ye within written Deed personally appeared & made Oath that he was present and did see Anne Richards John Foster & Benjamin Alford sign seal and Deliver the same as their Act and Deed And that he the Depont. & Joseph Eldredge subscribed their Names thereto as Witnesses at the same time
Attest Addington Davenport Cler

Plate 9. *Endorsements on the mortgage deed of William Smith to John Richards, 1687. The endorsements show how the mortgage deed, made out to Richards personally, was turned over by his executors to the Treasurer of Harvard College.*

were away for a quarter or more. Obviously some students got by on less than these averages, and some spent considerably more.

In addition to these charges, students had personal expenses including those for laundry, clothing, books, tips, and wood for their own fireplaces — charges which could be very small if the student lacked funds.

Some figures are available for English colleges. For example, James Master, Esq., was at Trinity College, Cambridge, in 1647. He seems to have been well provided with funds, and he was enrolled as a fellow-commoner. Quarterly charges he recorded in his expense book include £1 for chamber rent (sometimes shared and therefore cut to 10*s*.), £2 for tuition, amounts varying from 4*s*. ("being absent") to £4 to £6 16*s*. for commons and sizings, 10 *s*. for his cizar's wages (sometimes the cizar, too, was shared), 4*s*. for his charwoman for "dressing up" his chambers, 7*s*. for 14 weeks laundress work. These amounts, except perhaps commons and sizings, tend to be somewhat higher than those of Cambridge, Massachusetts Bay, but no doubt the style was different and it is hard to say how comparable conditions were.*

### THE COLLEGE'S RECEIPTS FROM STUDENTS

We might consider whether or not Harvard College actually collected this money. Little more need be said about the subject of commodity money, but we must remember that throughout this period, though in decreasing measure, payment was often made in commodities, and effective payment may not have been as large as that credited on the books. The College tried to simplify the Steward's problem by such laws as:

> That all such payments shall bee discharged to the Steward of the College either in Current Coine of the Country, or Wheat or Malt, or in

*James Master, Esq., "A Booke of my Expences," in Appendix of *The Flemings in Oxford; Being Documents Selected from the Rydal Papers in Illustration of the Lives and Ways of Oxford Men 1650–1700*, ed. John Richard Magrath (Oxford, 1904), Oxford Historical Society Series, pp. 379–382.

I am indebted to Mrs. Catharine Firman of the Oxford Collection, Honnold Library, Claremont, California, for this and other similar references.

HUA, Corporation Papers (1636–1660), has a MS. "Propositions Concerning the Colledg Business" (written in 1654 prior to the reorganization of the fees) which suggests "that every scollar do pay for his tuition quarterly 8*s*. pece which is much less than in England."

such provision as shall satisfy the Steward for the time being, and Supply the necessityes of the Colledge.

or

It is ordered that the steward shall not bee enjoyned to accept of above one quarter part of flesh meat of any person.[14]

Of course, when a commencement dinner was about to be arranged, almost anything to eat could be fitted into the menu and credited on the College account.

A rather more sizable than usual receipt is "a barne" taken in payment of £6 for Samuel Shepard, 1658, a son of the Reverend Thomas Shepard, fortunately a close neighbor of the College. One wonders who wore the "yallow and read cotten" worth 5*s.* 5*d.*, taken from one student, along with 9*s.* of "buttens" and 1*s.* 2*q.* of "ribine."[15] What "necessitye" of the College did they meet?

A statement of income received and expense year by year for the seventeenth century is a modern refinement that it is impossible to produce. However, we can make fairly good estimates from the accounts and fractions of accounts which have come down to us. An example of such an account appears in Plate 7 which shows Dunster's major receipts from students: those from commencement fees and from tuition. Plates 5 and 6 show some of the Steward's records.

Table 10 is a statement of average income from students for 1687 to 1712, figured from the Quarter-Bill Books. When there is a direct and offsetting charge, such as to pay the glazier, nothing appears in the column of net income. In other cases (food), items show in Column (2) only to the extent that they provided a net gain to the College. Occasionally there was a net loss or gain from food service, but usually, as we shall see later, the income about offset the expense in this essential area. Thus the major income to the College from students came from (1) tuition (paid to Tutors), (2) study and cellar rent, and (3) the net amount gained from all other services, fines, and fees. (We shall speak of scholarships under "expense" below.)

*Tuition Receipts.* The total tuition received by President Dunster from 1643 to 1652 was, as Plate 7 shows, £233 10*s.* 3*d.*, which was made up of amounts increasing from £10 12*s.* in 1643 to £50 17*s.* 4*d.*

*Table 10. Harvard College Mean Annual Income from Students, 1687 to 1712*

| | (1) Receipts, gross[a] | (2) Net income to College[b] | |
|---|---|---|---|
| Tuition[c] | £ 87 | £ 0 | |
| Detriments | 17 | 17 | |
| Study rent | 46[d] | 43 (Study rent & Cellar rent) | (Pres. house out) |
| Cellar rent | 3 | | |
| Commons & sizings | 386[e] (Commons & sizings & Absent Commons) | 21 | (C & S allowance) |
| Absent Commons | | 5 | |
| Punishments | 6 | 6 | |
| Glass-mending[c] | 6 | 0 | |
| Monitor[c] | 5 | 0 | |
| Wood & candles[c] | 1 | 0 | |
| Gallery | 2 | 2 | |
| Commencement (A.B. & A.M.) | 48 | 12 | (Fees less cost) |
| | £607 | £104[f] | |

*Source:* QBB.

[a] This is the same as the annual income from students shown in Figure 4 (page 125) at the end of Chapter VI, except that *contra* items for Sweep, Glass, Wood and Candles are omitted from Figure 4.

[b] Net income or gain after immediate expenses. The *net* income was turned over by the Steward to the Treasurer to be used for other expenses.

[c] *Contra* item: that is, came in and was paid out directly by Steward without going through Treasurer's books; for example, tuition went to Tutors.

[d] Of this £6 belonged to the President.

[e] Commons and Sizings includes a very small amount from others than students.

[f] Does not add to total because of rounding.

in 1652, and averaged £23 a year. Though the tuition rate was up, Dunster's receipts from tuition in 1653 were down to £47 3*s*., perhaps because of dispute over the length of the college course. We can estimate from Danforth's accounts that the annual tuition receipt from 1654 to 1668 was about £57 a year:[16] The average number of graduates each year from 1656 to 1668 was seven, whereas from 1642 to 1654 it had been six. However, there were more than the usual number of nongraduates in the classes of 1655 to 1658. Considering these facts and the small classes of 1655, 1670, and 1672, the estimate of a £57 average per year for the Danforth period is probably not more than five pounds off one way or the other. Similar reasoning would lead us to assume that the £57 average is as good an estimate as we can make for the next period, from 1669 to 1686, when the size of the average class graduated was six scholars; we have no Steward's records by which to check this further. Actual summation from the Quarter-Bill Book completes Table 11. From 1654 into the eighteenth century, tuition money was paid to the Tutors.

*Table 11. Estimated Average Annual Receipts from Tuition (for Four Quarters), Harvard College*

| Years | Amount |
|---|---|
| 1643–1652 | £23 |
| 1654–1668 | 57 |
| 1668–1686 | 57 |
| 1687–1693 | 79 |
| 1693–1712 | 89 |

From 1654 into the eighteenth century tuition money was paid to the Tutors.

*Rents.* The total amount received by the College for all rents was fairly substantial. Our early accounts of Dunster's administration show his receipt of what are called study rents; perhaps this meant purchase price, or perhaps some studies were rented in the 1640's. From October 1644 to 1646 he had £20 from this source, from 1647 to 1649 another £20, from June 1650 to June 1652 £19 14*s*. 5*d*., and from March 1653 to June 1654 six quarters' rent at £3 4*s*. a quarter, or £19 4*s*.[17] The receipts do not seem to go up as much as one might expect if a radical change in practice was instituted about 1650.

Danforth's accounts for 1654 to 1663 list study rents for three years only — amounting to £57 15*s*. His account for 1663 to 1668 shows five years' rents amounting to £150 6*s*. 6*d*.[18] What happened to the rents for the other six of the first nine years, and why did the average receipts increase so much in the second of his accounting periods? These questions probably arise from a change in the accounting practice. In 1654 the Corporation had ordered that all student charges be paid to the Steward, but the Steward may have turned them over to the Treasurer, or he may have disbursed them directly on the order of the Treasurer. Mr. Danforth made up these accounts to explain the disposition only of what went through his hands as Treasurer.

When Richards took over, the receipts from study rents no longer appeared on the Treasurer's College Books in the detail or in the summary, though the Laws of 1667, two years before the change from Danforth to Richards, specifically order the Steward to pay the study rents to the Treasurer. All this means is that the rents are credited to the College and balanced out by disbursements on the Steward's "Harvard College" account, which we do not have.

In 1687 we pick up study rents again in the Quarter-Bill Book; the average annual receipts from 1687 to 1712 were £40 6*s.*, excluding the President's House rent.*

There were two items of income or loss from students which did not appear on student bills: "Commons and sizings allowance" and "absent commons."

*Commons and Sizings Allowance.* A "Commons and Sizings Allowance" was set up by the Orders of 1686:

> The Steward shall be allowed for his Cost and Pains the whole sum that is charged in the Collumnes of Commons and sizings, supposing the Sum shall not amount to sixty Pounds per Quarter; and if the Said Sum shall amount to more, the Steward shall pay to the College Treasurer one sixth Part of the Excess, and accordingly if the Said Sum shall fall short of the fore mentioned Sum of sixty Pounds, the College Treasurer shall allow him one third of this Defect.[19]

By this provision, the College stood to gain if the total charge for commons and sizings in a quarter was over £60, which it usually was in the late eighties. In 1690 the two Fellows, Messrs. Leverett and Brattle, renegotiated arrangements with the Steward, and Richards recorded "that Aaron Bordman the Steward and Cooke is to allow to the Colledge treasurer Such a proportion of the profitt of his place by agreement which they will notify to me as it growes due."[20] From then on the Fellows from time to time "made up the accounts" with the Steward. In 1709 an agreement was made which lasted until 1713 that the Steward should allow the Treasurer one sixth of anything in the quarterly commons and sizings column which was over £80.[21]

From 1701 on there was a fairly regular allowance (called

* In September 1692 the Corporation decided that the peripatetic Mr. Mather, who was not occupying the President's House, was entitled to the rents of rooms there which were occupied by students. (*CSM* XV, 340.) Mather received £13 to £14 a year from this source for the rest of his term of office. (QBB, pp. 137, 143, *et passim.*) Willard did not receive these rents, but Leverett, when he took over in 1708, again benefited from this addition to a President's income.

"advance") to the Steward the first quarter, because there were fewer students in commons during the summer months. The College received the allowance the other three quarters. The average commons and sizings allowance (profit on food) credited to the College from 1687 to 1712 was £20 16*s*. a year.*

*Absent Commons*. The Orders of 1667, setting forth the duties of the College servants, included the provision that "The Buttler shall take a distinct Account of the commons of those schollars that are absent from meales, which shall be reserved for the Colledge use."[22] Mr. Morison feels that "Absent commons presumably meant the detriments,"[23] but it appears to me that though both are derived from students' not being in attendance, absent commons are a different thing from the payments by students when they were not in residence. The next mention of absent commons after 1667 was at a Corporation meeting in May 1685 where it was ordered that "out of the absent Commons of bread and bear shalbe allowed to the Buttler Thirty Shillings on account of washing the Trenchers."[24] Then in 1686 in the Rules and Orders of that year we find, "The Butler shall allow to the College for the absent Commons quarterly 10*s*."[25] Thereafter this flat quarterly charge which the Butler allowed the College was raised to 20*s*. in 1691 (effective 1693), and varied between 20*s*. and 40*s*. to 1713, going to 50*s*. in 1719. It appears in the Steward's account as a flat credit to the College.[26] In April 1725 the Corporation voted that "In Consideration that so great a Number of Students have been out of Commons this Year and the Butler had great Loss by Cyder . . . the Butler be abated five pounds of what he is Obliged by Law to pay to the College for absent Commons this year."

The crucial evidence that absent commons are not detriments is that *both* appear in the College accounts in the Steward's Book of 1703 on and sometimes earlier, for example the account shown in Plate 6. It seems from the wording of all the above rulings that originally the Butler was thought to gain from students' absence

* This came out of an average receipt from the students of £386 a year for commons and sizings, a large sum compared with other receipts. In the early years the intention was that two thirds of the price of parts should be spent on actual foodstuffs and the other third should be used to cover disbursements such as for fuel, utensils, and special expenses connected with feeding, plus some salaries. (Orders of 1650, *CSM* XV, 32.) Thus it was not expected that there should be much profit to the College.

from bevers (and meals) and after 1685 a flat average rate was required of him to permit the College more readily to share in the gain. When cider took the place of some of the beer, the Butler seems usually to have suffered a loss from student absences, and then the College forgave him some of the absent commons charge.*

We have considered income from the obvious sources in the modern view: that is, from tuition, rents, food. Table 10 shows four other sources of revenue: detriments, fines, gallery money, and commencement fees, which we can see are of some consequence, netting among them some £37 a year. In summary, from Table 10 we find that the net income from all these Stewards' operations in 1687 to 1712 was about £104 a year. Chapter VII will show how this was spent.

### ECONOMIC COMMENT

For this analysis we have been heavily dependent on the books of Steward Chesholme and the Bordmans, which show not only detail but changes over the years. For us it is fortunate that records for these particular years have been preserved, for they cover very interesting times from the general economic point of view and enable us to separate at least some of the effects of economic conditions in Massachusetts Bay from the specifically Harvard economics.

It is clear that the greatest variations in the value of the currency of the Colony took place at two times — the first when the mint was established in 1652, and the second after the first four or five years of the eighteenth century, when, as a result of the issue of paper currency, the money of account depreciated. Possibly we should add the years of King Philip's War as a third time of variation. To these major movements can be added the results of the political complications of the end of the seventeenth century when the practically autonomous colony became a royal province. There were also small fluctuations in prices from year to year,

* The drawing of cider seems to have been a frequent source of loss to the Butler, for his accounts with the College are often adjusted because of it. Cf. *CSM* XV, 75, 80; XVI, 422, 520.

The Stewards' records, giving as they do weekly charges for commons and sizings, throw no light on how the Butler took care of brief absences. It is not clear to me exactly how the Butler stood to gain if the student was charged only for what he consumed. The Butler's Book for 1722 to 1750 does not give me any further clues.

but they did not affect Harvard's economy as much as did the larger financial or political changes:

That there was dissatisfaction with the handling of the finances of Harvard in the early 1650's is especially clear from a Committee Report to the General Court on May 3, 1654.[27] At least some of the trouble with such matters as inadequate food may well have been due to rise in prices which took place when the debased N.E. shilling went into circulation. And the increase in the various charges effective in the College Laws of 1655 bears what must be a more than coincidental relationship to the amount by which the money was debased: the value of the English shilling rose to 120 per cent and then later to 135 per cent of the N.E. shilling; tuition charges went from 80*d.* a quarter to 96*d.* — 20 per cent increase; commons, the price of parts, went from 6*f.* to 9*f.* — up 50 per cent. We hope that the administration, the faculty, and the students got some benefit from the raises in charges, but the charges may have just barely kept up with prices.

When, during King Philip's War, the Indians were raiding not far from Cambridge, and when the tax rates to pay for the war were more than ten times what they had been, it would have taken a strong president indeed to have kept the Harvard youth content with academic pursuits. We have told something of President Hoar's difficulties; we know little of the financial details of his short administration or that of Oakes, but we can surely assume that these outside economic and political happenings had a considerable effect in the 1670's. If we checked on the location of the homes of students of that day, graduates and nongraduates, it is conceivable that we might find that the students remaining at College were those from very close to Cambridge, whose expenses would have been lower and whose homes would not have been in so much danger.

When the Dominion was established, the Governor and his Council apparently felt that one way to make possible improvement at the College was to raise the fees. I have no evidence that the raise was caused by price rises; rather, any change in the price level was in the other direction — a depression caused by political troubles. Therefore the increase in College income in the 1690's was due to the deliberate decision to raise fees, and to a slight increase in the number of students, but not to an increase in prices, as had been more or less the case in the fifties. And the tuition increase did contribute to tutors' staying and therefore to a better educational product. There may well have been temporary shortages of food-stuffs, with assaults on Canada being mounted from Boston, but any resultant rise in prices was reversed again by the end of the century; the inflation of prices due to paper money does not seem to have been much felt until, at the earliest, 1707.

## SUMMARY OF INCOME FROM STUDENTS

In summary we can say that, as Table 9 shows, the money cost of an education at Harvard was remarkably steady during the Puritan Period.* Figures for the years before 1653 are not comparable with the others shown because they cover a three-year college course instead of four, and also because there was a definite change in the value of money in the mid 1650's. That the four-year total money cost on our rough average basis rose from £57 a man only to about £65 after fifty to sixty years is surprising, and there is no evidence that there were large fluctuations in the intervening years. Some of the increase, too, was caused by what we might call an improvement in the product, such as when it became possible to spend six shillings a year for wine-cellar rent! And this total charge of £57 to £65 was larger — one cannot say than any man paid, but one can say it was half again as large as the £41 the average student actually paid, ignoring scholarships.

For the average four-year cost, that is for £41, a man could, in the Puritan Period, purchase a small house "38 × 17 and 11 foot stud," clapboarded, with three chimneys.[28] Or one could hire (if he could find him) an ordinary laborer for two years. Thus it took the full pay of a laborer for two years, or half to a third of the annual salary of a college president, to send a boy through four years of college. These are slim bases for comparison, but the figures do not sound extremely different from now.

From the economic view it is significant that tuition then cost so much less than board and room. The fees at a residential college are made up of three very different variables — agricultural goods

* But we leave this subject at 1712, when a bad inflation was getting under way and really beginning to distort prices.

for food, manufactured goods (such as books), and what economists call "services." The relative value of these component parts may vary, but it is possible, and it seems very roughly to have been the case, that over even 300 years the *total real* cost of a Harvard education has stayed nearly constant.

Fortunately the College had some other sources of income, for it is clear that the tuition, study rent, and the net other Stewards' receipts we have mentioned were nowhere nearly sufficient to pay the President, provide him with assistance, or do much toward the erection or maintenance of buildings.

# V

# GOVERNMENT AID

In the relatively small colony the Court and the people were in closer communication than they are today. Hence any description of direct aid by the Court must also recognize government-*sponsored* gifts. From the time of the founding of the colonies the people were familiar with the idea of sharing in the support of public officers and with subsidizing activities which otherwise could not get started, and though most of them had themselves not had the privilege of a college education, the colonists were convinced of the need of educated leaders for their churches and their government; they therefore favored doing all that was possible to further "the Colledge." That this was considerable is attested by the summary of government aid in Table 18 on page 104. Because over the years there has been disagreement about the amount of help from the Colony, we shall describe it here in some detail.

## THE ORIGINAL £400
## 1636–1650

When the College was authorized in 1636, the Court had promised £400 as an initial grant. It was some time before any money was forthcoming. Hugh Peter seems to have had some money to purchase property in Marblehead when he was projecting a college there,[1] but the only amounts we know were paid to the College before Dunster's time totaled £79 3*s.* 3*d.* (net of losses); this was paid to Eaton and Shepard from the Watertown and Cambridge rates* by order of the Colony Treasurer. As of May 16,

* A "rate" was a tax levy; multiples of the basic "rate" were voted each year or more frequently by the General Court. The "Country" was the Colony.

1644, Mr. Ting, the then Colony Treasurer, gave an account of the Country's dealings with the College as shown paraphrased in Table 12. Since Dunster's personal account and the Massachu-

*Table 12. The College Account with the Country, 1644*

| Due the College | £ | *s.* | *d.* |
|---|---|---|---|
| Mr. Harvard's Estate lent to the Country | 175 | 3 | 0 |
| Due the College from money raised by Weld & Peter[a] | | | |
| The original grant | 400 | 0 | 0 |
| | 575 | 3 | 0 |
| Paid the College | | | |
| Rates paid to Eaton and Shepard | 79 | 3 | 3 |
| Cambridge rate paid to H. Dunster | 62 | 12 | 6 |
| Money paid to Dunster | 8 | 7 | 6 |
| In boards paid for by the Country | 10 | 0 | 0 |
| £40 plus £16 to H.D. from Mr. Weld & Mr. Peter | 56 | 0 | 0 |
| | 216 | 3 | 3 |

*Source:* Ting's account is given in College Book I, *CSM* XV, 21.

[a] Weld and Peter's fund-raising mission will be described in the next chapter. No amount was shown here in the original manuscript.

setts Bay Colony Records,[2] show that Ting's final item of £56 was considered to have been allowed President Dunster personally, we have £79 3*s*. 3*d*. plus £81, or £160 3*s*. 3*d*., as the total received from the Country by 1644, and £414 19*s*. 9*d*. due.

Dunster appealed to the Court on behalf of the College and of himself, and as a result the Court voted £150 in November 1644 toward the President's Lodge and another £100 in November 1646.[3] The Court actually ordered the Colony Treasurer to pay these amounts; Mr. Morison feels that we have no reason to think that the Treasurer did *not* pay,[4] but we have no specific evidence that he did. If £250 was paid, £164 19*s*. 9*d*. was left in 1646. However, on October 27, 1647, again in answer to Dunster's request, the Court voted an acknowledgment that it owed the college

| | | |
|---|---|---|
| Given by several donors in England (Weld-Peter) | £133 | 0*s*. |
| Upon the country's gift | £190 | 16*s*. |
| Due the President personally for annual salary | £ 56 | 0*s*.[5] |

Thus the Court acknowledged owing £190 16*s*. and not £164

19*s.* 9*d.* This would indicate either that the two grants of £250 *were* paid and some other small debt incurred (such as a gift deposited with the Country Treasurer), or that something (£25 16*s.* 6*d.*) less than the £250 had been paid. At the time of this accounting the Court stated, "We conceive it reasonable" that the £190 16*s.* should be paid, but they did not then order it paid. They provided, however, that if what appeared due from the Country was not paid forthwith, eight per cent must be allowed on it so long as it remained unpaid.

On September 14, 1650, the Court finally ordered that the current Cambridge rate should be turned over to the College Steward to cover any remaining unpaid balance due the College, and that "any overplus" of the rate should "remayne as the colledge stocke."[6] The next month, October 1650, £100 was voted and ordered paid with interest from 1648.[7]

All of the above serves to indicate that the total direct grant paid to the College to the end of Dunster's time as President was no more than the original £400 of 1636. We have, however, some reason to believe that the £400, as well as John Harvard's gift, which Treasurer Ting said had been "lent to the Country," were actually paid to the College.* From this time on the only claim

* President Quincy did not believe that these amounts ever were fully paid, but Quincy was writing at a time when he was having trouble with the General Court (1840) and he was inclined to minimize the Country's contribution. He points out that the £150 grant was voted out of Weld-Peter monies raised in England. Josiah Quincy, *The History of Harvard University* (Cambridge, 1840), 2 vols. The final Weld-Peter account, however, lists £291 3*s.* 10*d.* as paid for the College, but it includes £162 16*s.* 4*d.* for the Mowlson fund, which was still due the College at the end of the century and was paid only in 1713. Thus there was not £150 additional in the Weld-Peter College account to have covered the £150. Or we could say the £291 Weld-Peter less £150 paid gives £141 due on Weld-Peter (not £133), and then assume that the Mowlson fund had been temporarily forgotten.

Mr. Morison says the £133 in the Court's acknowledgment is a misstatement of Mowlson money (*FHC*, p. 295). But what of the £56 we know Dunster received from Weld-Peter? If the £150 was paid from Weld-Peter funds of £291 3*s.* 10*d.*, £291 less £56 less £150 gives £85, insufficient to have been Mowlson (see *Quincy*, pp. 41–42 and Appendix VII, p. 473; also the Weld-Peter account in HUA, College Papers, Vol. I, Item 5).

The discussion of payment of the Country's £400 has not yet referred to an "abridgement" of some College and Dunster accounts found in "Corporation Papers, 1636–1660." There, in the College account, receipts from the Country are lumped with "gifts" to list a 1640–1652 total of £797 2*s.* 7*d.* We have shown that in *Dunster's* time the College in all likelihood received £431 from the Country (£81 on Ting's account plus assumed grants of £350), and it should have had at least an additional £64 19*s.* 9*d.* from the Cambridge rate to clean up the Country and John Harvard made against the Country for money overdue was in connection with a scholarship given by Lady Mowlson, which was the balance of money raised in England by Weld and Peter.

We find from Dunster's personal accounts[8] that the total he himself received in *direct* Country grants to 1652 was £50, if we consider the Weld-Peter £56 to have come from private sources. As we shall see later, the Country also granted the College the income of the Charlestown ferry, and Dunster did receive this personally, but the Court did not seem to take full responsibility for the salary of the first president.

## THE COLLEGE CORN
## 1644–1655

One of the most important and best-known early gifts to Harvard from the Country was the "College corn." Thomas Shepard, the pastor of the Cambridge church, had the College's welfare very much in mind. In September 1644, seeing that Dunster was not faring too well with the Massachusetts General Court, he presented a proposition to the Commissioners of the United Colonies of New England that

> Although hitherto God hath carryed on that worke by a speciall hand, . . . yet, . . . for want of some externall supplys, many are discouraged from sending their children (though pregnant and fitt to take the best impression) thereunto; . . . And those who are continued not without much pressure generally to the feeble abillities of their parents or other private frends who beare the burthen therein aloane . . . .

Shepard therefore suggested that "but the fourth part of a bushell of Corne, or somethinge equivalent thereunto" be given yearly by every family in New England "which is able and willing." The

accounts left in 1650. This leaves £301 2*s.* 10*d.* to have been received from gifts or other Country payments. To check this — we shall show in Chapter VI (Table 19) that there is record of £382 17*s.* 6*d.* of gifts made before 1654, not including Mowlson or John Harvard. From this we may deduct £56 which Ting said was paid *Dunster* (personally) from Weld-Peter funds, and, *if* these gifts were all made in Dunster's time, we have £326 17*s.* 6*d.* of gifts available to Dunster for College expenses. This is more than the £301 2*s.* 10*d.* we had left in the abridgement account for gifts, and we appear to have assumed £25 14*s.* 8*d.* too much payment by the Country. This reasoning would throw some doubt on whether or not the Country did pay the full £350 of the grants; perhaps it was £25 16*s.* 6*d.* less, as shown on page 87. (Some amounts which look like gifts were payment of taxes. See *CSM* XV, 17 and 21.)

One can see that the number of "if's" makes all such refinements precarious.

Commissioners fully approved this suggestion and agreed that it should "be comended to the severall generall Courts as a matter worthy of due consideracion and entertainement. . . ."[9]

Massachusetts, Connecticut, and New Haven General Courts took action on this recommendation for scholarship assistance to "poor, pious, and learned"[10] students, commended it to the various towns for action, and set up systems for the collection of the corn or its equivalent. Plymouth Town acted, but not Plymouth Colony. Table 13 shows the record of receipts from these gifts, made mostly at the rate of a peck of corn or 12*d.* per family.* We know that the effective amount received was reduced by £12 6*s.* 6*d.* for freight charges.[11] The College corn money was used for payments to Fellows and students and certainly was a substantial contribution.

Toward the end of the eight-year period the annual amounts given decreased. In 1647 Dunster had written again to the United Colonies with some questions about the use of the money, the suggestion that the contributions be made a more regular voluntary tax, and a request for support of the President and the library, but there had been no financial response to his appeal.[12]

The President and Fellows appealed again to the Commissioners of the United Colonies in September 1651, and the Commissioners agreed to use their influence to encourage the continuation of gifts of corn.[13] Then in the first item of business of the session on October 19, 1652, the Massachusetts Court made a special order that each town should appoint an officer to accept individual gifts and turn them over to the College for maintenance of the President, Fellows, and poor scholars.[14] The University Archives contain a file of the returns of this second general subscription, listing the names of donors, with amounts given, and commenting upon the difficulties of procuring the money.[15] This group of papers gives one of the most graphic pictures of what it meant to the Colonists to support the "Universitie" as they did.

On May 14, 1653, twenty-five individuals in Wenham signed that "There is ingeaged six pound and ten shillings to be payd at wenham att this next harvist come twellve month." Twenty-three

* The corn of the "College corn" is wheat, English corn. Corn as we think of it in this country today was in the seventeenth century usually called "Indian Corn" or just "Indian."

*Table 13. Value of Eight Years' College Corn from the Towns, 1644 to 1653*

| | | £ | s. | d. | ob. | £ | s. | d. |
|---|---|---|---|---|---|---|---|---|
| *Massachusetts* | Boston | 84 | 18 | 7 | 2 | | | |
| | Charlstown | 37 | 16 | 2 | 0 | | | |
| | Lyn | 1 | 0 | 0 | 0 | | | |
| | Ipswich | 5 | 0 | 0 | 0 | | | |
| | Dorchester | 4 | 6 | 0 | 0 | | | |
| | Concord | 8 | 17 | 4 | 0 | | | |
| | Dedham | 4 | 6 | 0 | 0 | | | |
| | Cambridge | 2 | 15 | 3 | 2 | | | |
| | Brantrey | 5 | 4 | 3 | 0 | | | |
| | Glocester | | 12 | 0 | 0 | | | |
| | Mauldon | | 12 | 6 | 0 | | | |
| | Rowley | 7 | 8 | 7 | 2 | | | |
| | Roxbury | 16 | 18 | 3 | 0 | | | |
| | Newbury | 1 | 10 | 0 | 0 | | | |
| | Woburne | 5 | 13 | 7 | 2 | | | |
| | Sudbury | 1 | 4 | 3 | 0 | | | |
| | Springfield | 3 | 0 | 0 | 0 | 191 | 3 | 5 |
| *Hartford* | Hartford | 30 | 17 | 0 | 0 | | | |
| | Saybrook | 2 | 9 | 0 | 0 | | | |
| | Windsor | 5 | 15 | 0 | 0 | 39 | 1 | 0 |
| *New haven* | New haven | 17 | 11 | 9 | 0 | | | |
| | Millford | 10 | 15 | 6 | 0 | | | |
| | Stratford | 6 | 14 | 0 | 0 | 35 | 1 | 3 |
| *Plimouth* | Plymouth Town | 4 | 13 | 0 | 0 | 4 | 13 | 0 |
| | | | | | | 269 | 18 | 8 |

*Source:* Rearranged from *CSM* XV, 179–180. See also *CSM* XV, 175.

in "Wooburne" planned to make gifts of from £5 to 5*s*., in all totaling £28 14*s*. 6*d*. Thirty-three in Yorke, up on the coast of Maine, signed for contributions totaling £9 10*s*. 6*d*., ranging from £1 to several of 2*s*., "to be paid in boards the yeare, but not yearly."

Daniel Poore, Constable of Andover, writes to Collector Nowell:

Upon the note I received from your Selfe and the rest of your Comittee for the Colledge, I called our Inhabitantes together and acquainted them therewith, who well approves of the care of the Court for the advancement of Learning and are willing to be helpfull according to their ability: but by reason our Towne is very small consisting of about 20 poore familyes (few whereof have corne for their owne necessity) they found themselves unable to give any considerable summe to the case aforesaid. Yet to shew their willingness to forward so good a worke, they have generally agreed to give a pecke of wheat this year for the least family, others two, some a bushell. What it will exactly Come to I cannot yet tell; we hope God will enable us to doe the like hereafter. . . .

A later list shows "about £2" as Andover's total, which, at 12*d.* a peck, was more than they could have expected.

Mr. Increase Nowell of Charlestown is addressed November 28, 1653, by Mr. Joshua Hubbard of Hingham:

> I received your Letters, though they were long before they came to my hands, insomuch as I could not get fit opportunity to impart the desires, and good motions (there in specified) unto the Towne before this present day. Wherein I have not onely certified them of your just and laudable proposalls, but have also labored to my utmost to effect something therein that might be satisfactory to your worships who are intrusted with these affaires, and also beneficial unto learning, and for the honor of God. And truely our Towne stands very well affected toward Learneing . . .

and would much like to support the proposals also "by reason of the respect they beare to the honored Court, and your selves who are the authors of this present design, . . ." but the town "cannot answer fully your expectations" because of great expenses, many scholars leaving the country, and other reasons. Mr. Hubbard would like to talk with their worships to learn arguments to use with the town. (The matter of Harvard graduates leaving the colonies was a complaint which frequently interfered with support.) The incomplete list we have does not tell us what Hingham finally gave.

Cambridge itself, where one of the two collectors appointed by the town was Thomas Danforth, promised gifts of £150 over the next two years — a really notable sum, especially since the Cambridge rate was often assigned to the College by the Country and Cambridge people were better able than average to see that the General Court was doing something for the institution. But no doubt Cambridge was also better able to appreciate the benefits from the College.

Concord carried out Dunster's earlier suggestion: the "Company of sayd towne and church" agreed to give five pounds per annum "to be leavyed upon the same town after the same manner as the other rates are leavyed" for seven years, to be renewed "if it shall appeare that it may be improved for good. . . ." This order was to be recorded in the Court. There were forty-two signatures, four made by mark.[16] According to the Committee which had reported to the General Court on May 3, 1654, two other towns, Charlestown and Ipswich, promised annual gifts, the first £10 a year, the second £8 a year for seven years.[17]

The Committee reported that the total of this subscription promised was £572 3*s.* 11*d.*, plus the £23 a year for several years. How much of this was actually collected, we do not know.*

## PRESIDENTIAL SALARY GRANTS

## 1654–1712

We can see that the magistrates, ministers, and other leading citizens were during Dunster's presidency frequently pressed to arrange financial support for the College, either through official action by the "country" or by sponsoring voluntary giving from individuals. We can see, too, some signs that these frequent appeals were tending to wear out the College's welcome, even though all agreed that the work of the institution was essential. Increase Nowell, as Secretary of the Colony, and also as collector of the 1652 to 1655 subscriptions, and finally as chairman of the General Court's committee which reported on the College in 1654, was in an especially good position to understand the situation. The Nowell Committee had based a large part of its solution of the problems on the continuation of the contributions; but by October 18, 1654, experience being that "nothing have binn hitherto obteined from severall persons and townes, although some have donne very liberally and freely,"** the General Court decided that a different

* See also *HCSC*, p. 30, n. 5.

It is obviously not entirely correct to say that the College Corn or this subscription was a gift of the Country. It was, however, due in large measure to Court action, and later the Court provided that the 1652–1655 subscriptions for salaries and scholarships could be deducted from taxes paid.

** The full quotation from the Court is worth reading: "Whereas wee cannot but acknowledg the great goodnes of God towards his people in this wildernes in raysing up schools of learning, and especially the colledge, from whenc there hath sprung many usefull instruments, both in church and commonwealth, both to this and other places: and whereas at present the worke of the colledge have binn severall wayes obstructed, and seemes yett also at present, for want of comfortable mainetenance for the incouragement of a president: this Court, taking the same into theire serious consideration, and finding that though many propositions have binn made for a system was necessary and came to an important decision: to allow the President and Fellows £100 a year besides the ferry. The £100 was to be added to the regular Colony tax levy and to be paid by the Colony Treasurer to the College Treasurer, who should distribute the money between President and Fellows as the Overseers determined. Anyone who had subscribed to the College voluntarily since about 1652 could deduct his contribution from his future tax.

On Mr. Chauncy's accepting the presidency the Overseers voted that the full £100 should go to the President, and when Hoar was made President the Court raised the amount to £150, to "be continued untill the Generall Court or overseers shall finde some other way for making it good."[18]

With this vote we enter calmer waters for financial relations between the College and the Court. Though the College and its friends from time to time over the decades made special appeals to the Court for aid, in general it seemed to be assumed that the Court was responsible for the President's salary and for special building needs, but that the rest of the College's support must come from other sources.

What, then, did the Court provide of the Presidents' salaries? The best we can gather from College and Court records is shown in Table 14.*

## THE PISCATAQUA BENEVOLENCE
## 1669–1677[19]

Towns along the Piscataqua River in New Hampshire (long a part of Massachusetts) were established in the early 1630's and shortly became quite prosperous through fishing and lumbering. The largest Piscataqua town was Portsmouth, originally called Strawberry-Bank. On May 20, 1669, the inhabitants of that town authorized John and Richard Cutt and the Reverend Joshua Moody (Harvard A.B. 1653) to write the General Court:

---

voluntary contribution, yett nothing have binn hitherto obteined from severall persons and townes, although some have donne very liberally and freely, and fearing lest we should shew ourselves ungratefull to God, or unfaithfull to posteritie, if so good a seminary of knowledg and virtue should fall to the ground through any neglect of ours, It is therefore ordered by this Court . . . ." *Mass. Bay Recs.* IV, i, 205.

* For full discussion of the Presidents' salaries, see below pages 129–130.

That seeing by your meanes (under God) wee injoy much peace and quietnes, and very worthy deeds are donn to us by the favorable aspect of the government of this colony upon us, we accept it alwaies and in all places with all thankfullnes; and though wee have articled with yourselves for exemption from publique charges, yett we never articled with God and our oune consciences for exemption from gratitude, which to demonstrate, while wee were studying, the loud groanes of the sinking colledg in its present low estate, came to our eares, the releiving of which wee account a good worke for the house of our God, and needfull for the

*Table 14. Harvard Presidents' Receipts from the Country to 1712*[a]

| President | Payments | Total | Notes |
|---|---|---|---|
| Dunster | £50 | £50 | Plus ferry. |
| Chauncy | £58 | | 1st year salary (fraction). |
| | £30[b] | | 1655. *Mass. Bay Recs.* IV, i, 237. |
| | 17 × £100 | | 17 years' salary. |
| | £20 | 1808[c] | 1666 gratuity. *Mass. Bay Recs.* IV, ii, 314. |
| Hoar | 2 × £150 | | |
| | 1 × £100 | 400 | 3 years' salary (*Salary continued in 1675, after resignation. Mass. Bay Recs.* V, 31.) |
| Oakes | 5 × £100 | | |
| | 1 × £150 | 650 | 6 years' salary. |
| Fellows | £50 | 50 | Acting as President. *Mass. Bay Recs.* V, 352. |
| Rogers | 2 × £150 | | |
| | £37 | 337 | $2\frac{1}{4}$ years' salary. |
| Fellows | 1 × £100 | 100 | Acting as President. *Mass. Bay Recs.* V, 479. |
| Mather | —[d] | | June 1685 to June 1692. |
| | 1 × £100[e] | | 1692–1693. *A&R* VII, 452. Corporation Papers. |
| | 7 × £50 | | Salary 1693–1700. |
| | 1 × £110 | 560+ | 1700–1701, *A&R* VII, 645. |
| Willard | 1 × £72 | | 14 months. *A&R* VII, 362, 742. |
| | 5 × £60 | 372 | 5 years' salary. |
| Leverett | 4 × £150 | | 4 years' salary to July 1712. *A&R* VII, 257. |
| | 2 × £30 | 660 | Voted 1711 and 1712. *A&R* IX, 214, 267. |
| | | £4987 | |

*Source:* The figures represent a consensus of not only the public records referred to in "notes" but also College records in *CSM*, as well as *FHC* and *HCSC*.

[a] This exhibit does not include Court payments for any housing.

[b] On May 23, 1655, the new President's funds had run out and he, "standing in neede of present supplies," was voted £30 by the Court — to be repaid from the ferry rent. *Mass. Bay Recs.* III, 388; IV, i, 237. Chauncy *may* have repaid it.

[c] In addition the Court paid £10 a year for several years toward the support of Chauncy's invalid son after the father's death. Cf. John Langdon Sibley, *Biographical Sketches of Graduates of Harvard University* (Cambridge, 1873), I, 528–529.

[d] There seems to be no available source of knowledge concerning possible payments by the Country to Mather during this period. It seems to me improbable that there were *no* such payments.

[e] The record for this year is confirmed by our having in HUA the original order for payment to Mather as President of the College and Mather's endorsement that he received payment.

perpetuating of knouledge, both religious and civil, among us, and our posterity after us; . . . therefore, . . . wee have made a collection in our toune of sixty pounds per annum (and hope to make it more), which said summe is to be paid annually for these seven yeares ensuing, to be improoved, at the discretion of the honoured overseers of the colledge, for the behoofe of the same and the advancement of good litterature there, hoping withall that the example of ourselves (which have been accounted no people) will provoke the rest of the country to jealousy (wee meane an holy emulation to appeare in so good a worke), and that this honoured Court will, in their wisdomes, see meete vigerously to act for the diverting the sad omen to poore New England, if a colledge, begun and comfortably upheld while wee were litle, should sinc, now wee are groune greate, especially after so large and proffitable an harvest that this country and other places have reaped from the same . . . .[20]

On June 3, 1669, the Overseers met to appoint John Richards Treasurer of the College, and they also voted that £34 of the first year's Piscataqua gift should be distributed among the three fellows and the balance be used for the "Encouragement of Schollars."

"The loud groanes of the sinking colledg" had been heard, and Richards came into office under good auspices. But the receiving and disposing of the "Piscataqua benevolence" probably caused Treasurer Richards more work and bother than did any other account which he handled for the College; a very high proportion of the entries in his book in the next seven years were concerned with its management. The gift was paid in boards and barrel- and pipe-staves,* sent by ship from Portsmouth to Richards' wharf where most of them were sold to Bostonians who needed them.

Though there may have been lumber to the value of £60 a year put on board ship in Portsmouth, there was many a possible slip between the loading and the spending of the money for salaries and scholarships in Cambridge. The first shipment arrived on July 16, 1670, supposedly "all merchantable," but much was inferior; 24*d.* had to be paid for "culling and piling." On July 2, 1672, one transaction was completed by the receipt of money from John Man in payment for some iron which Belcher had received from Pool in exchange for 5000 feet of boards which were sold to Kimball. The Treasurer's mother bought some of the boards, as did the

* Staves were pieces of wood, usually oak, suitable for the making of barrels or wine casks, which were much in demand for the European and West Indian trade.

Town of Boston for the construction of a school house, and the College itself used 500 feet to build fences. In August 1674 "that Great Storme" broke Richards' wharf "all to peeces, by two vessels which drove against it; and all those boards . . . were lost . . . beaten to peeces and driven along the Shoar." Three thousand four hundred and fifty-six feet of lumber was lost, but some was recovered.[21] What with these losses and deductions, and charges for freight, landing, piling, and wharfage, the net annual proceeds were not £60.

The attractions of making this sizable gift had somewhat dimmed for some of the townspeople of Portsmouth, too, for we find the Portsmouth general town meeting of March 13, 1673, voting that the subscriptions of those who had not paid should be levied against them in the town rate.[22] Richard Cutt's interest in the College was steadfast, for he had subscribed a full third of the £60, and in his will of May 10, 1675, he provided for the payment if he died with any balance outstanding. September 12, 1676, Richards received boards on this account from Mrs. Elinor Cutt.[23]

Richards shows all these transactions in detail. Table 15 gives the final results. Even allowing for the losses in the storm and differences in valuation, this amount is far from £60 times seven, but it is all I can find on the College books. Nonetheless, the people of Piscataqua had made a notable gift and one which helped and cheered the College when it was badly in need of both help and cheer.

*Table 15. Harvard College Piscataqua Benevolence, 1670 to 1677*

| Year | Gross receipts | | | Net of expenses | |
|---|---|---|---|---|---|
| | £ | s. | d. | £ | s. |
| 1670 | 34 | 18 | 6 | 31 | 10 |
| 1671–72 | 41 | 15 | 6 | 35 | 10 |
| 1672–73 | 31 | 5 | 6 | 26 | 4 |
| 1673–75 | 49 | 10 | 6 | 46 | 6 |
| 1676–77 | 32 | 11 | 0 | 28 | 4 |
| | 190 | 1 | 0 | 164 | 4 |

*Source:* Richards, pp. 43, 44, 57.

## RECEIPTS FOR BUILDINGS

## 1638–1715

We have seen the small amounts provided by the Country for the first Harvard College. This first building built expressly for the College did not hold up very well, for President Dunster frequently from 1647 on appealed to the Court and to the Commissioners of the United Colonies for help in repairing it. In 1650, after such an appeal, the General Court replied, "For the desire of enlargment of buildinge, the Courte, beinge so farre in debt, are in no capacitie at present to encourage it, as otherwise they would."[24] The Commissioners, while agreeing that the buildings were in bad shape, did not provide any funds.

At the same time as the extension of the corn was being promoted, the Massachusetts General Court, perhaps as a result of the Corporation's appeal to the United Colonies, went on record as suggesting to the College that it try to raise money for building repairs by asking the town ministers to arrange personal giving to the College for that purpose. College Book III (Danforth) shows £250 5*s*. 6*d*.[25] as having been given for repairs in 1654 and 1655, and very possibly this money was the result of such an appeal.

On May 9, 1655, the Corporation, despite repairs made, drew up "A briefe Information of the present necessityes of the Colledg which the Corporation do desire may by the concurrence of the Overseers be presented to the Consideration of the Generall Court with earnest desires of their speedy and effectuall help for supply," and they included the following paragraph concerning one of the two most important needs:

> The Colledge building, although it be new-groundsilled by the help of some free Contributions the last year, yet those ceasing and the worke of Reparation therewith intermitted, it remains in other respects, in a very ruinous condition. It is of absolute necessity, that it bee speedily new-covered, being not fitt for Scholars long to abide in, as it is. And without such Reparation some time this Summer both the whole Building will decay, and So the former charge about it be lost, and the Scholars will be forced to depart. So that either help must be had herein, or else (we fear) no lesse then a Dissolution of the Colledge will follow. And it is conceived that it will need a Hundred pounds to set it in Comfortable Repair.[26]

There is no evidence that the Country responded to this forceful appeal, but since the first Harvard College continued in use for over twenty years, we judge the £100 turned up from somewhere.

The time did come, however, when the old building had to be replaced. President Chauncy in August 1671, six months before his death, joined the Fellows and the Overseers in another urgent letter to the Court and had the satisfaction of seeing the Council the next month vote to promote a drive throughout the Colony to raise funds to build a new brick or stone building.[27] This turned out to be by far the most successful general appeal made during the Puritan Period. All parts of Massachusetts, including the outlying regions, under the leadership of the ministers and the local town authorities, answered by promising a total of £2280 3*s.* 3*d.* by 1672.[28] Even the students gave. President Hoar had every reason to be very hopeful when he took office in December of that year.

Collection of the subscriptions went only fairly well, but the Overseers appointed a committee to supervise and two Stewards to manage the work of construction, which began in 1674. Unhappily, King Philip's War, starting in July 1675, threw the whole of New England into confusion and made extremely heavy financial demands in taxes;[29] collection of the College's funds lagged. In 1675 the General Court issued an order "for the quickening of the several townes," and in 1677 Secretary Rawson of the General Court sent letters to all towns which had not lived up to expectations.*

* To the ministers and selectmen of towns which were behind in payments, Rawson wrote, "Gentlemen:

"Upon motion of this Court formerly for the erecting a new aedifice for the colledge at Cambridge, wee received from your tounes subscriptions of considerable value, at which time wee suppose there was upon yow a serious sence of so good a worke, which procured so free a promise from your selves; but so it is that the overseers of that worke, who were entrusted to receive the same, make complaint that you are yet behind considerably of your engagements on that behalfe, whereby the building is obstructed. The want of some supply makes the house wholly useless, and frustrates the donors' intentions and the country's just expectation. Wee entreate and expect that you hasten within two months to compleat your full summs, and remitt the same to Mr. Maning and others of Cambridge betrusted in that matter, that the worke may be finished, and this Court prevented further trouble of taking the same by distresse. Herein you will comply with your owne duty. This is all I am comanded at present.

"Edward Rawson. Secretary

"In the name and by order of the Generall Court."

To Ipswich and Salem, which had not yet subscribed anything, he included that

Commencement was held in the new — second — "Harvard College" in 1677, though it was far from complete. There were excellent reasons why some of the gifts had not come in: King Philip's warriors had scalped some of the prospective donors, burned out others, and otherwise ravaged the lands of many. The amount collected to May 1682 was the large sum of £1969 14*s*. 9*d*., and not more than £100 came in later.

No further general College buildings were built with the Country's help in the Puritan Period,* but the Court did make some provisions for the Presidents' Houses.

President Dunster had some help from the Country in building his lodge — £150 was granted by the Court in 1644 for that purpose and credited against the £400 original promise. In 1672 the Court, to encourage President Hoar, allowed not over £300 of the subscriptions for the new Harvard Hall to be used to repair and improve Dunster's old Lodge.[30] Richards' accounts show no sign of this receipt or expense; however, the Stewards of Harvard Hall kept separate accounts and they may have repaired the President's Lodge from Harvard Hall money.

We know that Hoar did not stay long in the President's House and that Acting President Oakes did not live there. Then, when he was made President in 1680, Oakes required new lodging, and a new President's House was built at the direction of the Court to facilitate "his more constant and convenient Attendance of his place" and because the old Lodge was found to be "so defective that it is not worth repayring."[31] It looks as if any money spent in 1672 was largely wasted.

Financial provision for this 1680 construction was ambiguous; the Court authorized using "such or part of the Colledge Estate

---

the Court "desire you to consider that Scripture, 1 Chronicles, 29, especially from verse 10 to 17, wherein David and the people of Israell gave liberally unto a good worke, praysing God that he had given them hearts to offer so willingly, acknowledging that all their substance came from God, and that of his owne they had given him, verse 13. But wee shall add no more, but committ you to God, and remaine,

"Your loving friends, the Generall Court of the Massachusetts."

*Mass Bay Recs.* V, 143–144; see also pp. 32, 156, 195, 255, 268, 380, 445–446.

* In 1713 repairs costing about £150 were made to Harvard Hall with the approval of the Governor, but President Leverett made it a practice to consult Governor Dudley (presumably as an Overseer) on many matters, and this does not prove that the Court made any financial contribution to this charge. *CSM* XV, lxxxix–xci. I find no record of payment by the Court for this at least up to 1715.

or Stocke as may attayne the ends proposed, provided they meddle not with any thing that is given to particular Uses; and in case that shall not fully attayne the ends, the Treasurer is hereby ordered to make payment of so much as shalbe wantinge for the finishing." The total cost was not to exceed £200. They directed that the Stock be "inquired into" to see "howmuch may be had there, . . . to know what bills to draw upon the Country Treasurer for further supply if need be. . . ."[32] It is clear the Country did not pay for *all* of the cost, but how much it paid is hard to say.

For most of the next twenty years there was no President living in the House, and it was used for students. When Mather agreed to move to Cambridge, and did so for a few months, the Court in 1701 authorized the Governor and Council to pay £150 for more repairs.[33] This does not appear to have been put through Brattle's books, but it looks as if this amount was spent.

On November 2, 1708, President Leverett wrote the Court that, "It having bin but little Inhabited, the house is gon again much to decay, and unless repaired is in Danger of being soon in dispair." Again the Court agreed, and several small sums were paid in 1709 and 1710.[34] This house was demolished when Massachusetts Hall was built in 1720.

*Table 16. Cost of Buildings at Harvard College Granted or Sponsored by the General Court to 1715*

| | Grants | | | Subscriptions sponsored | | |
|---|---|---|---|---|---|---|
| | £ | *s.* | *d.* | £ | *s.* | *d.* |
| First Harvard College (of the original £400) | 160 | 3 | 3? | | | |
| President's Lodge, 1644 (of the original £400) | 150 | | | | | |
| Gifts for repairs, 1654–1655 | | | | 250 | 5 | 6 |
| Second Harvard College, 1671–1685 | | | | 2000 | | |
| President's House repairs, 1672 (included in above) | | | | (300) | | |
| New President's House, 1680 | 100? | | | | | |
| President's House repairs, 1701 | 150 | | | | | |
| President's House repairs, 1709–1710 | 40? | | | | | |
| | 600 | 3 | 3 | 2250 | 5 | 6 |

Despite all this periodic agitation and sympathetic attention to the state of Harvard's buildings, we find, in summary, that direct grants by the Country for buildings were not very substantial, but the Court's influence in support of the College building was extremely important, as Table 16 shows.

### THE CHARLESTOWN FERRY

One of the most important grants from the Colony to the College was the income of the Charlestown ferry, the oversight and rent of which were in 1640 turned over to Harvard College with the thought that the College would relieve the Court of direct responsibility for keeping this essential public utility operating, and that the College in turn, in the manner of beneficiaries of the Crown of England, would have the use of a substantial and regular revenue.

This grant, like most benefits to early Harvard, was not without its complications. Perhaps the most bothersome to Dunster, and to the ferrymen, was the practical necessity of accepting wampumpeage in payment of the small fare; moreover, the peage that came to them was the "refuse" of the business community. The Court tried to improve matters with a provision that the franchise to the fur traders was contingent on their accepting £25 worth of peage a year from the College,[35] but the problem continued.

As wampum came to be used less, that part of the problem was solved, but not the basic difficulty of "Wante of small money for change," which forced the ferrymen "to trust those whome we cary over, And many times never have our pay, but doe our Labour for Noe thing, which is more than we cane beare, And is very unComefortable in many respects." The ferrymen therefore requested that the Court consider coining twopenny and fourpenny pieces. They also found that the £40 per annum they paid to the College was too much rent after the construction in 1662 of the Cambridge Bridge (where the Lars Anderson Bridge now is) cut into their business; so, to "maintayne our familyes, and pay Such publicke Charges to Church and Common wealth which god and the Laws require of us," they needed an abatement.[36] The Court was sympathetic, and the College received less for a few years.

Business on the ferry improved and the £40 fee was reinstated by 1674, and later the rents were gradually increased. In 1695, when the contract was renewed at £60 a year, the Treasurer also exacted a "fine" of £10 for the renewal privilege. This practice

*Table 17. Annual Rents of the Charlestown Ferry*

| Date | Rent |
|---|---|
| | £ |
| 1640 | 40 |
| 1654 | 40[a] |
| 1654–1663 | av. 37 |
| 1663–1668 | av. 27 |
| 1669–1674 | 27½ |
| 1674–1681 | 40 |
| 1681–1695 | 50 |
| 1695–1702 | 60[b] |
| 1702–1709 | 70[b] |
| 1709–1716 | 72[b] |

*Sources* include Danforth in *CSM* XV, 213, 215; Richards, pp. 12, 54, 55, 71, 74; Brattle, pp. 35, 45, 68, 107, 95, *et passim*.

[a] See footnote 36 of this chapter.

[b] In addition, there was a "fine" of £5 a lessee when a new lease was made: £10 in 1695, £10 in 1701, £10 in 1707, £5 in 1710 (for ⅓), in all £35. Brattle, pp. 35, 68, 69, 94, 107.

was continued on most subsequent renewals. The 1702 contract (£70 a year) was the first to require the boatmen to give bond for their rent, and Brattle duly recorded the names of the eminent citizens who guaranteed the "Payment of the rent, and performing the Covenants expressed and reserved in said Lease."[37] The ferry continued for many years to pay the College a very welcome revenue, as shown in Table 17.

## LAND AND OTHER GRANTS

## 1638–1715

The General Court, not having the funds to make the rewards and allowances it thought deserved, frequently made grants of land to public servants and to institutions. The Court made grants of land to Harvard College and to the College Presidents, but these lands produced little revenue for the College in the period we are studying.[38] For obvious reasons, grants made to the College by the Town of Cambridge met with better success.

The first land granted by the Town for the College was a tract of two and two-thirds acres in the Old Ox Pasture, set aside on May 11, 1638, for "the professor."[39] The tract included the land where the Littauer Center now is. The Town also at the same time made two allotments to Eaton personally.

The site of Shawsheen, now Billerica, was granted by the Colony to the Town of Cambridge, and in 1649 Cambridge in turn made a grant there of 400 acres to President Dunster personally and 100 acres to the College.[40] Dunster shortly gave 100 of his 400 acres to the College. This "farme at Billerica" brought in a small annual income for many years.[41]

A government that wishes to encourage an institution or an activity within its confines may do so by making grants of money or other property, or it may allow what we might call corporate "fringe benefits." Early Massachusetts, in the College Charter of 1650, ordered liberal exemptions from taxes and services for the College and its employees and students.

To some extent the Weld-Peter 1642 fund-raising mission was sponsored by governments in England: Parliament seems to have appointed collectors, and the Lord-Mayor of London backed the collection.[42]

## SUMMARY OF GOVERNMENT SUPPORT

We have seen that the government of Massachusetts Bay Colony, and sometimes those of other New England colonies, wished to support Harvard College and higher education. For Dunster and his successors in the seventeenth century, government aid was a major source of income; but then as now receipt of government assistance was not without attendant pain. Moreover, from the earliest days and throughout the seventeenth century, the administration of fiscal matters in Massachusetts was so inept that actual *payment* of grants suffered. We can refer again to Governor Winthrop:

> Mr. Winslow being now to go for England, etc., the court was troubled how to furnish him with money or beaver (for there was nothing in the

*Table 18. Government Financial Aid to Harvard College, 1636 to 1712*[a]

| Dates | Purpose | Grants | Sponsored subscriptions | | | |
|---|---|---|---|---|---|---|
| | | £ | £ | *s.* | *d.* | |
| 1636 | The original grant | 400 | | | | |
| 1640 | President Dunster, salary | 50 | | | | |
| 1644–1653 | The College corne | | 269 | 18 | 8 | |
| 1652–1655 | Extension of corne[b] | | (572 | 3 | 11 | plus £23 each of several years) |
| 1655–1712 | Other Presidents' salaries[c] | 4937 | | | | |
| 1669–1677 | Piscataqua benevolence | | 164 | 4 | 0 | |
| 1640–1712 | Ferry[d] | 3299 | | | | |
| 1650–1712 | Capitalized land rent[e] | 27 | | | | |
| | Buildings (other than elsewhere in this table) | | | | | |
| 1654–1655 | Gifts for repairs[f] | | 251 | 15 | 6 | |
| 1671–1685 | Second Harvard College and President's House repairs | | 2000 | 0 | 0 | |
| 1680 | President's House | 100? | | | | |
| 1701 | President's House repairs | 150 | | | | |
| 1709–1710 | President's House repairs | 40? | | | | |
| | | 9003 | 2685 | 18 | 2 | |

[a] This table should be read keeping in mind the reservations throughout this chapter. The table does not show lands unless they provided money income in this period. Grants include only money from Country or Town funds and not amounts from Weld and Peter or other sponsored gifts.

[b] The Court allowed this to be credited against future taxes, so we do not know how much of it was actually paid. Since the taxes were to cover the President's salary and the latter had presumably been paid in full to 1655 as due, it may well be that in so far as this gift was paid by 1655 it may not have been claimed as a tax deduction and should be included in this list. See *HCSC*, p. 30, and n. 5.

[c] Plus Mather's salary, if any was paid by the Country, from 1685 to 1692.

[d] The Ferry estimate is based on

| | | |
|---|---|---|
| £40 × 14 | for | 8/40–5/54 |
| 37 × 9 | | 8/54–5/63 |
| 27 × 5 | | 8/63–5/68 |
| 27½ × 6 | | 8/68–5/74 |
| 40 × 7 | | 8/74–5/81 |
| 50 × 14 | | 8/81–5/95 |
| 60 × 7 | | 8/95–5/02 |
| 70 × 7 | | 8/02–5/09 |
| 72 × 33 | | 8/09–5/12. |

Actual rate changes sometimes took place a quarter or more after the theoretical date of change and therefore give a sum a little less than the theoretical. This is just about offset by the £35 total fines received but not included here.

[e] This includes £7 for one half of the Billerica farm, £16 for Menotomy land, and £4 for Cambridge Neck Land (all gifts of Cambridge Town).

[f] £127 15*s.* 6*d.* repairs list from Danforth's accounts. *CSM* XV, 213–214; £20 from Pastor Wilson; £104 from or via Richard Saltonstall.

treasury, the country being in debt one thousand pounds, and what comes in by levies is corn or cattle), but the Lord stirred up the hearts of some few persons to lend one hundred pounds, to be repaid by the next levy.[43]

Despite such mechanical deficiencies, the support which the Colony and the Province did manage to give the College was extremely important to the institution's survival and effectiveness. So far as we can now tell, the total financial help actually realized was as shown in Table 18.

This description does not fully recognize the extent of government aid. Especially in the first days of the Colony, the members of the Court of Assistants (Governor's Council) and the Chamber of Deputies (House of Representatives) were so very closely in touch with the townspeople, directly or through their ruling elders, that a suggestion from the Court that the College needed support usually resulted in some individual gifts to the institution—and individuals also gave very material financial aid to the College.

# VI

# *INCOME FROM GIFTS AND FROM ENDOWMENT, AND SUMMARY OF ALL INCOME*

In addition to collective action taken through governments or at their suggestion, friends of Harvard made individual gifts to the College, and some individuals in England responded to the fund-raising drives conducted there for the New England college's benefit.

Gifts to the College may be considered in four categories: (1) money, including easily negotiated commodities, which was available for immediate use, (2) annuities — that is, money payable annually coming from capital funds not held by the College, (3) gifts of land which produced an annual rent, and gifts of buildings and of land that was either unimproved or for other reason produced no income, and (4) gifts of equipment and for related activities. Each of these categories can be split up to show the amounts received under the four Treasurers' periods, as well as whether each gift was from a living donor or a bequest, and if the donor lived in England or in America. Table 23 on page 121 summarizes all gifts.

Table 19 shows the gifts in the first category — money immediately available. Here we can mention only the very largest or best-known cases.

### INDIVIDUAL GIFTS OF MONEY, EXCEPT ANNUITIES

The first recorded gift to the College from an individual was the bequest in 1638 of £779 17*s.* 2*d.* by the Reverend John Harvard, and this was by far the largest amount given by one person for almost fifty years.

Then in 1641 the high-spirited and public-spirited Hugh Peter was asked by the General Court to leave his parish in Salem and go with the Reverend Thomas Weld and William Hibbins on a fund-raising mission to England for the Colony and the College. Winthrop records that the emissaries were sent, "but with this caution, that they should not seek supply of our wants in any dishonorable way, as by begging or the like, for we were resolved to wait up on the Lord in the use of all means which were lawful and honorable."[1]

The mission met with moderate success in Puritan England, where it was to some extent backed by Parliament and by the Lord-Mayor of London. Weld and Peter stayed in England, preaching in churches and talking to anyone who would listen. Weld continued for some time to promote giving to New England, but Peter shortly went off to join the army of Parliament. Their promotion leaflet, "New Englands First Fruits," seems to have fascinated English donors as much as it fascinates us with its descriptions of the state of the Colony in 1640. The total of the contributions they gleaned came to £1553 4*s.* 2*d.*, including £231 specifically designated for the College, £874 9*s.* 2*d.* for transporting poor children to New England, some funds for the "Common Stock" of the Colony, money for "the Godly poore," and gifts for educating and converting the Indians, a favorite project of Old England.[2]

The largest single gift to the College from the Weld-Peter mission was Lady Ann Radcliffe Mowlson's £100 for a permanent scholarship fund (Plate 2). The Mowlson £100 and a £50 legacy from Mr. Francis Bridges of Clapham, with "other small gifts" — totaling in all £162 16*s.* 4*d.* — was lent, willingly or not, to the Country, which from 1649 on seems to have allowed the College "annually £15 for 4 Schollarships that being the Intent of the donors."[3]

It will not be surprising to anyone that, despite our having Weld's account of the mission from the time of its landing in England until April 10, 1647, it is not too clear what the College actually received from this source, but we may reasonably conclude from Weld's and the College's records that the Weld-Peter

*Table 19. Gifts and Bequests Recorded by Harvard College, 1636 to 1712 (not*

| | 1636–1654 | | | | | 1654–1663 | | | | | 1663–1668 | | | |
|---|---|---|---|---|---|---|---|---|---|---|---|---|---|---|
| | | | £ | *s.* | *d.* | | | £ | *s.* | *d.* | | | £ | *s.* |
| GIFTS | | | | | | | | | | | | | | |
| *American* | | | | | | | | | | | | | | |
| | M | E. Ting | 9 | 10 | 0 | MB | Paines | 30 | 0 | 0 | | | | |
| | MB | T. Eaton | 40 | 0 | 0 | | Colbran | 5 | 0 | 0 | | | | |
| | B | Jackson | 10 | 0 | 0 | | Penelton | 5 | 0 | 0 | | | | |
| | MB | Russell | 9 | 0 | 0 | | Willoughby | 16 | 0 | 0 | | | | |
| | | Pooll | 10 | 0 | 0 | | | | | | | | | |
| | | Weles | 10 | 0 | 0 | | | | | | | | | |
| | | Six others | 27 | 0 | 0 | | | | | | | | | |
| American gifts | | | 115 | 10 | 0 | | | 56 | 0 | 0 | | | | |
| *Eleutheran* | | | 124 | 0 | 0 | | | | | | | | | |
| *English* | | | | | | | | | | | | | | |
| | MSP | Mowlson | 100 | 0 | 0 | M | Saltonstall | 294 | 5 | 7 | | | | |
| | | "Other small gifts" | 12 | 16 | 4 | | For Indians | 37 | 7 | 0 | | | | |
| | | Weld-Peter | 81 | 0 | 0 | | | | | | | | | |
| | | | 47 | 7 | 6 | | | | | | | | | |
| | | Stranguish | 10 | 0 | 0 | | | | | | | | | |
| | | Latham | 5 | 0 | 0 | | | | | | | | | |
| English gifts | | | 256 | 3 | 10 | | | 331 | 12 | 7 | | | | |
| *All gifts* | | | 495 | 13 | 10 | | | 387 | 12 | 7 | | | | |
| BEQUESTS | | | | | | | | | | | | | | |
| *American* | | | | | | | | | | | | | | |
| | (M) | Harvard | 779 | 17 | 2 | M | Keayne | 100 | 0 | 0 | | Rouse | 2 | 10 |
| | | | | | | | J. Ward | 72 | 0 | 0 | | Wines | 4 | 0 |
| | | | | | | MP | Webb | 50 | 0 | 0 | | Peirce | 1 | 0 |
| | | | | | | | [J. Ward-lost | 22 | 0 | 0] | M | Sprague | 30 | 0 |
| | | | | | | | | | | | M | Keayne house | 160 | 0 |
| American bequests | | | 779 | 17 | 2 | | | 222 | 0 | 0 | | | 197 | 10 |
| *English* | | | | | | | | | | | | | | |
| | S | Bridges | 50 | 0 | 0 | | | | | | MP | Hopkins | 100 | 0 |
| English bequests | | | 50 | 0 | 0 | | | 0 | | | | | 100 | 0 |
| *All bequests* | | | 829 | 17 | 2 | | | 222 | 0 | 0 | | | 297 | 10 |
| GIFTS AND BEQUESTS | | | | | | | | | | | | | | |
| American & Eleuth. | | | 1019 | 7 | 2 | | | 278 | 0 | 0 | | | 197 | 10 |
| English | | | 306 | 3 | 10 | | | 331 | 12 | 7 | | | 100 | 0 |
| SUM | | | 1325 | 11 | 0 | | | 609 | 12 | 7 | | | 297 | 10 |

*Source:* Harvard University Archives and other documents. All are discussed in detail in my thesis (1958).

[a] Money available in 1687, bequest 1683–1686.

[b] Before 1715.

[c] Plus bequests probably received 1682–1686: J. Browne and Ashurst.

*including real estate, annuities, or money granted or sponsored by governments)*

| 1669–1682 | | | | | 1686–1693 | | | 1693–1712 | | | | Sum | | |
|---|---|---|---|---|---|---|---|---|---|---|---|---|---|---|
| | | £ | *s.* | *d.* | | | £ | | | £ | *s.* | £ | *s.* | *d.* |
| B | Building | 9 | 0 | 0 | | | | M | Hutchinson | 120 | 0 | | | |
| | Smedley | 10 | 0 | 0 | | | | | | | | | | |
| M | Widdow Sprague | 20 | 0 | 0 | | | | | | | | | | |
| M | Hull | 100 | 0 | 0 | | | | | | | | | | |
| | | 139 | 0 | 0 | | | | | | 120 | 0 | 430 | 10 | 0 |
| | | | | | | | | | | | | 124 | 0 | 0 |
| | Ashurst *et al.* | 100 | 0 | 0 | | | | | Gunston | 65 | 0 | | | |
| | Henly | 27 | 0 | 0 | | | | | | | | | | |
| | For Indians | 20 | 0 | 0 | | | | | | | | | | |
| | Others | 24 | 0 | 0 | | | | | | | | | | |
| | | 171 | 0 | 0 | | | | | | 65 | 0 | 823 | 16 | 5 |
| | | 310 | 0 | 0 | | | | | | 185 | 0 | 1378 | 6 | 5 |
| | Wilson | 10 | 0 | 0 | | Trusedale | 40[a] | M | J. Richards | 100 | 0 | | | |
| | Clark | 50 | 0 | 0 | MSP | W. Browne | 100 | M | Sprague | 426 | 18 | | | |
| M | Russell | 31 | 13 | 4 | | | | MSP | B. Browne | 200 | 0 | | | |
| | Scarlett | 10 | 0 | 0 | | | | | Anderson | 5 | 0 | | | |
| | Finch | | 14 | 6 | | | | MFP | [T. Brattle-1713 | 200 | 0[b]] | | | |
| (M) | Mrs. Richards | 5 | 0 | 0 | | | | | | | | | | |
| | [E. Browne-lost | 100 | 0 | 0] | | | | | [T. Richards-1715 | 30 | 0[b]] | | | |
| | [J. Browne-? | 100 | 0 | 0] | | | | | | | | | | |
| | | 107 | 7 | 10 | | | 140 | | | 731 | 18 | 2178 | 13 | 0[c] |
| M | Holworthy | 1234 | 2 | 6 | | [Thorner] | | P | Hulton | 130 | 0 | | | |
| M | [Ashurst? | 128 | 0 | 0] | | | | | | | | | | |
| | | 1234 | 2 | 6 | | | 0 | | | 130 | 0 | 1514 | 2 | 6[c] |
| | | 1341 | 10 | 4 | | | 140 | | | 861 | 18 | 3692 | 15 | 6 |
| | | 246 | 7 | 10 | | | 140 | | | 851 | 18 | 2733 | 3 | 0 |
| | | 1405 | 2 | 6 | | | – | | | 195 | 0 | 2337 | 18 | 11 |
| | | 1651 | 10 | 4[c] | | | 140 | | | 1046 | 18 | 5071 | 1 | 11[c] |

Key: M, Merchant; (M), Merchant connections; P, Permanent fund; B, Buildings; F, Faculty salaries; S, Scholarships; [ ], not received or uncertain mission produced £291 3*s.* 10*d.* for the College, including the Mowlson money.

The income from the Mowlson fund stopped with 1685, after the Colony charter was vacated. The President and Fellows petitioned the Court in 1693, and again frequently until April 29, 1713, when Thomas Brattle made almost the last entry in his book before his death. It must have given him great satisfaction:

> Cash received of mr. Taylor, province Treasurer, £426 10*s.* 4*d.*, being £162 16*s.* 4*d.* of it the principal remaining due of monies borrowed by the late Colony of the Massachusetts Bay of the College, and £263 14*s.* being for Interest for said Summe at 6 per Cent per annum from the year 1685 to this time; less paid Mr. Addington for a Warrant to the Treasurer to pay me said Summe, pursuant to a resolve of the General Court at their last Sessions in March last, 2*s.*
>
> Memorandum. This £162 16*s.* 4*d.* was what was due from my Lady Moulson's etc.'s gift to our College, lent the Country anno 1648, and they paid Interest for till 1685.

At this point the Mowlson Fund disappears from the books — it does not show at all in the 1715 account — and it was many years before the money was dug out and the permanent fund reestablished. Ann Radcliffe herself is not likely soon again to be forgotten, for Radcliffe College has been named in her honor.

In 1650 the church members of Massachusetts Bay sent a gift of "several hundred pounds' worth of provisions and other necessaries" to the Colony of Eleuthera in the Bahamas, which through shipwreck and other casualties was in a pitiable state. By return ship the Eleuthera colonists sent all they could provide — ten tons of brazil-wood, which was to be for the use of Harvard College, "that wee may expresse how sensible wee are of Gods love and tender Care of us manifested in yours; and avoid that foule sin of ingratitude so abhorred of God, so hatefull to all men. . . ." The wood brought £124, which was put to good use by President Dunster.[4]

To make any administrator or alumnus of a 1962 college feel right at home in the seventeenth century, it is necessary only to tell of Mitchell's Modell. About 1663 Jonathan Mitchell, who had been a Tutor under Dunster and had become a non-teaching Fellow, a member of the Corporation, drew up a "Modell" based on Poole's English Model for maintaining teaching fellows who were scholars at the universities of Oxford and Cambridge. Mitchell quotes ecclesiastical authority for a good six pages. Then,

> Finding therefore that the want of needfull Maintenance for fellows and of somewhat to enable other scholars to continue at the Colledge till they be well and thoroughly furnishd for publike service (the whole Charge whereof but few parents among us are able or willing to beare of themselves) is a cause of the languishing of that society, and is like to enforce a decay of Learning among us if not timely remedyed,

he suggests that

> It is earnestly desired that what persons shall please to give they would doe it in Annuall way for 7 or eight years, or if it may be for ever: which will be deservedly looked upon as a noble and eminent act of Charity and which present and future Ages may have Cause to Blesse God for. Yet if any shall contribute any thing in any other way It will be Acceptable.
>
> That the name of every Contributor be fairly written in a Book appointed for the purpose together with the summ which it shall please Him to contribute to this work.[5]

Mitchell goes on to state that some of the money might well be used also for building and Library needs, and he ends with a section of objections to the scheme and gives his answers. No gifts can be traced directly to the Modell, but it may well be that Mitchell's softening inspired some of the gifts which were received in the next few years.

Bequests in this period were important. Captain Robert Keayne of the Ancient and Honorable Artillery Company of Boston was a merchant whose struggle between his apparent business interests and his conscience have become well known. Because of familiarity and sympathy with the needs of the College, and no doubt as part of salving his conscience, Captain Keayne, who died in 1656, included in his will provisions under which the Puritan institution received £100 in cash before 1663 and by 1668 a house in Boston valued at £147. He stated that he wished the money to "be improved, not about the buildings or repairs of the College, for that I think the Country should do and Look after," but to add to the income of "poor and hopefull Scholars whose parents are not able comfortably to maintain them there," or to help "the poorer Sort of Fellows or Tutors," or for "an Enlargement of the Commons of the Poorer Sort of Scholars, which I have often heard is too Short and bare for them." His next provision must have appealed to the administration:

> Because I have Little insight in the true Ordering of Scholars and other things thereto belonging in a College-way, and so possibly may dispose my gift where there is less need, and that it may do more good if it had bin imployed in Som other way, I am willing to refer it to the President and Feoffees and Overseers that are intrusted with the Care and Ordering of the College and Scholars or Students with the things thereto belonging. Still taking in the Consent of my Executors, and of such of the Overseers of this my Will as shall then be alive. . . .[6]

Another leading merchant, whose shop was only two doors down from that of Robert Keayne, was Henry Webb; he died in 1660, leaving Harvard £50 and a house in Boston ". . . that both it and the House above mentioned may be and continue as a Yearly Income for the Ends aforesaid forever."[7] The Webb property still belongs to the University and, with the buildings now there, is valued on the June 30, 1961, books at $164,604.79.* "Forever" is a powerful word.

The largest gift in the seventeenth century, as the plaque on Holworthy Hall now states, came by bequest from Sir Matthew Holworthy, merchant-ship-owner of Bristol and London. Sir Matthew prospered under the Puritans, and he also managed to get along nicely under the Restoration. When Sir Matthew died in October 1678 he left a will written with the admirable generality or flexibility common to many other donors of the time: He gave £1000

> unto the Colledg, or University, in, or of, Cambridg, in New England . . . to bee payd and made over to the governours and directors there of, to bee disposed of by them as they shall judg best for the promoting of learning and promulgation of the Gospell in those parts, the same to bee payd within two years next coming after my decease.[8]

As soon as Treasurer Richards received the money (increased to £1234 2*s.* 6*d.* NE), he promptly "lett it out" at the going eight per cent on twenty-one bonds in amounts from £10 to £270.[9] Some of this money was spent for current needs as the bonds came due,

* The address is 254–256 Washington Street. *Financial Report to the Board of Overseers of Harvard College,* 1960–1961, p. 35.

but these securities formed the backbone of the College's investments for many years. No separate fund was set up, and, except for the many grateful people who profited from his generosity in the seventeenth century, Sir Matthew's name was forgotten for a while, but it was revived and is prominent now in the hall named for him in 1812.

An active force for the dissemination of the Harvard "gospel" in England was the peripatetic Reverend President Mather. While traveling primarily on Province business, he lost no opportunity to make or solidify a friend for Harvard. English connections maintained and established by Mather and others were valuable for many years.

Treasurer Richards, too, traveled on Country business, and his period as Treasurer was broken by a trip to England in 1682. Acting Treasurers were therefore appointed: first Thomas Danforth and then Samuel Nowell. Richards picked up the books again in 1686. Dividing Richards' total incumbency into two periods, before and after he was away in England, we notice a great difference between the recorded receipts: there were *no* gifts from England or America entered on the books from 1686 to 1693, and the only bequest paid during that period, according to the record, was Mr. William Browne's. Neither was there any fund drive, government-sponsored or otherwise. The most obvious reason for this was that after the Colony was abolished and when the Province was young the government and legal status were completely upset. No one was confident about what would happen to his money if he did give it to the College. This feeling was intensified by the fact that the College could not seem to get a permanent resident president. Had they not been able to use some of Holworthy's large gift, there is no telling how the institution would have fared. There is, of course, the possibility, which we shall discuss later, that gifts *were* made, as well as payments on other obligations due, and that they were not entered on the books lest Sir Edmund Andros and others of the Crown's agents interfere with their use.

Although political matters had calmed somewhat by 1693 and the colonists were becoming more accustomed, if not reconciled, to living in a province under a royal governor, there were only two gifts of free money made to Harvard by living persons in the twenty-year period 1693 to 1712, during most of which the College's charter was in doubt. There were, however, several bequests, including sizable ones from Treasurers Richards and Thomas Brattle.

The generosity of all these people and many others over the years adds up to the very substantial assistance for the College shown in line (3) of Table 20. If we wish to see any tendencies

*Table 20. Outright Gifts and Bequests Recorded by Harvard College, 1636 to 1712 — in New England Pounds*[a] *(not including real estate or annuities, or money granted or sponsored by the government)*

| | From Americans | | | From England | | | From Eleuthera | Totals | | |
|---|---|---|---|---|---|---|---|---|---|---|
| | £ | *s.* | *d.* | £ | *s.* | *d.* | £ | £ | *s.* | *d.* |
| (1) Gifts | 430 | 10 | | 823 | 16 | 5 | 124 | 1378 | 6 | 5 |
| (2) Bequests | 2278 | 13[a] | | 1642 | 2 | 6[a] | 0 | 3920 | 15 | 6 |
| (3) Totals | 2709 | 3 | | 2465 | 18 | 11 | 124 | 5299 | 1 | 11 |
| (4) Bequests (2) without Harvard and Holworthy | 1498 | 15 | 10 | 408 | | | 0 | 1906 | 15 | 10 |
| (5) Totals (3) without Harvard and Holworthy | 1929 | 5 | 10 | 1231 | 16 | 5 | 124 | 3185 | 2 | 3 |
| (6) Sponsored Subscriptions | 2685 | 18 | 2 | | | | | 2685 | 18 | 2 |
| (7) Total (3) and (6) | 5395 | 1 | 2 | 2465 | 18 | 11 | 124 | 7985 | | 1 |

[a] Assuming Joseph Browne's £100 and Henry Ashurst's £128 were received.

in these figures, it is of interest to show them with the two largest legacies deducted, the reduced bequests in line (4), and the reduced totals in line (5). It is evident comparing line (5) and line (1) that in America legacies (£1498 excluding Harvard's) account for a much larger proportion of outright giving than gifts from living persons (£430), but that except for Mr. Holworthy's £1234, in England there was more given by the living (£823) than by bequest (£408). In total, legacies amount to about three times gifts from the living; even with the John Harvard and Holworthy bequests excluded, the total of bequests is half again as large as that of other gifts. The line (3) figures show individuals in England giving almost as much as those in America.

But this is just part of the picture. First, we should consider not only the support by taxation in America, but also especially the government-sponsored giving. If to the totals we add the £2685 given by individuals through Court-promoted collections we get new totals in line (7). Moreover, there were gifts of annuities and of rent-producing or other property which are not included above. The next section will show what these annuities and rents meant to seventeenth-century Harvard.

### GIFTS OF ANNUITIES

The modern generation of alumni and alumni fund-raisers may think they invented "annual giving" to their alma mater, but this is far from the case; annual giving at Harvard started more than three hundred years ago. And anyone who reads the records of seventeenth-century Harvard is acutely conscious of how much the faculty and administration of that time counted on their annual gifts and rents, few though they were.

The first annual gift was promised before the College had any income-producing endowment at all. In the fact that £5 a year was promised to continue in perpetuity, this annuity differed from the modern concept of giving annually in amounts which vary from year to year.* The merchant John Newgate of Boston on June 11, 1650, made out an elaborate instrument stating that Harvard College should receive "five pound per Annum forever." Newgate would pay it during his lifetime, and after his death it should be paid out of the revenue of his farm at Rumney Marsh.[10]

* But some government-sponsored gifts described in Chapter V include the feature of annual variation according to ability.

Newgate had been on the Boston committee which collected the extension of the College corn in 1652 to 1654, and he continued his interest in the College until his death in 1665. Thereafter the various owners of the Rumney Marsh farm paid the annuity fairly regularly, and back payments were eventually made up.[11]

John Glover, another Boston merchant, sent his son John to "the Universitie" and paid a good proportion of his fees in shoes at from two to four shillings a pair. When John, Senior, died in 1654 he left an annuity of £5 forever, charged upon his "Housing and Tanpitts" in Boston, the annuity to begin on the death of his wife, "and if my beloved Wife can Spare to give the said £5 a year in her Life time, I doubt not but she will give it."[12] Mrs. Glover apparently could not spare the £5, but the College saw that son Habakkuk Glover, who inherited the tan-pits, was reminded of the annuity in 1669 when his mother died. The annuity was paid as of 1671 on, though in 1686 reduced, as Newgate's was, to £4 for payment in money instead of commodities. In 1686 or before, Habakkuk's account shifted to that of Rebecca Smith, which in turn was taken over by Thomas Clark in 1693. For the Glover annuity as well as Newgate's, the College accepted a capital sum in lieu of equivalent income in the nineteenth century.[13]

An English benefactor whose money came over irregularly but did come over was Mr. William Pennoyer, a very successful London operator in merchant-shipping and trading who was a member of the Society for the Propagation of the Gospel in New England and had business interests as well as relatives in New England.[14] Pennoyer died in 1670, leaving the rent of a farm in Norfolk, England, to Harvard College after deducting payment of £10 a year to the Corporation for Propagation of the Gospel in New England. The annuity was to start on the death of his wife and came due sometime before April 1678. The farm then paid £44 sterling a year; Harvard's share, £34, was to provide for scholarships and tutors' salaries. The total received in our period was £680 12*s.* 8*d.*, which, though it may not have been all the donor intended, was a large sum indeed.[15]

In order to evaluate what the receipt of annuity income meant to Harvard, and to be able to combine this evaluation with statistics of other giving, we show in our summaries an estimate of £373 as the total capital value of the Newgate, Glover, and Pennoyer annuity gifts on the date the first income payment of each was made. These are the only annuities appreciable income of which was clearly used for the College in the Puritan Period. This value is figured by assuming that the income is 8 per cent of the capital, and on this basis calculating the principal the College would have needed to have produced the income it received. No such capital was ever actually taken onto the College books, but we shall use it in making breakdowns of the sources of College receipts. We shall not consider the *income* from these funds as gifts at all but as endowment income.*

## GIFTS OF LAND AND BUILDINGS FROM INDIVIDUALS

Gifts of land and buildings may be divided into three categories: (1) rent-producing, (2) usable, but not rent-producing, and (3) not used in our period, that is, given before 1715 but not acquired by that time, and "unimproved" or unclaimed. As we said above about annuities, ordinarily the capital value of this property was not taken onto the College books. The one exception to the College's practice in this regard was in the case of the Keayne house, where the value *was* listed by Danforth as a receipt; then the sales value was also listed as a receipt when the house was sold in 1696. The confusion arose, of course, because there is no separate capital account on the books.

The capital values of rent-producing real estate are shown in Table 21.

Gifts and real estate, usable but not rent-producing, were three: an orchard for the Fellows, the "Indian College," and Stoughton College. (We might, of course, say that the buildings produced income in the form of net study rent.)

In 1655 to 1656 Commissioners for the United Colonies provided for the building of what was known as "the Indian College." In so doing they were acting as agents for the English corporation known as the "President and Society for Propagation of the Gospel in New England." Whether the Commissioners paid for half or all

* This would be dubious practice in some cases in actual accounting, but here I think it makes sense. In the cases where we so capitalize annuities, the College later received settlement for more capital than we use here.

*Table 21. Capital Value of Rental Property Given to Harvard College by Individuals from 1636 to 1712 (including only property which produced rent during this period)*

| | Donor | Year Given | Year Probable first rent | Bequest or gift | Description | Gross rent | Estimated capital value[a] |
|---|---|---|---|---|---|---|---|
| M | Sedgwick | 1647 | 1647 | gift | shop | 10*s*. to £1 | lost |
| | Dunster | 1649 | 1650[b] | gift | 100 acres | ½ of 10*s*. to £1 | £6 |
| M | Coggan | 1652 | 1652 | gift | marsh | £4 to £3 to £10 | £50 |
| M | Webb | 1660 | 1661 | bequest | house | £12 to £15 | £160 |
| M | Keayne | 1656 | 1669 | bequest | house | £10 to £12 | [sold for £160 in 1696] |
| | Hayward | 1672 | 1683[b] | bequest | 24 acres Watertown | £1 5*s*. to £1 10*s*. to £1 | £16 |
| | S. Ward | 1680 | 1683[b] | gift on death | Bumpkin Island | £2 5*s*; £4 in 1701 | £35 |
| | E. Rogers | 1701 | 1701 | bequest | Rowley land | £4; £6 5*s*. in 1710 | £50 |
| M | W. Stoughton | 1701 | 1703 | bequest | Dorchester land | £4 3*s*. 6*d*. | £52 |
| | Champney | 1669 | 1707 | bequest | 40 acres Newton | £1 | £13 |
| Total from individuals | | | | | | | £382[c] |

M, Merchant.
[a] Based on an early year and on 8 per cent income.
[b] Possibly rent was paid earlier outside the books.
[c] Plus Keayne £160 listed among gifts.

of the building, we do not know, but it cost about £300 to £400 and provided lodgings and studies for about twenty students.[16] There were very few Indian students, and from 1656 on the Commissioners gave yearly permission to use the building for English students. Also the printing press was lodged there. In 1693 the Harvard Corporation, having secured the approval of the local Commissioners for Propagating the Gospel (most of whom were on the Board of Overseers), ordered that the decrepit old building be torn down. On agreement that all Indians should have free rent thereafter, the bricks were sold for £20 to the builder of Stoughton College.

Three years before his death, Lieutenant-Governor Stoughton, Harvard A.B. 1650, personally paid the full cost, which was around £1000, of erecting a new "college" to house some of the increasing student body. The Corporation paid for the cellar — £20. The building began to need repairs by 1710, but it was used for many more years after that.[17]

There is a modern tendency for colleges to ask donors who provide buildings to take care of endowing their maintenance; in Stoughton's day it was different. In his will the Lieutenant-Governor exercised the right previously agreed upon by the Corporation that the donor should be allowed the disposal of "some part of the Incomes of that Building."[18] He directed that for five years £20 should go to Elijah Danforth, son of the pastor in Dorchester, and that thereafter £10 a year be reserved forever for "some poor scholar," preferably a minister's son, next a student from Dorchester or Milton, but in any case Stoughton's relatives to have preference.

During the seventeenth century several individuals made gifts of land which for one reason or another did not come to use by the College during our period. One of the major difficulties was the same as in the case of government grants — it was not simple to claim and hold land at a distance from Cambridge. But the loss of some of the tracts can be set down only to negligence on the part of the College in following up the claims.

Table 22 lists these gifts of land and buildings.

### GIFTS OF EQUIPMENT OR FOR RELATED ACTIVITIES

If Harvard College had had to spend money for the books and equipment which were given to it directly, it is likely the students and faculty would have done without. Teaching and learning would have been very different from what it was.* We find President Dunster in 1648 writing to Dr. Christianus Ravius, Professor of Oriental Languages, to thank him for the gift of some books:

> So if Gods providence put an opportunity into your hand that you help us with books of those languages from some able hands and willing hearts (for from your selfe it were unreasonable to expect any more then such books as your selfe are personally the Author of), then should wee be

* Undergraduates did not use the library books very often. College Laws, *passim*.

*Table 22. Real Estate Given to Harvard College but Not Availed of by 1715*

| | Donors (all American) | Year | Bequest or gift | Description | Notes | Reference |
|---|---|---|---|---|---|---|
| | I. Stoughton | 1645 | Bequest | 100 acres at Blue Hill<br>200 acres at Neponset | On first board of overseers<br>Father of William<br>Land not laid out | *CSM*, p. 176<br>*FHC*, p. 323<br>Winthrop II, 220 |
| | Nathaniel Ward | 1646 | Purchase & gift? | 600 acres at Andover (Court grant) | For son's expense<br>Not laid out | *CSM*, pp. 283, 176 |
| | Robert Cooke | 1652 | Gift | 800 acre Court grant | Not laid out | *CSM*, p. 284 |
| (M) | Rev. D. Russell | 1678 | Bequest | 1000 acres in Maine | Resolved later | *CSM*, pp. 272–5<br>A. Eliot, pp. 165–9 |
| | Edward Jackson | 1681 | Bequest | 400 acres at Billerica (Cambridge grant) | Not claimed | *CSM*, pp. 284–5 |
| M | Judge S. Sewall & wife (Hull) | 1696 | Gift | 500 acres in Narragansett | For scholarships<br>No rent by 1715 | *CSM*, pp. 272, 846<br>Brattle, p. 43 |
| M | T. Danforth | 1699 | Gift and bequest | Three tenements in Framingham | Received 1724 | *CSM*, pp. 281–2, 842 |
| | T. Atkinson, feltmaker | 1701 | Gift on death | 20 x 20 rods in South Boston | "Gave away more than had" | *CSM*, p. 285 |

M, Merchant; (M), Merchant connections.
*Source:* Some of the sources are listed above under "Reference." The *CSM* XVI Index will lead to more information, as will HUA, Land Papers I.

very glad and evermore thankfull to you and them. . . . A wonderfull impulse unto these studies lyes on the spirits of our students, some of which can dextrously translate Hebrew, and Caldee, into Greek. . . .[19]

How could people resist him? They didn't.

Such gifts amounted to an extremely important and sizable financial and educational aid. The College published a Library Catalogue in 1723 which listed 3516 volumes. A major proportion of these had come from gifts, for we know of gifts by 1715 of around 1500 volumes plus others valued at about £900.

The College received not only books, but also building material and various sorts of equipment to use, not sell; and gifts were made as well to the printing press which the College ran until 1702.

## SUMMARY OF GIVING

We are now in a better position to list donations made before 1715 by individuals (Table 23 and Figure 2).

Of the funds listed in Table 23, some were designated for particular purposes; and of the designated and undesignated funds, some were firmly stipulated to be for permanent endowment.*

* Table 19 indicates which outright gifts of money were so restricted. In collecting these amounts, I have included only those which from the terms of the gifts (according

*Table 23. Donations by Individuals to Harvard College Availed of from 1636 to 1715 (not including books and equipment)*

| | Money | | | Capitalized annuities and rent | Stoughton Hall and Indian College | Sponsored subscriptions | | | Sum | | | Sum | | |
|---|---|---|---|---|---|---|---|---|---|---|---|---|---|---|
| | £ | s. | d. | £ | £ | £ | s. | d. | £ | s. | d. | £ | s. | d. |
| American | | | | | | | | | | | | | | |
| Gifts | 431 | 0 | 0 | 154 | 1000 | 2685 | 18 | 2 | 4270 | 18 | 2 | | | |
| Legacies | 2278 | 13 | 0 | 351 | | | | | 2629 | 13 | 0 | | | |
| | | | | | | | | | | | | 6900 | 11 | 2 |
| English | | | | | | | | | | | | | | |
| Gifts | 823 | 16 | 5 | | 350(?) | | | | 1173 | 16 | 5 | | | |
| Legacies | 1642 | 2 | 6 | 250 | | | | | 1892 | 2 | 6 | | | |
| | | | | | | | | | | | | 3065 | 18 | 11 |
| Eleuthera | 124 | 0 | 0 | | | | | | 124 | 0 | 0 | 124 | 0 | 0 |
| Sum | 5299 | 11 | 11 | 755 | 1350 | 2685 | 18 | 2 | 10 090 | 10 | 1 | 10 090 | 10 | 1 |

*Sources:* Tables 19, 20, 21; and pp. 116–117 for annuity capital.

In most cases the amounts included here are gross, that is the full amount is included without deducting transportation costs, which appear as expense. On the other hand, some amounts may never have been collected, but this is in the nature of an investment loss — when an estate paid a bequest, but the College did not get all this money to use.

We find that of the £10,090 shown in Table 23 as given by individuals before 1715, £4782 was designated for specific purposes, and £5308 was not so designated; £4705 was absolutely without restriction; £1628 was for permanent endowment. Many of the donors were merchants and came from merchant families. A few were of the gentry, and some had themselves been at Harvard or at a university, but the great majority were not college men. Some were yoemen, or craftsmen, or — "widowes." Many in Old England gave, but the major support for their "Universitie" came, and rightly, from New England people.

---

to the information I have) seem firmly, and practically unquestionably, to belong in these categories. Another person might interpret the wordings somewhat differently. There are many other funds where the donor expressed a preference but left the ultimate use to the Corporation, in the knowledge that needs change and only the Corporation is in a position to keep up with the changes. In full realization and appreciation of the fact that the Corporation is meticulous in respecting these expressed preferences where possible, I do not include these "somewhat designated" amounts among the designated, my thought being that in an extremity the Corporation would have the legal right to use them for other purposes.

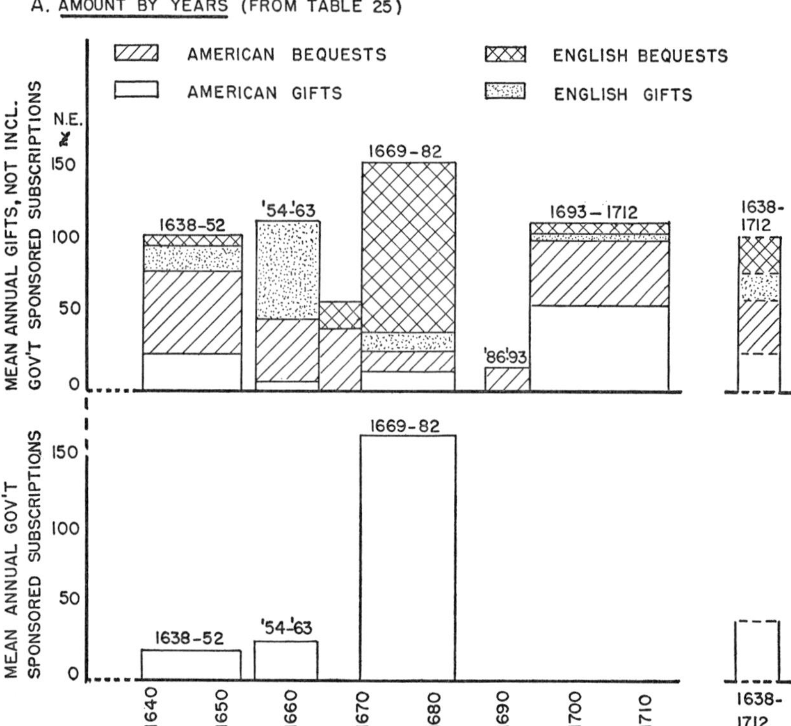


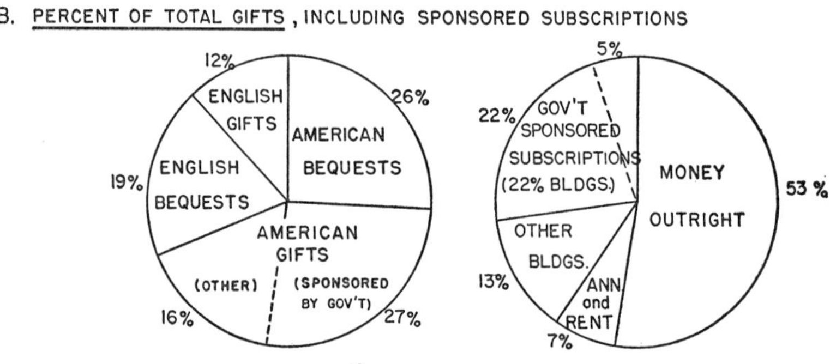


Figure 2. *Source of gifts to Harvard College, 1638 to 1712, including capitalized rents, annuities, and buildings.*

## INCOME FROM ENDOWMENT

By the end of the seventeenth century the College's growing investments in bonds and mortgages and its annuities and rents were producing the substantial sum of about £156 a year, an amount which would have seemed astronomical to President Dunster. Of this about two fifths came from rents and annuities, the balance from bonds and mortgages.

Commencing especially with the time of Sir Matthew Holworthy's bequest, the Treasurers of Harvard College had a good-sized sum of money to invest which they "lett out" on personal bonds or mortgages, or, very occasionally, unsecured. Frequently a small bond or mortgage would originate in overdue interest or rent, and sometimes such bonds reached relatively sizable amounts. The growth of these funds will be discussed in Chapter VIII below. The income appears in Table 24.

The legal interest rate on loans was 8 per cent to 1693, when by law it was changed to 6 per cent. Additional book profits accrued after the turn of the century from exchange of heavy for lighter coin, but these we have not considered earned endowment income;

*Table 24. Harvard College Gross Endowment Income from Rents, Annuities, and Interest — 1636 to 1712 (excluding 1652 to 1654, 1682 to 1686)*

| | 1636–1652 | 1654–1663 | 1663–1669 | 1669–1682 | 1686–1693 | 1693–1712 | Totals |
|---|---|---|---|---|---|---|---|
| | £ | £ s. | £ s. d. | £ s. d. | £ s. d. | £ s. d. | £ s. d. |
| Rents | 4 | 52 3 | 123 17 6 | 288 0 0 | 160 0 1 | 661 1 9 | 1289 2 4 |
| Annuities including Pennoyer | 8 | 43 15 | 25 0 0 | 205 7 6[a] | 144 10 0 | 520 2 1 | 946 14 7 |
| Rents and annuities | 12 | 95 18 | 148 17 6 | 493 7 6 | 304 10 1 | 1181 3 10 | 2235 16 11 |
| Interest | | 138 19[b] | 184 18 8[b] | 259 2 6 | 342 0 0 | 1789 4 10 | 2714 5 0 |
| Mowlson | 60 | 150 0 | 75 0 0 | 195 0 0 | 0 | 0 | 480 0 0 |
| Totals | 72 | 384 17 | 408 16 2 | 947 10 0 | 646 10 1 | 2970 8 8 | 5430 1 11 |
| Average income per year | £18[c] | £40 | £79 | £74 | £96 | £156 | £81[d] |

[a] Uneven receipt of income.

[b] This is Danforth's "Advance" (adjusted for accounting errors), which probably is not all interest and was not all collected. It includes amounts put in "Gain on Stock" in Tables 25 and 32. Mowlson income *may* be counted twice in 1663–1669.

[c] 1648–1652.

[d] 1638 on.

they were necessary to keep the real value of the assets from declining.

The accumulation of the figures in Table 24 and Figure 3

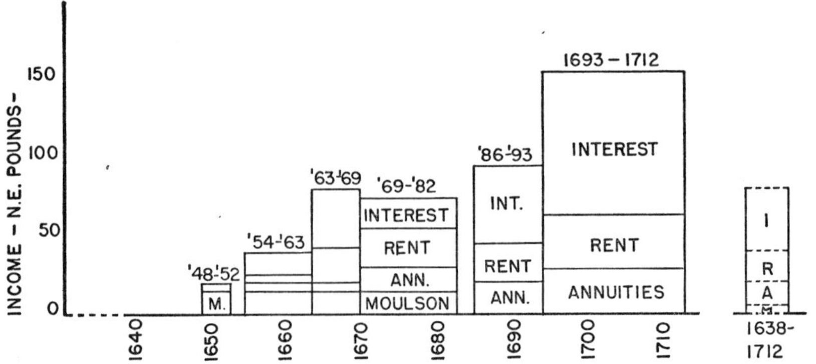


Figure 3. *Mean annual endowment income of Harvard College, by years, 1638 to 1712, not including the ferry. From Table 24.*

shows what we all know — that small figures can over the years add up to make an important contribution when compared with other sources of income. The average figures give a better idea than the totals, for the varying lengths of the periods are confusing. We see that there was steady progress, despite the falling away of the Mowlson money in 1686. This table shows as nearly as possible *actual* payments and not payments due, though Danforth's accounts received interest and rent as it became *due* and therefore include some amounts never actually received. Thus the Newgate annuity, which was unpaid in Richards' last years, appears in a lump sum of back payments in Brattle's period. But both Richards' and Brattle's periods here lack the Mowlson money, which was made up in 1713.

### SUMMARY OF INCOME FROM ALL SOURCES

### 1636–1712

Table 25 shows the summary of Chapters IV through VI; it brings together income from students, government, gifts, and endowment. Since we do not have all the Stewards' accounts, section

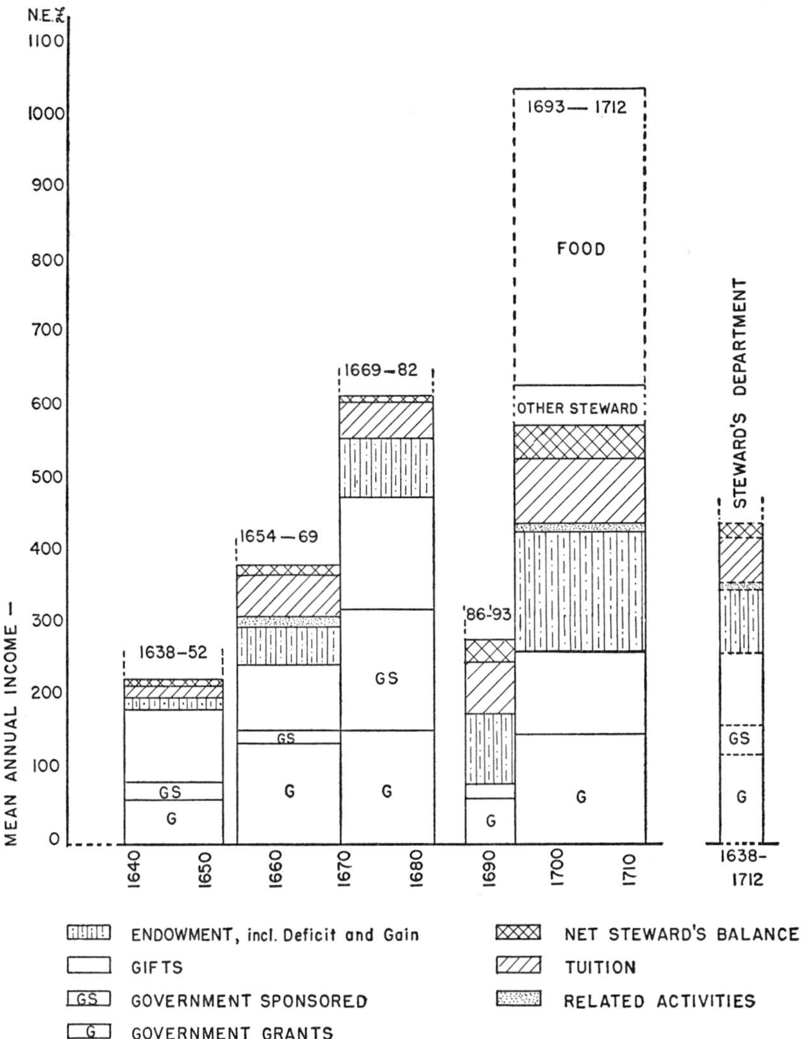


Figure 4. *Income according to source, 1638 to 1712.* (Not *operating income — includes plant and capital.*) *From Table 32.*

I, "Income from Students," is notably incomplete, but the *net* income to the College is there. We do have Stewards' records from 1687 on, and Table 25 includes in italics the figures obtained from Bordman's Quarter-Bill Book. Inclusion of the additional

## Table 25. Harvard College Income in the Puritan

| Source | Oct. 1636– May 1652 | | | 1652–1654 (incomplete) | | | 1654–1663 | | |
|---|---|---|---|---|---|---|---|---|---|
| | £ | s. | d. | £ | s. | d. | £ | s. | d. |
| I. From students | | | | | | | | | |
| Tuition | 233 | 10 | 3 | | | | 550 | 0 | 0 |
| Food charges | | | | | | | | | |
| Room and cellar rent[a] | 59 | 14 | 5 | | | | 75 | 5 | 8 |
| Services, fines, fees, and Monitor | 54 | 0 | 0 | | | | — | | |
| Net balance paid by Steward on order or in cash | | — | | | | | — | | |
| | 347 | 4 | 8 | | | | 625 | 5 | 8 |
| II. From government | | | | | | | | | |
| Grants — General and building | 400 | 0 | 0 | | | | | | |
| Capitalized rents | 11 | 0 | 0 | | | | | | |
| Salary | 50 | 0 | 0 | | | | 958 | 0 | 0 |
| Ferry | 440 | 0 | 0 | 100 | 0 | 0 | 328 | 10 | 0 |
| Sponsored subscriptions | 269 | 18 | 8 | | | | 249 | 15 | 6 |
| | 1170 | 18 | 8 | | | | 1536 | 5 | 6 |
| III. From individuals' gifts | | | | | | | | | |
| American gifts[c] | 239 | 10 | 0 | | | | 56 | 0 | 0 |
| bequests[d] | 779 | 17 | 2 | | | | 244 | 0 | 0 |
| English gifts[e] | 143 | 7 | 6 | | | | 294 | 5 | 7 |
| bequests[e] | 50 | 0 | 0 | | | | | | |
| Of college buildings | | — | | | | | 350 | 0 | 0? |
| Capitalized annuities and rents | 231 | 16 | 4 | | | | 160 | 0 | 0 |
| | 1444 | 11 | 0 | | | | 1104 | 5 | 7 |
| [Including scholarship income of] | [162 | 16 | 4] | | | | | | |
| IV. From endowment | | | | | | | | | |
| Annuities, including Mowlson | 68 | 0 | 0 | 30 | 0 | 0 | 193 | 15 | 0 |
| Rents | 4 | 0 | 0 | | | | 52 | 3 | 0[f] |
| Interest | | — | | | | | | | [f] |
| Gain on Stock (including "advance") | | — | | | | | 138 | 19 | 0[g] |
| "Deficit" (capital availed of) | 53 | 11 | 6[h] | | | | | | |
| Total from endowment | 125 | 11 | 6 | | | | 384 | 17 | 0 |
| [Including scholarship income of] | [60 | 0 | 0] | [30 | 0 | 0] | [150 | 0 | 0] |
| V. From related activities | | | | | | | | | |
| Press | 88 | 11 | 1 | | | | 20 | 0 | 0 |
| Indians | | | | | | | 37 | 7 | 0 |
| Books sold | | | | | | | | | |
| | 88 | 11 | 1 | | | | 57 | 7 | 0 |
| VI. Cash brought forward | 0 | | | | | | 0 | | |
| TOTAL INCOME | 3176 | 16 | 11 | | | | 3708 | 0 | 9 |

For assumptions involved, see text.

*Note:* Items in italics 1687 to 1712 come from the Steward's Harvard College account in the Quarter-Bill Book. Similar records are not available for earlier periods except that students' rents are included for most of the years 1636–1669. The italicized figures do not include *contra* of glass, wood and candles, sweeper. Totals in italics include only figures in italics.

[ ] = included in other figures shown.

[a] Room rent or commencement fee received by Treasurer. Note that rents are incomplete, especially from 1669 on. See p. 78 above.

[b] President's study rents paid to President not included.

[c] Including Eleuthera. Classification is imperfect when a gift is both annuity or real estate and gift or bequest,

*Period (including capitalized rents and annuities)*

| 1663– Feb. 1669 £ | s. | d. | June 1669– 1682 £ | s. | d. | (1682–1686) (incomplete) £ | s. | d. | 1686–1693 (Italics 1687–1693) £ | s. | d. | 1693–1712 £ | s. | d. | Totals (*not* including 1652–54 & 1682–86) £ | s. | d. |
|---|---|---|---|---|---|---|---|---|---|---|---|---|---|---|---|---|---|
| 248 | 0 | 0 | 741 | 0 | 0 | | | | 545 | 0 | 0 | 1694 | 9 | 0 | 4011 | 19 | 3 |
| | | | | | | | | | *1872* | *7* | *5* | *7784* | *16* | *9* | — | | |
| 150 | 6 | 6 | | | | | | | 20 | 0 | 0 | 134 | 8 | 0 [b] | 439 | 14 | 7[a] |
| | | | | | | | | | *223* | *17* | *0* | *820* | *3* | *0* | — | | |
| 2 | 14 | 5 | — | | | | | | — | | | 3 | 0 | 0[a] | 59 | 14 | 5 |
| | | | | | | | | | *123* | *9* | *3* | *254* | *7* | *0* | — | | |
| — | | | 20 | 13 | 0 | | | | 176 | 19 | 0 | 687 | 9 | 10 | 885 | 1 | 10 |
| 401 | 0 | 11 | 761 | 13 | 0 | | | | 741 | 19 | 0 | 2519 | 6 | 10 | 5396 | 10 | 1 |
| | | | | | | | | | *2219* | *13* | *8* | *8859* | *6* | *9* | — | | |
| | | | 100 | 0 | 0? | | | | | | | 190 | 0 | 0? | 690 | 0 | 0 |
| | | | | | | | | | | | | 16 | 0 | 0 | 27 | 0 | 0 |
| 550 | 0 | 0 | 1400 | 0 | 0 | 437 | 0 | 0 | 100 | 0 | 0 | 1492 | 0 | 0 | 4550 | 0 | 0 |
| 135 | 0 | 0 | 475 | 0 | 0 | 225 | 0 | 0 | 337 | 10 | 0 | 1258 | 0 | 0 | 2974 | 0 | 0 |
| 2 | 0 | 0 | 2164 | 4 | 0 | 0 | | | 0 | | | 0 | | | 2685 | 18 | 2 |
| 687 | 0 | 0 | 4139 | 4 | 0 | | | | 437 | 10 | 0 | 2956 | 0 | 0 | 10926 | 18 | 2 |
| | 10 | 0 | 139 | 0 | 0 | | | | | | | 120 | 0 | 0 | 555 | 0 | 0 |
| 37 | 10 | 0 | 107 | 7 | 10 | 140 | 0 | 0? | 100 | 0 | 0 | 731 | 18 | 0 | 2000 | 13 | 0[d] |
| | | | 151 | 0 | 0 | | | | | | | 65 | 0 | 0 | 653 | 12 | 8[e] |
| 100 | 0 | 0 | 1234 | 2 | 6 | 128 | 0 | 0? | | | | 130 | 0 | 0 | 1514 | 2 | 6 |
| 0 | | | 0 | | | | | | 0 | | | 1000 | 0 | 0 | 1350 | 0 | 0 |
| 160 | 0 | 0 | 361 | 0 | 0 | | | | 0 | | | 115 | 0 | 0 | 1027 | 16 | 4 |
| 298 | 0 | 0 | 1992 | 10 | 4 | | | | 100 | 0 | 0 | 2161 | 18 | 0 | 7101 | 4 | 11 |
| | | | [100 | 0 | 0] | | | | [100 | 0 | 0] | [252 | 0 | 0] | [614 | 16 | 4] |
| | | | | | | 12 | 0 | 0 | | | | | | | | | |
| 100 | 0 | 0 | 400 | 7 | 6 | 204 | 2 | 10 | 144 | 10 | 0 | 520 | 2 | 1 | 1426 | 14 | 7 |
| 123 | 17 | 6[f] | 288 | 0 | 0 | 30 | 2 | 2 | 160 | 0 | 1 | 661 | 1 | 9 | 1289 | 2 | 4 |
| 51 | 1 | 0[f] | 259 | 2 | 6 | | | | 342 | 0 | 0 | 1789 | 4 | 10 | 2441 | 8 | 4 |
| 133 | 17 | 8[g] | | | | | | | | | | 165 | 13 | 10 | 438 | 10 | 6 |
| 97 | 11 | 2 | | | | 474 | 19 | 8 | | | | 0 | | | 151 | 2 | 8 |
| 506 | 7 | 4 | 947 | 10 | 0 | | | | 646 | 10 | 1 | 3136 | 2 | 6 | 5746 | 18 | 5 |
| [75 | 0 | 0] | [212 | 10 | 0] | [121 | 10 | 0] | [9 | 0 | 0] | [271 | 16 | 0] | [778 | 6 | 0] |
| | | | | | | | | | | | | | | | 108 | 11 | 1 |
| | | | 20 | 0 | 0 | | | | | | | 136 | 5 | 2 | 193 | 12 | 2 |
| | | | | | | | | | | | | 30 | 0 | 0 | 30 | 0 | 0 |
| — | | | 20 | 0 | 0 | | | | — | | | 166 | 5 | 2 | 332 | 3 | 3 |
| 0 | | | 0 | | | | | | 0 | | | 16 | 16 | 0 | 16 | 16 | 0 |
| 1892 | 8 | 3 | 7860 | 17 | 4 | | | | 1925 | 19 | 1 | 10 956 | 8 | 6 | 29 520 | 10 | 10[a] |

[d] American bequests differ from those in Tables 19 and 20 because
Ward +£ 22 lost, is included here.
Keayne −£160 house is below in capitalized annuities and rent.
Trusedale −£ 40 is not here except in 1682–1686.

−£178 more in Table 19.

[e] English gifts in Tables 19 and 20 include £57 7*s.* which is in "Related activities" of Table 25. Bequests include Bridges; rest of Mowlson is in annuities. In general Table 23 shows gifts as intended by donors, Table 25, III, as received.

[f] Danforth "receives" interest and rent as *due*. Later Treasurers do not.

[g] Danforth's "Advance of Stock" seems to have included gain on turnover and some income.

[h] This deficit must have been covered by Steward's balance due, not otherwise included here.

amounts in italics facilitates evaluating the estimated Treasurers' figures, which are those in standard type.*

The significance of this income can be better understood if we postpone further comment on it until the end of the next chapter, on disbursements. Also in that chapter we shall discuss further the Stewards' net balance and the meaning of the figures in italics in Table 25.

Meanwhile, Figure 4 gives a picture of the sources from which the increasing income was funneled into the College's coffers. The income and the relative importance of sources of income obviously vary considerably according to whether the period studied involved a large gift (Holworthy in 1678) or a major new building (second Harvard College, 1672; Stoughton College, 1700).

* I have also estimated and included receipts from tuition from 1654 to 1682. There is an inconsistency in treatment of study rents: gross study rents are included from 1641 to 1652 and 1660 to 1669, but are not included in Treasurers' figures thereafter, though they do appear in italics from 1687 on. Thus the total income includes most study rents to 1669, but not thereafter. If study rents and odd fees were deducted before 1669, the figures would be more consistent. In this case it is perhaps better to follow the Treasurers' practice, and the error is not large. As we shall see in the next chapter, the net Stewards' balance covers any *gain* from study rents. Table 25 also undoubtedly misses some minor receipts (*contra*) through the Steward in years to 1669.

# VII

## *ANALYSIS OF DISBURSEMENTS*

THE way the College money was spent was in large part determined by the force of circumstances, including the way the money came in, but there was still an important measure of discretion left to the administrators. By the terms of the charter the approval of the Overseers was required "in great and difficult cases," and it is hard to picture the Corporation in the seventeenth century making such a major change as, for example, in the tuition rate, without the approval of the larger board. However, the recommendations of the Corporation, while by no means always followed by the General Court or the Overseers, carried great weight since the President and Fellows were responsible for the daily operations. In President Leverett's time there was a tendency to consult the governor of the Province before taking any important steps, and getting his advance approval seems to have been thought good policy even on smaller matters. Earlier Presidents, too, were in frequent contact with the leaders of the Colony's civil and religious affairs, and it may be assumed that under the Colony government there was full sympathy and understanding between the College officers and the community.

### SALARIES

*The President's salary.* The outstanding fact about salaries is that after Dunster's time the Court definitely assumed responsibility for paying the President.* There were also occasional small supplemental allotments to Presidents by the Corporation, and there were some allowances for expenses.

But in the second decade of the Colony's existence President Dunster's salary was not yet forthcoming from "the Country" with

* See above, pages 92–94.

any regularity.* Whoever prepared the figures for the Committee report of May 3, 1654, which is the basis of our College and Dunster accounts of 1652, went to some length to show that Dunster's total receipts from the Country averaged about £55 a year. We conclude, however, that Dunster may have been promised £60 a year when he was first appointed, and that before the end of his term he may have averaged £62 9*s.* 2*d.* a year from all sources, at least for 1640 to 1652. The figure to 1652 is based on £40 a year from the ferry (some of it in "bad peage"), £50 in all from the Colony, £56 from the Weld-Peter moneys, and tuitions from Massachusetts and other students (£314 13*s.* 8*d.*), as well as some of the Commencement fees.

Besides his salary, Dunster had the President's Lodge and also his personal grant in Billerica from the Town of Cambridge.

With President Chauncy's arrival, the Court took over payment of presidential salaries. From Court and other records we can estimate amounts fairly well with the exception of President Mather's salary; records during the Andros period were so incomplete that we are left in considerable doubt about that.[1]

Because the Presidents of Harvard were only acting or part-time during most of the latter part of our period, a table of compensation actually paid does not represent the rates which were considered suitable for full-time presidents. The "suitable" rate showed a fairly steady increase, varying to some extent with the experience of the incumbent. Dunster had about £60 and Chauncy about £100. After that, £150 was the basic rate for the full-time position, but the distinguished Mr. Mather was at times offered as much as £250 if he would devote himself exclusively to this work. Table 26 shows an estimate of the actual compensation received by the major persons who held the President's position.

*The Fellows' salaries.* On December 10, 1643, at a meeting of the

* Dunster described his troubles collecting College money in his letter to the Colony Treasurer, September 18, 1643: ". . . pervailing intreaties of some poore neighbours that thought themselves overcharged [on their taxes] and so have got partly some releases, and many whole forbearance even to this day: this disconvenience hath been distractive that I was to receive it at so many mens hands, and albeit the constables should have saved mee this labour, yet our neighbors knowing I should receive it inevitably appealed from them to myself: . . . where in they in a sort both blamed myselfe because they received not satisfaction at my hands immediately . . ." (*FHC*, p. 298, citing *Mass. Archives*, CCXL, 58.)

*Table 26. Average Total Annual Compensation Received by Harvard Presidents, 1640 to 1712 (in addition each usually received either a house or, after 1693, rents of £13 a year)*

| President | Annual compensation | (plus) Average commencement fees[a] |
|---|---|---|
| Dunster | £ 62 | |
| Chauncy | 110 | £ 7 |
| Hoar | 133 | 3 |
| Oakes (Acting 5 of 6 years) | 108 | 6 |
| Rogers | 150 | 1 |
| Mather (part-time) | 80 | 11 (when not in England) |
| Willard (part-time) | 60 | 11 |
| Leverett | 165 and some tuition[b] | 13 |

[a] It is not certain that the President always had these fees.
[b] Leverett kept a class when he had trouble finding Tutors.

Governors of the College it was ordered "that 2 Batchelours shall be chosen for the present helpe of the president, to read to the Junior pupills as the president shall see fitt, and be allowed out of the Colleadge Treasury £4 per Annum to each of them for their paines." Thus Dunster had his first assistance, and Harvard College its first faculty members other than the President. From that time on in our period the College had usually two teaching Fellows, sometimes three, and very occasionally four for a brief period. In the earliest years these men were candidates for the A.M. degree (for which the requirements were minimal), and they seldom stayed on at the College after completing their own studies. Obviously their stipend in the first decade, though it increased somewhat, hardly paid the Fellows' own expenses at the College. Dunster wished that the Tutors could have their students' tuition money, but tuition was in his time "a considerable part of the President's maintenance."[2]

The amount paid to the Fellows gradually increased, and in 1654 the three Tutors had £12, £11, and £10 a year respectively, and the tuition.* They paid for their board but had their chambers and studies rent-free. The bulk of the increase was the result of the

* See above, p. 78.

Country's taking over the payment of the President's salary and thus releasing tuition for the Tutors. Their total compensation from 1654 to 1669 must have averaged less than £35 a year, with somewhat smaller amounts coming with the declining enrollment at the end of these fifteen years, and the payment of anything beyond tuition varying according to what income came in to the Treasurer.

In 1666 the Overseers issued an order which no doubt confirmed the status quo:

> That such as are fellows of the Colledge, and have sallaryes payd them out of the Treasury, shall have their constant Residence in the Colledge, and shall Lodge therin and be present with the Schollars at meall times in the Hall, have their Studyes in the Colledge that so they may be better enabled to inspect the manners of the Schollars and prevent all unnecessary dammage to the Society.[3]

This order assured that the teaching Fellows should be resident and usually unmarried, and thus not called upon to support households of their own. Yet within the next decade the College had the first of its Tutors who stayed much beyond the time they received their own Masters' degrees — Thomas Graves (A.B. 1656) was a Tutor from 1666 to 1671, Alexander Nowell (A.B. 1664) tutored from 1666 to his death in 1672, and Daniel Gookin (A.B. 1669) taught from 1673 to 1681. The best known of the seventeenth-century Fellows, John Leverett (A.B. 1680) and William Brattle (A.B. also in 1680), both taught from about 1685 to 1697. These men lived with their students, and though they made occasional short excursions away from the College to preach or for other business, they had little life outside Harvard Yard.

Fellows John Leverett and William Brattle on June 2, 1690, presented some "Proposalls" (Plate 8) to the Corporation meeting, stating that in the year 1686 the President and Council had allowed them, besides the ferry, £58, with which they were satisfied, though it was considerably less than their predecessors had received, but for the years since then, they had "not received one Penny" besides the ferry, though, especially because of the absence of Mr. Mather, "whose presence very much Mitigated our Difficulties, and Alleviated our trouble and toyle," their work the last years had been harder than ever.

In answer to the proposals the Corporation agreed that the two Fellows should have £50 per annum for the years from 1687 through the summer of 1690, and ordered the Treasurer to pay the arrears "So as may not be prejudiciall to the Colledge Stocke." This the Treasurer fairly promptly did, and since the Governor's Council had raised the tuition rate to 10*s.* a quarter, making an average of £40 a year each from that source, the Fellows did not do badly. This £25 a year plus the ferry (which went to £30 each in 1695) and their tuitions provided Leverett's and Brattle's compensation until they resigned in 1697.

During the years 1693 to 1712 the payment of Fellows' salaries changed from the rather erratic process of assigning income to them as it came in, to the more methodical arrangement of voting the total payment by the College and total income of the teacher at the beginning of the year.

Thus, in these twenty years we see the evolution of a salary scale: As we have said, in 1693 Leverett and Brattle received tuition money from their own students, half the ferry money each, and a definite £25 each from the College starting as of 1687. The £25 was made up of Pennoyer funds, or credits with the Steward, or perhaps cash from Treasurer Thomas Brattle or from some other debtor to the College, such as the John Glover estate. When these two "old" Tutors* resigned in 1697 to go into law or the ministry, the two men who replaced them were paid £50 each, plus their pupils' tuition; the variable "ferry money," though still usually paid to the Tutors (and collected by them from the ferry-men), was not specifically stipulated to be part of their salary (and the *College*, not the Tutors, gained from the increases in the ferry rent). When there were two Tutors before 1703, the salary was as above, £50 each plus tuition; when there were three, the College paid £40 to the senior and £35 to each of the other two, and they all had their tuitions.** (Notice that three Tutors cost the College only £10 more than two.)

In 1703 another variation was introduced — the College said that it would pay £120 in all to the three men, but the amount to

* Often a Tutor took a class as Freshmen and kept it until it graduated. Some Tutors had two classes.

** "Tutor," "Fellow," and "Teaching Fellow" are used here interchangeably.

each varied according to his teaching load; each still received his own students' tuitions.[4] In 1705 the Corporation stipulated further that the total tuition was to be divided equally among the three — the only variation for teaching load was that made each year by the Corporation in dividing up the £120. In 1708 they reduced the £120 to £100, a cut in College expense, but gave each Tutor back the tuition from his own pupils. In 1710 to 1711 there were only two Tutors during the first part of the year and the President took one class; he received his own tuitions, as did the others; the two Tutors, and the third when appointed, were paid on the basis of the flat £120 again. In 1712 there was a real innovation: the Corporation set an all-inclusive salary scale, £80, £70, £50, to the three Tutors, with *no* additions of tuitions or any other compensation except free study and cellar rents. In 1715 there was an increase of £4 to each of the three.

So — a salary scale had evolved, a scale which, though it may not have stayed thereafter at its most "advanced" point, tried out in a short space of time many of the possible variations on the compensation theme. It is conceivable that this was indicative of a changing concept of the college teacher — from the English university Fellow who shared in profits (if any), to the salaried appointee. It is interesting also that this change occurred at a time when teaching Fellows were beginning to have a less influential place on the Corporation.* In Table 27 there is a summary of the evolution of the salary scale.[5] (In looking at the table we remember that inflation of the currency began to be felt shortly after the turn of the century.)

In summary, the approximate range of Fellows' income over the century is set forth in Table 28. On the whole, there is a rising rate. The fact of whether there were two or three Tutors is a major consideration. Though there appears to have been a great difference in the pay — and there was such a difference, between, for example, 1693 and 1708 — the cost to the College was often the same, exclusive of tuitions, and the total tuition intake did not differ much; the discrepancy between £99 for each of two Tutors in 1693 and £65 average for three in 1708 is due to the same number

* This latter development takes place after 1716.

*Table 27. Evolution of a Salary Scale at Harvard College, 1693 to 1715*

| Years | Number of Tutors | Tutor's compensation[a] | | Cost to College[b] | Comment |
|---|---|---|---|---|---|
| 1693–1695[c] | 2 | £25 each plus ½ ferry and own pupils' tuition | about £99 each | £100 | As of 1687, no more assigning income of separate funds except as part of the £25 |
| 1695–1697 | 2 | Same | about £100 | £105 | (Ferry rate up £5) |
| 1697–1699 | 2 | | | | No more ferry |
| 1699–1700 | 3 | When 2: £50 each plus tuition | about £93 | £100 | |
| 1700 (2 Q's) | 2 | When 3: £40–£35–£35, plus tuition | about £70–£65–£65 | £110 | |
| 1700–1702 | 3 | | | | |
| 1702–1703 | 2 | | | | |
| 1703–1705 | 3 | £120 for 3, by load, plus own tuitions | about £71–£66–£66 | £120 | Flat, plus tuition; vary with load |
| 1705–1708 | 3 | £120 for 3; tuition equally (£126 in 1705–1706) | about £82–£67–£62 | £120 | Flat, by load, but tuition equally |
| 1708–1711 | 3 | £100 for 3; own tuitions (£106 in 1710–1711) | about £77–£65–£53 | £100 | Cut; own tuitions |
| 1711–1712 | 3 | Basis £120 and own tuitions | about £82–£72–£62? | £120 | Cut restored |
| 1712–1714 | 3 | Inclusive £80–£70–£50 | £80–£70–£50 | £200 less tuition[d] | No more tuitions; all inclusive |
| 1714–1715 | 3 | Inclusive £84–£74–£54 | £84–£74–£54 | £212 less tuition | |

*Source: CSM* XV, 357–392, 397–398; XVI, 405, 421, 425; Brattle's journal, *passim;* QBB; Steward's accounts.

[a] Housing was also provided.

[b] Exclusive of tuition to 1712.

[c] Immediately before 1687 Tutors received tuition, ferry money, plus whatever was available that came in from endowment or gifts.

[d] Tuition was about £105.

*Table 28. Income of Members of the Faculty of Harvard College, 1643 to 1715*[a]

| Years | Approximate compensation, each Tutor | |
|---|---|---|
| 1643–1652 | £4 to £12 | |
| | *If 2 Tutors* | *If 3 Tutors* |
| 1654–1669 | | £25–£35 |
| 1669–1682 | £42–£72 | |
| 1686–1697 | £90–£100 | |
| 1697–1705 | £93 | £60–£70 |
| 1705–1708 | | £62–£82 |
| 1708–1711 | | £53–£77 |
| 1711–1712 | | £62–£82 |
| 1712–1715 | | £50–£84 |

[a] Housing was also provided.

of pupils' being cared for by more teachers.* Another factor is not only that Leverett and Brattle were experienced teachers, but also that they were a large part of the time acting *in loco praesidentis;* probably at no time before or since has the running of the College been left so completely and for such long periods to the teaching Fellows as it was to Messrs. John Leverett and William Brattle from 1685 to 1697.

We have seen that the *source* of Fellows' income varied over the years. After 1654 and until 1712 the Fellows received tuitions. They had almost all the ferry money, at least after 1669, though it was specifically ordered every quarter and their receiving it was not entirely automatic; from 1697 on the ferry rent was just one of the contributions to the salary and not voted as such to the Tutors. Part of the Pennoyer annuity always went to the Fellows, but this income was highly variable, and the proportion given to the Fellows also changed. The Glover £5 annuity was designated to the faculty, and it was so used. The Webb annual rent of about £13 was sometimes used in this way. These sources, and the College corn and Piscataqua benevolence, did cover the major part of the compensation of the Fellows. The small balance was made up out of general College funds.

*Salaries of the Treasurer, Steward, and other officers.* Our information is meager concerning salaries paid to other College officers, but a few such payments are mentioned in detail in the records.

The Treasurer under Dunster was inactive, and in Danforth's time his salary, if he received one, must have been included in that of "other College officers" shown in his accounts. Richards speaks of his "commission" which was paid him at the rate of £6 a year until 1682. We know that after August 1686 the Treasurer was paid £15 a year for his services as long as Richards filled the position.[6] Brattle was paid £30 a year throughout his encumbency, plus a payment of £10 in 1698, and an anniversary gift of £60 in 1713.[7] Of course these men were active merchants, and the Treasurership was only a small part of their work, but surely the records indicate that the effort they put into caring for the College was hardly recompensed by these retaining fees.

The Stewardship, at least after 1669 when Danforth took it over,

* This situation is not without relevance to 1962 problems.

was a position of some distinction. Danforth was Deputy Governor of the Colony; a subsequent Steward's daughter married the College President, and another's son (also Steward) married the daughter of such a leading citizen as the son of the Royal Governor.[8] During Steward Chesholme's time the salary of his office was £20 a year, and it was still £20 in 1667.[9]

In 1686 the College Orders established a different financial system for the Steward.[10] He was to run feeding (Commons and Sizings) on the basis that "for his Cost and Pains":

1) if the total Commons and Sizings receipts in the students' Quarter Bill ran under £60 a quarter, the Steward received the "total column" plus one third of the amount the total lacked of £60; or
2) if the column of Commons and Sizings in the Quarter Bill added to over £60, he "allowed" the College one sixth of the amount by which his receipts for this purpose exceeded £60.

The Steward was to provide raw food, fuel, and his own ordinary equipment, and to pay wages for preparing and serving food, excepting the Butler's wage.

"For his pains" the Steward made a good personal profit by this method — so good that the agreement was periodically renegotiated. But when prices of raw food rose he lost, and the College was obliged occasionally to make his "advance" more liberal. Moreover, the prices he charged the students, called "the price of parts, " varied. The Stewards' only real profit seems to have come from Commons and Sizings — or anything he was able to glean from his purchasing activities. There is no sign of a salary for him in the Bordman period.

In 1667 the Cook was paid £30 a year and his Commons. The Bordmans often held the offices of both Cook and Steward, and the family filled the Cook's position from 1667 to 1747. In 1686 the pay for the Cook's work went up to £40 a year.[11]

The job of being College Butler was ordinarily given to one of the older students as a "work scholarship." In 1660 the Corporation voted, for example, that "the stranger motioned by Mr. Norton is not thought fit for the discharge of the butler's place, in regard that so many schollars stand in need of such an helpe." In September 1670 the Butler's stipend was ordered from moneys given for "encouragement of poor scholars."[12] Though it seems to have been the usual practice throughout our period to give this position to the poorer scholars, there are some conspicuous possible exceptions in the Saltonstall family.

The Butler's rate of pay was fairly constant. In 1650 Jonathan Ince received £6 allowance a year, but by 1657 the rate had gone up to £12 a year, where it remained into the eighteenth century.[13] Normally the Steward paid this money out of his receipts and charged the College, but very occasionally we find such a payment by the Treasurer.

By the Orders of 1667 a student was given the responsibility of ringing the bell (except for meals), keeping the clock, and calling the President for prayers. For the punctual performance of these duties the Steward paid him £5 a year. Later these tasks were added to those of the Butler, who all along had had charge of the bell to announce meals.[14]

The duties of the Library-Keeper are first described in the Orders of 1667. In March of that year, Solomon Stoddard, who was then a teaching Fellow, was voted Library-Keeper It is not clear that the position was always filled officially, but when it was, the incumbent was usually a Fellow or an A.M. candidate. The first Library-Keeper to be paid as such (£3 a year for 1689–1690)[15] was Henry Newman, A.B. 1687, who later was active in the College's behalf in London. The position paid £5 a year from 1693 to 1698, £8 from 1698 to 1702, £10 (to Vice-President Willard's son) in 1702 to 1703, and £6 thereafter in our period.[16] The Library-Keepers were usually paid by the Treasurer.

This completes the roster of most College officers.

## SCHOLARSHIPS

Scholarship funds may be considered a form of College expense if endowed scholarship money is considered income. It is clear that the source of scholarships at Harvard during the Puritan Period was, for practical purposes, gifts and endowment income, not the College operating funds.

One of the earliest gifts to Harvard College was the £100 fund given for scholarships by Lady Ann Radcliffe Mowlson. Though the Mowlson money was given to the College in 1643, it may not have benefited the College until 1648, and the earliest scholarships paid came from the College corn. Of the corn money, about a third was awarded as scholarships or financial aids in the form of paid jobs. The President also allowed a few pounds to "poor scholars," and other individuals made gifts to help defray expenses of the first two decades' students; but practically all the help the "feeble abilities of their parents or other private frends"[17] received up to 1660 came from Thomas Weld's Mowlson fund and Thomas Shepard's College corn.

Dunster's 1647 petition to the Commissioners of the United Colonies posed the age-old scholarship problem: First, there is not enough money; and second, there is the question whether what money there is should be used for "the maintenance of schollars" or for "the Society," that is, for only the "poor, pious, and learned," or for "all the schollars in general." He expressed the view, too, that if the graduates did not serve the Country, and if they did not stay in the colonies, they should "be engaged in convenient time to repay what they have received from the Colonies."[18] The tendency in the seventeenth century was definitely, though not exclusively, to subsidize the older students who had proved themselves, and their scholarships were sometimes renewed for one or two years and even carried into their years of graduate study. Certainly Dunster's scholars were useful to the Country, though the same can be said of a great majority of the seventeenth-century Harvard graduates; especially notable scholarship students were Urian Oakes, future President of the College, John Eliot, the apostle to the Indians, Samuel Nowell, future magistrate and Treasurer of Harvard.

The College corn ran out, but Mowlson income continued into the eighties. The next addition to funds used for scholarships was the rent of the Webb House, which as of 1661 on was spent, as its donor prescribed, "for the best Good of the College," and usually, as he had thought suitable, "for the Maintenance of Some poor Scholars."[19] "The Scholarships" (Mowlson) and Webb were the mainstay of the scholarship program until the Pennoyer income started in 1679.* When Brattle took over, the Mowlson income had stopped, but Pennoyer did fairly well and other funds began

* The Overseers had in 1669 ordered that £34 of the promised £60 a year from Piscataqua be spent for Fellows' salaries and "the Remainder to be for the Encouragement of Schollars as the Overseers shall see meet to order," but only three pounds of this money was ever spent on scholarships; the receipts from Piscataqua just about covered the votes for salaries. *CSM* XV, 219; Richards, pp. 43–44.

to come in. Treasurer Brattle in nineteen years paid out or ordered £672 19*s*. 6*d*. for scholarships.

An important part of this scholarship money was from the earliest days used to support what might be called "work scholarships," and its use for this purpose ties in with the practice of making grants to the more responsible and usually older students. Danforth's accounts of 1663 to 1669 list payments to "Scholars of the House," whose duties were described in the College Laws of 1667. They shall

take a strict Account of all the buildings, Chambers, Studyes, and fences belonging to the College and shall give an account quarterly to the Treasurer what dammage the Colledge hath susteyned in any of the aforementioned particulars and by whom.

No Schollar shall enter into or leave the possession of any Chamber or Study untill Some one of the Schollars of the house have viewed the State thereof, which they shall represent unto the Treasurer.*

— A precursor of student government. For carrying out this not too pleasant duty, two to six men were, after the late 1660's, paid from £3 to £6 a year.

In addition to the Scholars of the House, there was the rather lucrative job of Butler (about £12 a year), and those of Monitor (£3 a year largely for keeping track of late-comers to church), Bell-ringer (£2 a year in 1654, later £5 a year until taken over by the Butler in 1686 or shortly before), and Waiter in the Hall (£4 to £2 10*s*. a year).[20] A mother in the year 1712 attests the importance of this allowance:

Mrs. Pierpont setting forth . . . the great difficulties she Labours under with respect to her son now at College, and that she would be obliged to take him, not being able to Support him, unless he might be restored to his place of a Waiter, The President consented that he should be restored, and Sparhawk be dismist, not for any fault, but out of Charity to his Kinsman, who needed it more than He.[21]

Some of the students added odd small sums to their incomes by "writing" for the officers.

It is difficult or impossible for much of the seventeenth century

* Sometimes this position was given to holders of the A.M. degree who were at the College exercising their graduates' privilege of residence.

to make figures such as colleges now publish showing the percentage of students in college who received scholarships in any one year.* A few sample years, however, indicate that from one quarter to one third of the men did have such assistance each year. For example, the average amount "allowed" to the 16 out of 49 undergraduates in the year 1710 to 1711 was £4 9*s.*, which would have been about £18 over a four year period — assuming the scholarship was received every year. This, if a man was very economical, might have covered over half his expenses, perhaps more — and this average does not ordinarily include pay he may have received for jobs. Moreover, the students who worked as waiters or butlers spent less money on food, for they could pick up what had been prepared for those who were absent. Thus it was possible for an occasional student to earn his way completely, and in some years as many as half of those who graduated had had help at some time. The situation sounds in many respects much like the present.

### THE STEWARD'S ACCOUNT**

The Steward's account of his collections and expenses for the College other than food was his "Harvard College account," "H. C. Account," and on it he credited the College with its net gain, if any, on food, with commencement dinner gain, absent commons, receipts from study and cellar rents, detriments, punishment, and gallery money (see Plate 6). He debited the College

* It is possible to make some estimates of a larger figure, the percentage of the students who *at some time* while in college received aid. Appendix B presents such figures.

** The finance of any modern educational institution involves sundry "auxiliary enterprises" which show in the annual report of the institution only through net balances or by means of supplementary accounts. Activities sometimes treated in this way include, for example, a faculty club, of which the net loss is absorbed in the institution's expenses, but the total expense and disbursements are not added to the accounts of the parent operation; or, more importantly, sometimes dormitories and feeding are treated separately, with only their balance listed; commonly separate foundations or research projects are accounted for in this way. Treatment of auxiliary enterprises constitutes a possible major weakness in any totals of educational accounts and is one of the reasons it is difficult to compare finances of educational institutions — there is as yet no accepted and generally followed practice for this accounting.

For early Harvard we might classify all the Stewards' operations as an auxiliary enterprise; at least they were carried on outside the Treasurers' books. Largely outside the books also were several non-student sources of income and their expenditure, including the Country's payment of Presidents' salaries, major building projects, the ferry, the Piscataqua benevolence, and parts of Pennoyer income — all these we have added into the accounts to reach our estimates of income and disbursements.

for salaries of the Butler and College laundress, its own glass-mending costs, minor repairs, and any orders from the Corporation to pay College bills. Tuition and half-tuition, paid to the teachers, did not appear. *Contra* items for monitors' and sweepers' pay and students' glass-mending charges were taken on both sides of the account, received and disbursed. Commencement returns were sometimes shown gross and sometimes net. The net balance of the Harvard College account was kept up or down, as needed, by varying the number of "orders to pay" sent to the Steward by the Corporation.

The payments by the Steward on Corporation order added to sizable sums. In Brattle's period, the pay of Scholars of the House consumed £244 of the College balance, and other scholarships ordered by the Treasurer on the Steward totaled £353 10*s.* 8*d.* (The deduction for scholarships from the College's balance with the Steward was offset by endowment income which the Treasurer received.)

One of the important sources of a positive balance was the Commencement fee.[22] In 1689, for example, the Steward took in 16 fees of £2 each — £32 — and spent £18 19*s.* 7*d.* on the dinner; in 1690 there were 31 Commencers, total fees £62, but the dinner cost only £25 3*s.* 1*d.* In 1691 the allowance to the Steward for his Commencement pains and expense was set at one quarter of the cost of provisions used — a good device for assuring an ample feast, but perhaps not conducive to restraint of expenses. The fluctuation in the College balance over a year because of this annual fee was good reason not to balance the books and try to clear out the balance very frequently.

We see, then, that (1) the Steward ran a food concession for the College, with a variable proportion of the receipts going to the College, but a minimum clearance guaranteed to the Steward; and (2) the College's profits on this, and other College moneys collected by the Steward, were expended by the Steward as agent. The net balance of (2) was kept small by varying the amount of orders for payment out of these receipts. Because the Steward collected all student fees, besides food charges, he cared for many regular College expenses, such as repairs. Only if we knew the total of all the Treasurers' standing and special orders for payment and added them to the Treasurers' accounts would we know all the College expenses. We have little idea of these amounts before 1687; for later years I have made estimates which appear in some of the summary tables (25 and 31 to 34), but they could be incomplete if *contra* items have been variously treated.*

### BUILDINGS

We know little about the costs of the College's first major building, the first "Harvard College." Eaton and Shepard left lists of expenditures totaling £572 19*s*. 6*d*. which we assume represents money spent on this building. Dunster's expenses that were specified for building or that we deduce were for that purpose bring the total up to £900 7*s*.; this appears to be a maximum figure according to the accounts we have. Mr. Morison arrives at a similar amount (£965) by a different route.[23] Considering what we know of the building and comparing it with other buildings of which we have the cost, it is safe to assume that expenditures for the first Harvard College were in the neighborhood of £900.

Earlier discussions of gifts, government grants, and sponsored subscriptions have described the costs of other buildings with the exception of Goffe College. This "college," on a lot adjoining that of Harvard College, was originally owned by Edward Goffe and was purchased by the Corporation to house the overflow of Harvard College in about the year 1651. Apparently the President used a good part of the gift which came from the island of Eleuthera to provide this needed dormitory space.

Table 29 summarizes major expenditures for buildings. Table 30 lists amounts shown on the Treasurers' books for repairs.

* For those determined readers who wish to follow the detail of this adjustment, I show in Appendix C the results of analysis of the Stewards' books from 1687 to 1712. From the Quarter Bills we know the Stewards' receipts. The "food cost" was allowed the Steward; this I have made by subtracting Commons and Sizings Allowance from Commons and Sizings charges. From Treasurers' memoranda we estimate the amount paid out on Corporation order. The Steward paid the Butler and the Monitor. The balance of his expense covers repairs and other small, fairly regular charges; this is for us the balancing item of the account; it would be impossible to extract it in accurate detail from the Stewards' records, but we can see there of what it is composed.

Appendix C is the source of the figures in italics in Table 25, "The College Income in the Puritan Period." See also Plate 6.

*Table 29. Capital Expenditures for Buildings, Harvard College, 1638 to 1712*

| Dates of use | Building | Cost | Source |
|---|---|---|---|
| 1638–1641 | Peyntree House (First President's House) | Under £100 | |
| 1640–1679 | First Harvard College | Around £900 | Court, John Harvard, others |
| 1645–1680 | Second President's House | Around £150 | Court |
| 1650–1706 | Second Meeting House | Around £30 | Students (for gallery) |
| 1651–1660 | Goffe College | Under £124 | Eleuthera |
| 1655–1698 | Indian College | Around £350 | All or half from S.P.G.[a] |
| 1672– | Repairs President's House | Not over £300 | Country subscription |
| 1677–1764 | Second Harvard College (burned) | Around £1700 | Country subscription |
| 1680–1719 | Third President's House | £260 | £100? by Court |
| 1699–1781 | Stoughton College | £1020 | £1000 by William Stoughton |
| 1706– | Third Meeting House | £62 5*s.* | |
| 1711– | Brew-house | £58 2*s.* 6*d.* | |

[a] The Society for Propagation of the Gospel in New England, an English corporation.

*Table 30. Major Expenditures for Repairs, Harvard College, 1638 to 1712*[a]

| | | £ | *s.* | *d.* | *Source* |
|---|---|---|---|---|---|
| 1654–1663 | | 346 | 19 | 7 | (£250 5*s.* 6*d.* from subscription) |
| 1663–1669 | | 139 | 0 | 1 | |
| 1669–1693 | | 59 | 5 | 1 | |
| 1693–1712 | | 120 | 13 | 0 | |
| | plus | 190? | | | (from the Court for the President's House) |

[a] These figures come from the Treasurers' books and Court records. There were additional unknown but not large amounts paid out by the Stewards.

## MISCELLANEOUS DISBURSEMENTS

The expenses in this category are *very* "miscellaneous," but they are mostly self-explanatory. They include entertainment, funerals, travel and transport, fees, investment expense, the Press, Indians, and a few unidentified entries on the books. The amounts so expended are summarized in Table 31 insofar as we can find them in the Treasurers' records.

SUMMARY OF INCOME AND DISBURSEMENTS

Table 31 brings together the amounts of all the disbursements we have discussed. Figure 5 illustrates Table 31 in bar graphs.

Because of the varying lengths of the Treasurers' terms of office

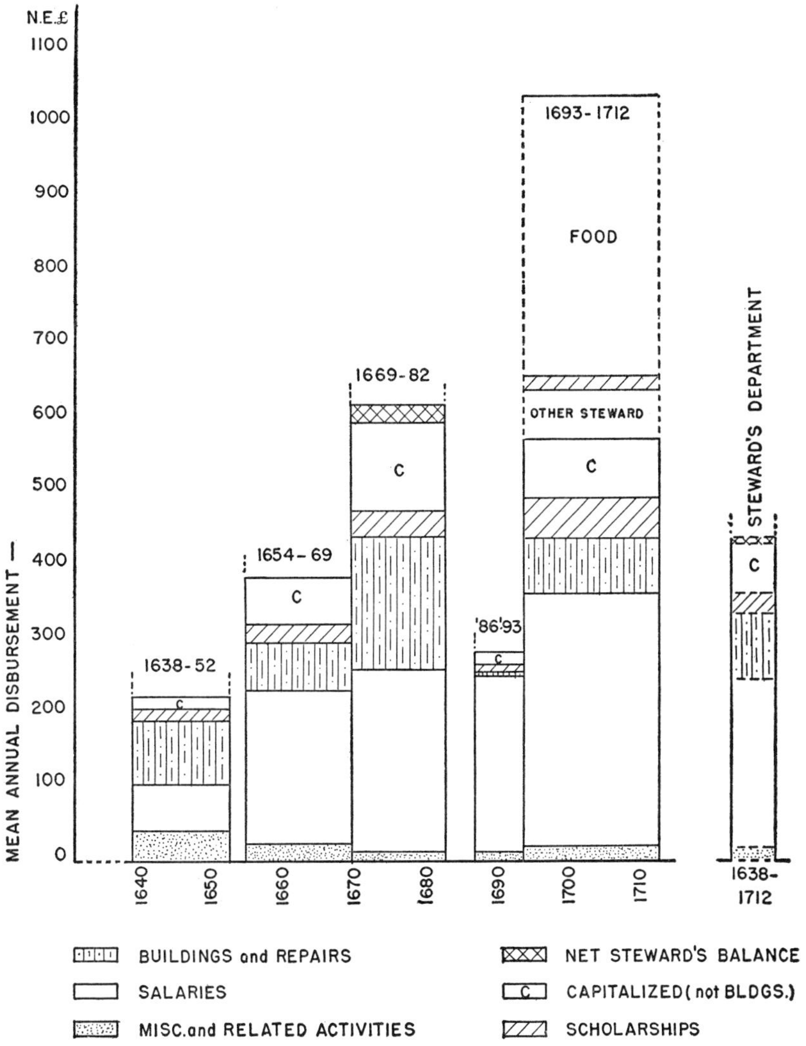


Figure 5. *Disbursements according to purpose, 1638 to 1712 (including plant and capital, but not turnover of investment accounts). From Table 32.*

| | 1636–1652 | | | (1652–1654) incomplete | | | 1654–1663 | | |
|---|---|---|---|---|---|---|---|---|---|
| | £ | *s.* | *d.* | £ | *s.* | *d.* | £ | *s.* | *d.* |
| I. Salaries and allowances | | | | | | | | | |
| President | 749 | 10 | 3 | 100 | 0 | 0 | 1018 | 0 | 0 |
| Fellows | 179 | 14 | 4½ | | | | 998 | 14 | 6[b] |
| Treasurer | | | | | | | | | |
| Librarian | | | | | | | | | |
| Other officers | 6 | 13 | 4 | | | | | | |
| | 935 | 17 | 11 | | | | 2016 | 14 | 6 |
| II. Steward's department (except tuition, Monitor and Butler) | | | | | | | | | |
| Cost of food (prepared) | | | | | | | | | |
| Balance of receipts from students, used for repairs and equipment, college glass, laundress, etc., and Corporation orders | | | | | | | | | |
| Net balance from Treasurer to Steward | 9 | 6 | 6 | | | | | | |
| | 9 | 6 | 6 | | | | | | |
| III. Buildings and repairs and equipment | | | | | | | | | |
| Capital construction and land | 1174 | 7 | 0 | | | | 370 | 10 | 0 |
| Cambridge meeting-house | 30 | 0 | 0 | | | | 0 | | |
| Repairs (more in Steward's miscellaneous and investment expense) | | | | | | | 346 | 19 | 1 |
| Equipment | 20 | 0 | 0 | | | | 18 | 11 | 0 |
| | 1224 | 7 | 0 | | | | 736 | 0 | 1 |
| IV. Scholarships | | | | | | | | | |
| From designated endowment | 60 | 0 | 0 | 30 | 0 | 0 | 150 | 0 | 0 |
| From undesignated endowment & gifts | 100 | 6 | 5 | | | | | | |
| For student work | | | | | | | | | |
| Scholars of the House | | | | | | | | | |
| Monitor | 60 | 0 | 0 | | | | | | |
| Butler | 3 | 0 | 0 | | | | | | |
| | 223 | 6 | 5 | | | | 150 | 0 | 0 |
| V. Miscellaneous | | | | | | | | | |
| Fees | | | | | | | | | |
| Investment expense[c] | 2 | 6 | 6 | | | | 1 | 0 | 0 |
| Miscellaneous[d] | 24 | 19 | 6½ | | | | 17 | 10 | 8 |
| Losses | 29 | 11 | 3 | | | | 62 | 16 | 11 |
| Unknown | 364 | 5 | 6 | | | | 66 | 13 | 8 |
| Related activities | | | | | | | | | |
| Press | 70 | 0 | 0 | | | | | | |
| Indians | | | | | | | 37 | 7 | 0 |
| Books | | | | | | | | | |
| | 491 | 2 | 9 | | | | 185 | 8 | 3 |
| VI. Capitalized gifts or income[f] | 0 | | | | | | 320 | 18 | 11 } |
| | | | | | | | 138 | 19 | 0 } |
| Capitalized rents and annuities | 292 | 16 | 4[h] | | | | 160 | 0 | 0 |
| | 292 | 16 | 4 | | | | 619 | 17 | 11 |
| VII. Cash on hand | 0 | | | | | | 0 | | |
| TOTAL DISBURSEMENTS | 3176 | 16 | 11 | | | | 3708 | 0 | 0 |

For assumptions involved, see text. Items in italics, 1686 to 1712, are additional amounts from the Steward's Harvard College account in the QBB (see Table 25 and Appendix C).

[a] President Mather was in England four years.

[b] Other officers included.

[c] Investment expense includes freight and insurance on gifts, repairs of houses rented. It may well be incomplete.

| 1663– Feb. 1669 | | | June 1669– 1682 | | | (1682–1686) incomplete | | | 1686–1693 | | | 1693–1712 | | | Totals (*not* including 1652–54 & 1682–86) | | |
|---|---|---|---|---|---|---|---|---|---|---|---|---|---|---|---|---|---|
| £ | s. | d. | £ | s. | d. | £ | s. | d. | £ | s. | d. | £ | s. | d. | £ | s. | d |
| 570 | 0 | 0 | 1571 | 6 | 8 | 437 | 0 | 0 | 305 | 3 | 0[a] | 1950 | 13 | 6 | 6164 | 13 | 5 |
| 533 | 7 | 3 | 1576 | 9 | 0 | 307 | 12 | 10 | 1192 | 10 | 0 | 3961 | 9 | 8 | 8442 | 4 | 9 |
| | | | 78 | 0 | 0 | | | | 108 | 2 | 2 | 580 | 0 | 0 | 766 | 2 | 2 |
| | | | 3 | 4 | 6 | | | | 6 | 0 | 0 | 120 | 0 | 0 | 129 | 4 | 6 |
| | | | 16 | 16 | 0 | | | | 32 | 10 | 0 | | | | 55 | 19 | 4 |
| 1103 | 7 | 3 | 3245 | 16 | 2 | | | | 1644 | 5 | 2 | 6612 | 3 | 2 | 15558 | 4 | 2 |
| | | | | | | | | | *1810* | *10* | *9* | *7324* | *17* | *8* | | | |
| | | | | | | | | | *317* | *2* | *11* | *1211* | *9* | *1* | | | |
| 36 | 8 | 11 | 253 | 7 | 11 | | | | 15 | 0 | 0 | 18 | 15 | 0 | 332 | 18 | 4 |
| 36 | 8 | 11 | 253 | 7 | 11 | | | | 15 | 0 | 0 | 18 | 15 | 0 | 332 | 18 | 4 |
| | | | | | | | | | *2127* | *13* | *8* | *8536* | *6* | *9* | | | |
| 0 | | | 2260 | 0 | 0 | | | | 0 | | | 1020 | 0 | 0 | 4824 | 17 | 0 |
| 0 | | | 0 | | | | | | 0 | | | 62 | 5 | 0 | 92 | 5 | 0 |
| 139 | 0 | 10 | 30 | 9 | 6 | | | | 23 | 3 | 3 | 353 | 9 | 0 | 893 | 1 | 8 |
| 14 | 8 | 0 | 52 | 19 | 11½ | | | | 5 | 8 | 0 | 7 | 14 | 8 | 119 | 1 | 7 |
| 153 | 8 | 10 | 2343 | 9 | 5 | | | | 28 | 11 | 3 | 1443 | 8 | 8 | 5929 | 5 | 3 |
| 75 | 0 | 0 | 212 | 10 | 0 | 121 | 10 | 0 | 9 | 0 | 0 | 271 | 16 | 0 | 778 | 6 | 0 |
| 61 | 0 | 0 | 168 | 2 | 8 | | | | | | | 401 | 3 | 6 | 730 | 12 | 7 |
| 75 | 0 | 0 | | | | | | | 53 | 10 | 0 | 342 | 3 | 0 | 470 | 13 | 0 |
| | | | | | | | | | *20* | *0* | *0* | *95* | *0* | *0* | 60 | 0 | 0 |
| | | | 5 | 0 | 0 | | | | *72* | *0* | *0* | *228* | *0* | *0* | 8 | 0 | 0 |
| 211 | 0 | 0 | 385 | 12 | 8 | | | | 62 | 10 | 0 | 1015 | 2 | 6 | 2047 | 11 | 7 |
| | | | | | | | | | | | | 30 | 3 | 6 | 30 | 3 | 6 |
| 40 | 12 | 0 | 36 | 0 | 2 | | | | 23 | 3 | 2 | 16 | 3 | 2 | 119 | 5 | 0 |
| 2 | 12 | 7 | 13 | 6 | 6 | | | | 3 | 8 | 0 | 12 | 0 | 0 | 73 | 17 | 3 |
| | | | 8 | 0 | 6 | | | | 3 | 17 | 6 | 31 | 18 | 0 | 136 | 4 | 2 |
| | | | 28 | 6 | 0 | | | | | | | 9 | 8 | 2 | 468 | 13 | 4 |
| | | | | | | | | | | | | | | | 70 | 0 | 0 |
| | | | | | | | | | | | | 136 | 5 | 2 | 173 | 12 | 2 |
| | | | | | | | | | | | | 42 | 11 | 11 | 42 | 11 | 11 |
| 43 | 4 | 7 | 85 | 13 | 2 | | | | 30 | 8 | 8 | 278 | 9 | 11 | 1114 | 7 | 4 |
| | | | | | | | | | | | | 165 | 13 | 10[e] | | | |
| | | | | | | | | | | | | 1291 | 15 | 5 | | | |
| 184 | 18 | 8[g] | 1185 | 18 | 0 | | | | 128 | 8 | 0 | 160 | 0 | 0 | 3576 | 12 | 10 |
| | | | | | | | | | | | | 131 | 0 | 0 | | | |
| 160 | 0 | 0 | 361 | 0 | 0 | | | | 0 | | | −160 | 0 | 0 | 944 | 16 | 4 |
| 344 | 18 | 8 | 1546 | 18 | 0 | | | | 128 | 8 | 0 | 1588 | 9 | 3 | 4521 | 9 | 2 |
| 0 | | | 0 | | | | | | 16 | 16 | 0 | 0 | | | 16 | 16 | 0 |
| 1892 | 8 | 3 | 7860 | 17 | 4 | | | | 1925 | 19 | 1 | 10956 | 8 | 6 | 29520 | 10 | 10 |

[d] Miscellaneous includes transportation, entertainment, "writing and printing," Fellow's funeral, College seal.

[e] Gain on money sold.

[f] This will be discussed further in Chapter VIII.

[g] Danforth's "advance of stock," adjusted for errors in adding and different valuation of Keayne house in *CSM* XV, 214–216.

[h] Including Mowlson.

*Table 32. Amount (and Per Cent of Total) of Average Annual Income, College, 1638 to 1712*

| INCOME | 1638–1652[a] £ | 1638–1652[a] % | 1654–1669 £ | 1654–1669 % | 1669–1682 £ | 1669–1682 % | 1686–1693 £ | 1686–1693 % | 1693–1712 £ | 1693–1712 % | 1693–1712 *% incl. Steward gross* | SUM[a] £ | SUM[a] % |
|---|---|---|---|---|---|---|---|---|---|---|---|---|---|
| Students | | | | | | | | | | | | | |
| Tuition (to teachers) | 17 | 7.4 | 55 | 14.2 | 57 | 9.4 | 81 | 28.3 | 89 | 15.5 | *8.6* | 60 | 13.6 |
| Food charges | | | | | | | | | +*410* | | *39.3* | | |
| Other[b] | 8 | 3.6 | 16 | 4.1 | | | 3 | 1.0 | 7 +*57* | 1.3 | *6.1* | 7 | 1.7 |
| Other — net balances[c] | | | | | 2 | .3 | 26 | 9.2 | 36 | 6.3 | *3.5* | 13 | 3.0 |
| Total | 25 | 10.9 | 71 | 18.3 | 59 | 9.7 | 110 | 38.5 | 133 +*466* | 23.0 | *57.4* | 80 | 18.3 |
| Government | | | | | | | | | | | | | |
| Building (& gen. in '40) | 29 | 12.9 | 0 | 0 | 8 | 1.3 | 0 | 0 | 11 | 1.9 | *1.0* | 11 | 2.4 |
| Salary (to President) | 4 | 1.6 | 104 | 26.9 | 109 | 17.8 | 15 | 5.2 | 79 | 13.6 | *7.5* | 68 | 15.4 |
| Ferry (to teachers) | 31 | 13.9 | 32 | 8.3 | 37 | 6.0 | 50 | 17.5 | 66 | 11.5 | *6.3* | 44 | 10.0 |
| Sponsored subscriptions | 19 | 8.5 | 17 | 4.5 | 169 | 27.5 | 0 | 0 | 0 | 0 | *0* | 40 | 9.1 |
| Total | 84 | 36.8 | 153 | 39.7 | 323 | 52.7 | 65 | 22.7 | 156 | 27.0 | *14.9* | 163 | 37.0 |
| Gifts | | | | | | | | | | | | | |
| Money | 87 | 38.9 | 51 | 13.1 | 127 | 20.8 | 15 | 5.2 | 55 | 9.6 | *5.3* | 71 | 16.2 |
| Buildings | 0 | 0 | 24 | 6.2 | 0 | 0 | 0 | 0 | 53 | 9.1 | *5.0* | 20 | 4.6 |
| Rent & annuities | 17 | 7.5 | 22 | 5.7 | 28 | 4.6 | – | – | 6 | 1.0 | *.6* | 15 | 3.3 |
| Total | 103 | 45.5 | 97 | 25.0 | 155 | 25.3 | 15 | 5.2 | 114 | 19.7 | *10.9* | 108 | 24.1 |
| Endowment | | | | | | | | | | | | | |
| Income | 5 | 2.3 | 36 | 9.3 | 74 | 12.1 | 96 | 33.6 | 156 | 27.1 | *15.0* | 77 | 17.5 |
| Gain | | | 19 | 4.9 | | | | | 9 | 1.5 | *.8* | 7 | 1.5 |
| Deficit[c] | 4 | 1.7 | 7 | 1.7 | | | | | | | | 2 | .5 |
| Total | 9 | 4.0 | 61 | 15.9 | 74 | 12.1 | 96 | 33.6 | 165 | 28.6 | *15.8* | 86 | 19.6 |
| Related activities | 6 | 2.8 | 4 | 1.0 | 2 | .3 | | | 9 | 1.5 | *.8* | 5 | 1.1 |
| Cash | | | | | | | | | 1 | .1 | *.1* | | |
| Total | 227 | 100 | 386 | 100 | 613 | 100 | 285 | 100 | 577 | 100 | | 440 | 100 |
| ***Total, including Steward*** | | | | | | | | | *1043* | | *100* | | |

NOTE: Caution is necessary in interpretation; see text, page 150 and note **.

Figures may not add to totals because of rounding. Figures in italics 1693–1712 represent additional amounts from the Steward's books; they are included in figuring percentages in italics.

[a] 1638 to 1654 is incomplete and atypical. 1652 to 1654 and 1682 to 1686 are excluded from the table and the total.

[b] Rent is included in the figures in italics for 1693 to 1712. See Note *e* of Table 2 and p. 78 above. Repairs were often paid from study rent and therefore the figure shown for repairs is incomplete. President's rents are not included.

*Including Capital Gifts, and of Disbursements Including Building, Harvard (see also Figure 6)*

| DISBURSEMENTS | 1638–1652[a] | | 1654–1669 | | 1669–1682 | | 1686–1693 | | 1693–1712 | | | SUM | |
|---|---|---|---|---|---|---|---|---|---|---|---|---|---|
| | £ | % | £ | % | £ | % | £ | % | £ | % | *% incl. Steward gross* | £ | % |
| Salaries | | | | | | | | | | | | | |
| President | 54 | 23.6 | 110 | 28.4 | 122 | 20.0 | 45 | 15.8 | 103 | 17.8 | *9.8* | 92 | 20.9 |
| Fellows | 13 | 5.7 | 106 | 27.4} | 123 | 20.1 | 177 | 61.9 | 208 | 36.2 | *20.0* | 126 | 28.6 |
| Others | .5 | .2 | | | 8 | 1.2 | 22 | 7.6 | 37 | 6.4 | *3.5* | 14 | 3.2 |
| Total | 67 | 29.5 | 215 | 55.7 | 253 | 41.3 | 244 | 85.4 | 348 | 60.3 | *33.4* | 232 | 52.7 |
| Steward | | | | | | | | | | | | | |
| Food (prepared) | | | | | | | | | *+386* | | *37.0* | | |
| Other (incl. repairs) | | | | | | | | | *+64* | | *6.1* | | |
| Other — net balances[c] | 1 | .3 | 3 | .7 | 20 | 3.2 | 2 | .8 | 1 | .2 | *.1* | 5 | 1.1 |
| Total | 1 | .3 | 3 | .7 | 20 | 3.2 | 2 | .8 | 1 *+450* | .2 | *43.2* | 5 | 1.1 |
| Buildings & repairs | | | | | | | | | | | | | |
| Capitalized | 86 | 37.9 | 26 | 6.6 | 176 | 28.8 | 0 | 0 | 57 | 9.9 | *5.5* | 73 | 16.7 |
| Repairs & equipment[b] | 1 | .6 | 36 | 9.3 | 7 | 1.1 | 4 | 1.5 | 19 | 3.3 | *1.8* | 15 | 3.4 |
| Total | 87 | 38.5 | 61 | 15.9 | 183 | 29.8 | 4 | 1.5 | 76 | 13.1 | *7.3* | 88 | 20.1 |
| Scholarships | | | | | | | | | | | | | |
| Endowed | 4 | 1.9 | 16 | 4.0 | 17 | 2.7 | 1 | .5 | 14 | 2.5 | *1.4* | 12 | 2.6 |
| Unendowed[d] | 7 | 3.2 | 4 | 1.1 | 13 | 2.1 | | | 21 | 3.7 | *2.0* | 11 | 2.5 |
| Work[d] | 4 | 2.0 | 5 | 1.3 | | | 8 | 2.8 | 18 *+17* | 3.1 | *3.4* | 8 | 1.8 |
| Total | 16 | 7.0 | 25 | 6.4 | 30 | 4.9 | 9 | 3.2 | 53 *+17* | 9.3 | *6.8* | 30 | 6.9 |
| Miscellaneous | 30 | 13.3 | 13 | 3.4 | 7 | 1.1 | 5 | 1.6 | 5 | .9 | *.5* | 12 | 2.8 |
| Capitalized | | | | | | | | | | | | | |
| Money (incl. spls.[c] & gifts) | | | 44 | 11.5 | 92 | 15.1 | 19 | 6.6 | 85 | 14.8 | *8.2* | 53 | 12.1 |
| Rent & annuities | 21 | 9.2 | 22 | 5.7 | 28 | 4.6 | | | −2 | −.3 | *−.1* | 14 | 3.2 |
| Total | 21 | 9.2 | 67 | 17.2 | 121 | 19.7 | 19 | 6.6 | 84 | 14.5 | *8.0* | 67 | 15.3 |
| Related activities | 5 | 2.2 | 3 | .7 | | | | | 9 | 1.6 | *.9* | 4 | 1.0 |
| Cash | | | | | | | 2 | .9 | | | | | |
| Total | 227 | 100 | 386 | 100 | 613 | 100 | 285 | 100 | 577 | 100 | | 440 | 100 |
| *Total, including Steward* | | | | | | | | | *1043* | | *100* | | |

[c] Figures may appear on both Income and Disbursement sides because this table is composed from accounts covering shorter periods.

[d] Most unendowed scholarships were paid from endowment income given preferably for scholarships

it is far easier to see what went on by considering average annual income and disbursements; those figures are presented in Table 32.* (Figure 6 on page 175 illustrates Table 32, as well as some additional ideas to be discussed below.)

There are very great limitations to the usefulness of parts of Table 32,** especially the percentages; nonetheless the table makes clear many important points.

These accounts are made up largely of receipts and offsetting (*contra*), or almost offsetting, disbursements:

> Tuition to 1654 went to the President (he taught); thereafter it went to the Fellows, and it constituted about half their pay — less than half in the last 19 years when endowment income and ferry rent were higher. The ferry rent was part of the President's salary to 1654, and thereafter provided about one third of the Fellows' income.
>
> The Court paid the President's basic salary after 1654.
>
> Food charges covered food costs and related services including work scholarships (1693–1712).

* The major difference between the total figures here and those in Table 2 at the end of Chapter II is that these include buildings and capitalized rents and annuities.

** I quote percentages in Table 32 only with great hesitation, for they are open to much misinterpretation for several reasons: First, classifications are arbitrary; for example, sponsored subscriptions might appear under either government or gifts. Second, the omission or not, of *contra* items can lead to very different results; a very clear instance occurs when in 1693 to 1712 food is included or omitted. Third, Table 32 shows *total* income, including amounts to be capitalized; this should not be confused with operating income, which we shall discuss later. Fourth, the percentage shows only the *relative* source of income or expenditure; if there is an extraordinary entry in one category, such as a building or a large gift, all the other percentages go down even though their absolute amounts may have increased; or, in years such as 1686 to 1693 when little else came in (not even President's salary), the percentages of income from tuition, ferry, and endowment income are inordinately large.

In the totals for the whole Puritan Period, however, the last difficulty — that percentages are only relative — largely averages out; the other troubles remain.

Shifts in percentages have much interest if we know enough detail to look behind them and see what caused the shift; they are misleading if we take them as an indication solely of a shift in the category which shows the change. If we tried to avoid these troubles by eliminating, for example, all capital expense, we would have little left in many years.

The totals of this particular table unhappily do not include 1682 to 1686, years when there was an unusually large deficit (see Chapter VIII).

Taking all these points into consideration it is obvious that percentages are of very dubious utility in making comparisons over time.

Study rents covered the upkeep of buildings and also related services.

Current capital drives or one large gift (Stoughton) provided new buildings.

Scholarships came from endowment income which the donors had designated either specifically or preferably for that purpose.

A very little endowment income went into faculty salaries — about three fifths of Pennoyer, and Glover except when his relatives had scholarships — covering about 5 per cent of the salaries.

Amounts added to capital, including buildings, total 32.0 per cent of disbursements in comparison with the 35.6 per cent of income that came from gifts of individuals, sponsored subscriptions, and government building grants. Of this, the cost of building (16.7 per cent) is about balanced by gifts and grants for buildings plus subscriptions (16.1 per cent) — leaving other capitalization (15.3 per cent) compared with other gifts (19.5 per cent); relatively few gifts were used for operating expenses in the long run.

As we look down the accounts in Table 32, going back and forth between income and disbursements, we see that the amount received for tuition increased sharply at two points — 1654 and 1686. In both years the rates went up, but not so much as the income increased.* The balance of the increase in tuition receipts is a reflection of the size of the student body.

On food from 1693 to 1712 the College made a slight gain, amounting to £24 a year, and to only £7 after the cost of work scholarships is deducted. The size of the food bill is over four times tuition and about eight times rent.

"Other" receipts from students include rent and fees mixed together to 1669, but rent is omitted from 1669 to 1693. However, the £57 "other" in the Steward account in 1693–1712 shows the

* Six shillings eight pence to 8*s*., 20 per cent, in 1655; 8*s*. to 10*s*., 25 per cent in 1687. Of course the 1638–1652 average is misleading, for there were not 14 full years of tuition collected.

proportion that rents and fees bear to all student payments — about 10 per cent.

The Stewards' balance was valuable to the College after the rate increase in 1686, though our enthusiasm for this change should be tempered by the possibility that the Steward may have paid for more repairs or other expenses before 1682. Expenses for repairs and equipment are largely hidden in the Stewards' account after 1669 — thus we miss them here from 1669 to 1693, but can see them in the Stewards' accounts of 1693 to 1712.

Students in 1693 to 1712 paid in only 57.4 per cent of the total receipts, including capital.

The Fellows' steady gain in total salary was due partly to an increase in tuition receipts, partly to the ferry. The percentage (salary of total expense) was unusually large from 1686 to 1693 because little else was paid out. The individuals did not have such an even gain because their pay varied with the number of Fellows. From 1686 to 1707 Fellows did much of the Presidents' work and more than earned the increase.

The Presidents' salary dips in the period 1686 to 1693, during four years of which Mather was away; the Government proportion of income is less when, from 1686 to 1708, Presidents were paid only for part time.

In 1669 to 1682 the account shows the beginning of salaries paid to "others," especially to the Treasurers, but also to a Librarian after 1690.

The fluctuation in Government payments is a major cause of the large variations in annual income. This category provides a large (37.0 per cent) part of the income, and gifts (24.1 per cent) provide another large part, especially when the gifts of buildings are included. This is still true if we switch the sponsored subscriptions (9.1 per cent) from government (then 27.8 per cent) to gifts (then 33.2 per cent). The only building to which the Government gave materially was the First Harvard College. Others came largely from sponsored subscriptions.

Under gifts, Holworthy stands out in 1681. The dearth from 1686 to 1693 is obvious. Fewer rental properties and annuities were given after 1682.

The percentages show clearly that endowment income early

played an important part — especially after 1654. After 1685 the £15 a year from Mowlson had stopped. Other scholarship income increases after 1693 (see Table 25). Few scholarships were awarded, at least through the books, from 1686 to 1693. Work scholarships are partly hidden in Stewards' accounts but show up after 1692.

The operating surplus, which appears in disbursements under money capitalized, offsets the deficit, but these accounts do not include the largest deficit, that under Nowell from 1683 to 1686.*

What we now call "related activities," such as the Press, were then unimportant.

Much of the large "miscellaneous" expense in 1638 to 1652 is disbursements which we cannot identify.

The totals are high for 1669 to 1682 because of the £2000 Harvard Hall and £1234 Holworthy gifts. The total was low in 1686 to 1693 — government unrest. It recovers in 1693 — more Presidents' salary, more gifts, more endowment income, a positive Stewards' balance.

In summary — the arithmetic of the seventeenth-century officers was simple after 1654: buildings usually came from the Court, as did the Presidents' salary; ferry rent and tuition money went to the Fellows; food and housing were self-supporting, except for the original cost of the buildings; scholarships were endowed. There was sometimes a slight balance in the Steward's account to cover small incidentals; occasionally the Steward ran a deficit. The budget for this deficit, any further salary payments, any extra expenses, *we* would say came out of gifts, or, later, endowment income; the mid-century officers would have said that there was little "budgeting" — expenses were incurred when money came in. Toward the end of the century the somewhat larger endowment income gave a flexibility which made planning more feasible. A large proportion of gifts was capitalized.

From Table 32 we can produce a preliminary summary of operating results (Table 33), which will be more meaningful after we have discussed the growth of Assets in Chapter VIII.

Also from Tables 32 and 33 we can readily make the traditional "Cost per Student" exhibit, though only for 1693 to 1712 when Stewards' costs are available. Table 34 indicates that for those

* Chapter VIII will describe it further.

*Table 33. Harvard College Operating and Total Annual Income, 1638 to 1712*

| | 1638–1712 | | 1693–1712 | |
|---|---|---|---|---|
| | Amount £ | Per cent of total income, including only net from Steward | Amount £ | Per cent of total income, including only net from Steward |
| Average annual income | 440 | 100 | 577 | 100 |
| Amount added to invested assets | 67 | 15 | 84 | 15 |
| Amount added to buildings | 46[a] | 10 | 47[b] | 8 |
| Average annual operating income = Operating expense | 327[c] | 75 | 446[d] | 77 |
| Steward's income (besides net) | ? | | 466 | |
| Operating income including Steward | | | 912 | |

[a] £73 of Table 32 less £27 depreciation, assuming buildings in 1712 worth £3000 and therefore depreciated by ⅜ of cost, or £27 a year.
[b] £57 less £10, assuming depreciation is equal to half repair expense.
[c] Includes scholarships of £30 (9% of operating income) and related activities £4.
[d] Includes scholarships of £53 (12% of operating income) and related activities £9.

nineteen years the average undergraduate non-scholarship student had a subsidy beyond his fees of 34 per cent of the actual operating costs including food and not including capital expense; for the average student including scholarship students, the subsidy was 40 per cent. If we assume that one quarter of the students received scholarships, the scholarship students had an average subsidy of 58 per cent. Of course the subsidy is a much larger percentage of costs if food is excluded.*

* See notes c, d, and e of Table 34. In Table 9 (page 66) we showed that in 1687 to 1712 the charge for a resident undergraduate who stayed four full quarters four years in residence could be about £65 (£16 a year) on a comfortable but not extravagant basis, but the actual average annual payment was around £41. Here we see in Table 34 that while in 1693 to 1712 the average operating cost *to the College* was about £17 a year, or £68 for four years, the average payment by the student was £11 a year, £44 for four years. This does not mean that the student who was "comfortable" paid his full cost; rather it restates (as indicated in Table 9) that the actual average cost was less than the full fees because few students were in residence four quarters four years, and also not all students were residents and some, especially those on scholarship, paid less for food than our standard resident. Actual payments were also less

*Table 34. Average Annual Cost to Harvard College, Total and per Student, Graduate and Undergraduate, Including Food, 1693 to 1712*

| | Cost in pounds per annum all students | Per cent of total cost, including Steward | Per cent of operating cost, including Steward: including schps. in total cost | Per cent of operating cost, including Steward: excluding schps. from total cost | Average annual cost in pounds[a]: per student grad. & u.g. (57 students) | Average annual cost in pounds[a]: per undergraduate (52 students) |
|---|---|---|---|---|---|---|
| Average annual income and disbursements (including Steward and scholarships) | 1043 | 100 | | | 18 | 20 |
| Money and buildings capitalized | 131 | 13 | | | 2 | 2½ |
| Average annual operating income and expense | 912 | 87 | 100 | | 16 | 17½ |
| Scholarships | 53 | 7 | 6 | | 1[b] | 1[b] |
| Average annual operating income and expense; scholarships out | 859 | 80 | 94 | 100 | 15 | 16½ |
| Gross fees of students | 599 | 57 | 66[c] | 70 | 10½ | 11½ |
| Operating income from other sources | 260 | 23 | | 30[d] | 4½ | 5 |
| Operating income from other sources, plus scholarships | 313 | 30 | 34[d,e] | | 5½ | 6 |

[a] We do not have the total expenses separated by graduate and undergraduate students. Therefore a more exact heading of the last column would be, "Total cost ÷ 52 undergraduate students." There were on the average 5 resident graduate students who paid no tuition. Thus the total cost should be divided by a number between 52 and 57 students, and the average fee paid is therefore about £11 a year.

[b] Average scholarship per student — *all* students — not average scholarship per scholarship student, which if one quarter of the students had scholarships was £4, if one third, £3. See pp. 140–141 and n., above.

[c] Average subsidy for *all* students is 40% if scholarships are included in expense: 100% of expense less net fees of students; that is, 100% less 60%, or 366/912.

[d] Subsidy for non-scholarship students is 34% (313/912) if scholarships are included in expense, 30% (260/859) if scholarships are excluded.

[e] Subsidy for scholarship students, assuming 25% of the students had scholarships, is 58% if scholarships are included in expense: $\frac{\frac{1}{4}(912) - [\frac{1}{4}(599) - 53]}{\frac{1}{4}(912)} = \frac{228 - 96.75}{228} = 58\%.$

According to Table 32, by the turn of the century the endowment provided more than half the operating subsidy. In the next chapter we attack the analysis of the growing assets which produced this income.

than the full operating cost to the College, and coincidentally the amount "saved" by each student who was not in residence all four quarters was just about equal to the (entirely different) part of the cost of his education paid for from sources other than his student fees and charges.

# VIII

## *ASSETS*

HARVARD'S investment problem in the seventeenth century was very different from that today. In the first place, they then had little money to invest; and, in the second place, there were no securities in the modern sense in which to invest. But very shortly after the College was founded it did have some endowment funds, and it was up to the Corporation to "lett them out" to produce income and conserve the capital.

The College's first permanent endowment was the Mowlson-Bridges Scholarship Fund, given in 1643. Thomas Weld sent the money back from England, and the College, as the Corporation said, "accommodated this colony" by leaving the money on deposit with the Colony Treasurer.[1] Whether or not this "accommodation," which lasted until 1713, was originally voluntary on the College's part we do not know, but since the money ultimately did return to the Corporation's care, and since the College received £15 annual income on £162 16*s.* 4*d.* until 1685 and 6 per cent thereafter, on the whole this early "investment" turned out well; but the trouble to the College involved in keeping the Country from forgetting about their deposit was sufficient to prevent their adopting this method of treatment for other funds.* Other means of investment had to be found.

But before we attempt any comment on Harvard's investment policy, we may well stop to consider in what ways the College might have invested its funds.

### INVESTMENT OPPORTUNITIES IN THE SEVENTEENTH CENTURY

The first Governor Dudley in 1631 wrote to the Countess of Lincoln: "If any come hither to plant for worldly ends, that can

* Leaving the John Harvard funds with the Colony had also proved to be a nuisance.

well live at home, he commits an error, of which he will soon repent him; but if for spiritual . . . he may find here what may well content him."[2] Those who did come here with excess funds were advised in 1638 to invest in raising cattle,[3] and farming was the only possible enterprise that was at all profitable for many years.

The acquisition of land would have seemed proper to the "foeffees" of an educational institution, for land was one of the major endowments of English universities; but land was valuable in England, and it was very cheap here. When Lady Holworthy's agent inquired about the disposition of Sir Matthew's bequest, Richards said, "It not being feasible to lay it out in Land here to yield an yearly rent (as he intimates) because the Incomes would be very little, it hath been put out at interest."[4] Rents for land were very low.* So the College hopefully held on to lands received as gifts or grants, but, especially when there was no inflation, there was little reason to use cash to acquire more such property.

Similarly, investment in town real estate was a different matter in the new small towns of Massachusetts, including Boston, from what it was in the well developed old, though growing, metropolitan areas of England. President Wilbur K. Jordan of Radcliffe, in his volumes on philanthropy in England to 1660, tells that large amounts of charitable endowment were very successfully invested in real estate there;[5] one might wonder that the seventeenth-century New England college did not put more of its money into this type of investment, rather than almost exclusively (except the Hopkins fund) in personal bonds and mortgages. The major reason was no doubt the different position of real estate in a new country.

In the first part of the century there was no securities market in America or in England, and when toward the end of the century such a market of an elementary sort did become available in London, ventures there were of a highly speculative nature.[6]

Mining, lumbering, fishing, shipbuilding, trading — all ordinarily needed individual enterprise or supervision, or they were too

* "The existence of new lands encouraged an attitude not unlike that of Alice's Mad Tea Party. When tea and cakes were exhausted at one seat, the most natural thing for the Mad Hatter and the March Hare was to move on and occupy the next seat. When Alice inquired what would happen when they came around to their original position again, the March Hare changed the subject. . . ." Norbert Wiener, *The Human Use of Human Beings* (Boston, 1950), p. 35.

large or too risky for Harvard College to undertake on its own. But most of such dealings, whether large or small, required capital, and no doubt Harvard had a second-hand interest in many of them through its policy of making loans secured by mortgages or only on personal bond. With the exception of produce in the earliest times, and of a few pieces of real estate given to the College, all of Harvard's investments in our period took the form of personal loans or mortgages. The College did not participate directly in development of New England business, but it was very much affected by the state of the local economy, and, in its position as a small money-lender, the College facilitated the affairs of many members of the community.

The loaning of money at interest, acting as a modern bank, was consistent with the Puritan theology. In accordance with these tenets, the Massachusetts legal rate of interest was set at 8 per cent, then reduced in 1693 to 6 per cent.[7] The record has a modern ring: "Forasmuch as the abatement of interest hath always been found beneficial to the advancement of trade and improvement of lands by good husbandry; and *whereas* the taking of eight in the hundred for interest of money tends to the great discouragement of ingenuity and industry in the husbandry, trade, and commerce of this province," taking of over 6 per cent is forbidden.[8]

In establishing Harvard's investment policy the early Corporation must have had in mind the practice in England. There was no business institution there which provided credit at low rates without excellent security. However, local charitable endowments supplied loans in many parishes, and guilds usually had funds available to members. Common in country places was the use of the parish "stock" for local credit, for it was not simple to find investments for the stock except in local enterprise or property.* Normally a formal document was signed by the borrower binding

* About the origin of this source of supply James says that in the late fifteenth and early sixteenth centuries "Some parishes owned livestock which were hired out to neighborhood farmers. . . . Later in the sixteenth century many charitable bequests provided for the purchase of a 'stock' of goods (such as wool) which was to be given to the poor to furnish them with employment. . . . Soon the term stock came to be applied to any sum of money possessed by a community that had been accumulated for charitable purposes, or even for schools and chapels." F. G. James, "Charity Endowments as Sources of Local Credit in Seventeenth and Eighteenth Century England," *Jour. Ec. Hist.*, VIII (1948), 160–161.

him for *twice* the amount of the loan, or else constituting a mortgage deed to his property if he failed to pay on time. According to James, the loans ranged in amount from £15 to £50 and up; they were made to "people of substance" in the parish. It was common for executors to hold on to the principal of a bequest and pay interest on it, but experience with such executors was not good. By the late eighteenth century this use of charitable endowments for personal loans was largely supplanted by banks or other financial institutions.[9]

Clearly, then, Harvard had precedent and ecclesiastical sanction for employing its funds in making personal loans. Let us see what the College's experience was.

## THE GROWTH OF HARVARD'S ASSETS

There is not perfect continuity in the story of Harvard's assets for the obvious reason that there are hiatuses about which we know little. The most annoying and the most intriguing such hiatus is that from 1683 to 1686, at the time Richards had gone to England and Samuel Nowell was acting as Treasurer. But considering the time that has passed, we get a remarkably clear impression of the way the assets developed. A summary of this process is shown in Tables 35 and 36, which, like all the tables in this book, must be interpreted in the light of their amplification in the text.

We shall consider the assets in two parts: first, cash, and securities, which in the seventeenth century were livestock and provisions, mortgages, and personal bonds and bills; and second, the ferry rent and other annual rents and annuities. To give an idea of the process involved we shall read along through Table 35 and speak of some of the "securities" by name, although the reader will not be familiar with all their circumstances.

Since the Mowlson Fund was for so long in the hands of the Country Treasurer, paying only income to the College, we classify it now as an annuity and will treat it later. Besides this asset, in 1654 there had apparently been a net balance of about £100 in the Steward's accounts.[10] Danforth starts his books with no assets, so we have not listed this £100 as "stock," nor do later Treasurers in our period list the Stewards' balance as an asset.

With the receipt of gifts from England and a building repairs

*Table 35. Harvard College Stock, 1636 to 1712*
*(see also Figure 7, page 176)*

| | May 3, 1652 | | | October 1654 | | | Feb. 1, 1669 | | | June 3, 1669 D to R | | |
|---|---|---|---|---|---|---|---|---|---|---|---|---|
| | £ | *s.* | *d.* | £ | *s.* | *d.* | £ | *s.* | *d.* | £ | *s.* | *d.* |
| Cash and "Securities" | | | | | | | | | | | | |
| *Cash | | | | | | | 0 | | | 0 | | |
| *Bills, bonds, mortgages | | | | [100][a] | | | 249 | 14 | 0 | 287 | 0 | 0 |
| *Grain and livestock due or on hand | | | | | | | 201 | 10 | 5 | 162 | 10 | 11 |
| *Old bills and bonds | | | | | | | 22 | 4 | 0 | 22 | 0 | 0 |
| Bequests due | | | | | | | | | | | | |
| Interest and rent due or overdue | | | | | | | 73 | 17 | 0[b] | 35 | 14 | 0 |
| Stock | | | | [100] | | | 547 | 5 | 5[b,d] | 507 | 4 | 11 |
| Capitalized Rents and Annuities | | | | | | | | | | | | |
| Annuities: Mowlson | 162 | 16 | 4 | 162 | 16 | 4 | 162 | 16 | 4 | 162 | 16 | 4 |
| Newgate | 63 | 0 | 0 | 63 | 0 | 0 | 63 | 0 | 0 | 63 | 0 | 0 |
| Glover | | | | | | | | | | | | |
| Pennoyer | | | | | | | | | | | | |
| Rents: Cambridge Neck | 4 | 0 | 0 | 4 | 0 | 0 | 4 | 0 | 0 | 4 | 0 | 0 |
| Billerica | 13 | 0 | 0 | 13 | 0 | 0 | 13 | 0 | 0 | 13 | 0 | 0 |
| Coggan | 50 | 0 | 0 | 50 | 0 | 0 | 50 | 0 | 0 | 50 | 0 | 0 |
| Webb | | | | | | | 160 | 0 | 0 | 160 | 0 | 0 |
| Keayne | | | | | | | 160 | 0 | 0 | 160 | 0 | 0 |
| Hayward | | | | | | | | | | | | |
| S. Ward | | | | | | | | | | | | |
| E. Rogers | | | | | | | | | | | | |
| Stoughton | | | | | | | | | | | | |
| Champney | | | | | | | | | | | | |
| Menotomy | | | | | | | | | | | | |
| Total Rents and Annuities | 292 | 16 | 4 | 292 | 16 | 4 | 612 | 16 | 4 | 612 | 16 | 4 |
| Capitalized ferry | 500 | 0 | 0 | 500 | 0 | 0 | 337 | 10 | 0 | 337 | 10 | 0 |
| Total assets without ferry | 292 | 16 | 4 | 292 | 16 | 4 | 1160 | 1 | 9 | 1120 | 1 | 3 |
| Total assets with ferry | 792 | 16 | 4 | 792 | 16 | 4 | 1497 | 11 | 9 | 1457 | 11 | 3 |

| | Oct. 1636 to May 1652 | | | Oct. 1654 to Feb. 1669 | | | Feb. 1669 to June 1669 | | |
|---|---|---|---|---|---|---|---|---|---|
| (1) [Change in "admitted" assets.*] | | | | [473 | 8 | 5] | [−1 | 17 | 6] |
| (2) Change in Stock above, including rents, interest, and bequests due | | | | 547 | 5 | 5 | −40 | 0 | 6 |
| (3) Change in Rents and Annuities above | 292 | 16 | 4 | 320 | 0 | 0 | 0 | | |
| (4) Change in all assets except ferry | 292 | 16 | 4 | 867 | 5 | 5 | −40 | 0 | 6 |
| (5) Change in ferry value — above | 500 | 0 | 0 | −162 | 10 | 0 | 0 | | |
| (6) Change in Stock from Receipts and Disbursements[i] (deficit out) | — | | | 547 | 5 | 5[d] | — | | |

* "Admitted" assets. D, Danforth; R, Richards; N, Nowell; B, Brattle.

[a] Not listed by Danforth. See page 159.

[b] Interest *due* was included by Danforth and is in this one figure. See Table 36, note e.

[c] In 1712 Brattle no longer listed rents and interest due as an asset. Therefore the change shown here for 1693 to 1712 is smaller than actual.

[d] In Danforth's accounts there is 13*s.* error in adding stock, 4*d.* error in adding receipts 1663–1669, and £5 10*s.* difference in value of Keayne house as received and listed in stock. £547 5*s.* 5*d.* shows these discrepancies corrected,

Table 35 *(Continued)*.

| Feb. 3, 1673 | | | Apr. 10, 1682 R to D | | | Mar. 5, 1683 D to N | | | Apr. 8, 1686 N to R | | | Apr. 29, 1693 R to B | | | July 4, 1693 | | | July 11, 1693 | | | July 1, 1712 | | |
|---|---|---|---|---|---|---|---|---|---|---|---|---|---|---|---|---|---|---|---|---|---|---|---|
| £ | *s.* | *d.* | £ | *s.* | *d.* | £ | *s.* | *d.* | £ | *s.* | *d.* | £ | *s.* | *d.* | £ | *s.* | *d.* | £ | *s.* | *d.* | £ | *s.* | *d.* |
| 102 | 9 | 10 | 7 | 6 | 0 | 0 | | | 0 | | | 56 | 10 | 2 | 16 | 16 | 0 | 19 | 18 | 6 | 330 | 1 | 1 |
| 336 | 13 | 0 | 1293 | 0 | 0 | 1335 | 6 | 0 | 1170 | 0 | 10 | 1232 | 15 | 4 | 1270 | 7 | 0 | 1595 | 0 | 0 | 2345 | 1 | 4 |
| 88 | 11 | 4 | 12 | 0 | 0 | 8 | 14 | 4 | 0 | | | 0 | | | 0 | | | 0 | | | 0 | | |
| 22 | 0 | 0 | 332 | 14 | 6 | 363 | 3 | 6 | 0 | | | 0 | | | 0 | | | 0 | | | 277 | 0 | 0 |
| | | | 293 | 6 | 8 | 340 | 6 | 8 | 168 | 6 | 8 | 168 | 6 | 8 | 168 | 6 | 8 | 168 | 6 | 8 | 168 | 6 | 8 |
| 72 | 18 | 6 | 140 | 14 | 2 | 251 | 19 | 4 | 19 | 18 | 5 | 241 | 16 | 6 | 277 | 18 | 10 | 180 | 13 | 0 | — | | [c] |
| 622 | 12 | 8 | 2079 | 1 | 4 | 2299 | 9 | 10[e] | 1358 | 5 | 11[f] | 1698 | 18 | 8 | 1733 | 8 | 6 | 2063 | 18 | 2 | 3120 | 9 | 1 |
| 162 | 16 | 4 | 162 | 16 | 4 | 162 | 16 | 4 | 162 | 16 | 4 | 162 | 16 | 4 | 162 | 16 | 4 | 162 | 16 | 4 | 162 | 16 | 4 |
| 63 | 0 | 0 | 63 | 0 | 0 | 63 | 0 | 0 | 63 | 0 | 0 | 63 | 0 | 0 | 63 | 0 | 0 | 63 | 0 | 0 | 63 | 0 | 0 |
| 60 | 0 | 0 | 60 | 0 | 0 | 60 | 0 | 0 | 60 | 0 | 0 | 60 | 0 | 0 | 60 | 0 | 0 | 60 | 0 | 0 | 60 | 0 | 0 |
| | | | 250 | 0 | 0 | 250 | 0 | 0 | 250 | 0 | 0 | 250 | 0 | 0 | 250 | 0 | 0 | 250 | 0 | 0 | 250 | 0 | 0 |
| 4 | 0 | 0 | 4 | 0 | 0 | 4 | 0 | 0 | 4 | 0 | 0 | 4 | 0 | 0 | 4 | 0 | 0 | 4 | 0 | 0 | 4 | 0 | 0 |
| 13 | 0 | 0 | 13 | 0 | 0 | 13 | 0 | 0 | 13 | 0 | 0 | 13 | 0 | 0 | 13 | 0 | 0 | 13 | 0 | 0 | 13 | 0 | 0 |
| 50 | 0 | 0 | 50 | 0 | 0 | 50 | 0 | 0 | 50 | 0 | 0 | 50 | 0 | 0 | 50 | 0 | 0 | 50 | 0 | 0 | 50 | 0 | 0 |
| 160 | 0 | 0 | 160 | 0 | 0 | 160 | 0 | 0 | 160 | 0 | 0 | 160 | 0 | 0 | 160 | 0 | 0 | 160 | 0 | 0 | 160 | 0 | 0 |
| 160 | 0 | 0 | 160 | 0 | 0 | 160 | 0 | 0 | 160 | 0 | 0 | 160 | 0 | 0 | 160 | 0 | 0 | | | [g] | | | |
| 16 | 0 | 0 | 16 | 0 | 0 | 16 | 0 | 0 | 16 | 0 | 0 | 16 | 0 | 0 | 16 | 0 | 0 | 16 | 0 | 0 | 16 | 0 | 0 |
| | | | 35 | 0 | 0 | 35 | 0 | 0 | 35 | 0 | 0 | 35 | 0 | 0 | 35 | 0 | 0 | 35 | 0 | 0 | 35 | 0 | 0 |
| | | | | | | | | | | | | | | | | | | | | | 50 | 0 | 0 |
| | | | | | | | | | | | | | | | | | | | | | 52 | 0 | 0 |
| | | | | | | | | | | | | | | | | | | | | | 13 | 0 | 0 |
| | | | | | | | | | | | | | | | | | | | | | 16 | 0 | 0 |
| 688 | 16 | 4 | 973 | 16 | 4 | 973 | 16 | 4 | 973 | 16 | 4 | 973 | 16 | 4 | 973 | 16 | 4 | 813 | 16 | 4 | 944 | 16 | 4 |
| 500 | 0 | 0 | 625 | 0 | 0 | 625 | 0 | 0 | 625 | 0 | 0 | 833 | 0 | 0[h] | 833 | 0 | 0 | 1000 | 0 | 0 | 1200 | 0 | 0 |
| 1311 | 9 | 0 | 3052 | 17 | 8 | 3272 | 6 | 2 | 2333 | 2 | 3 | 2672 | 14 | 0 | 2707 | 4 | 10 | 2877 | 14 | 6 | 4065 | 5 | 5[g] |
| 1811 | 9 | 0 | 3677 | 17 | 8 | 3897 | 6 | 2 | 2958 | 2 | 3 | 3505 | 14 | 0 | 3540 | 4 | 10 | 3877 | 14 | 6 | 5265 | 5 | 5 |

| June 1669 to Apr. 1682 | | | Apr. 1682 to Mar. 1683 | | | Mar. 1683 to Apr. 1686 | | | Apr. 1686 to July 1693 | | | July 1693 to July 1712[c] | | |
|---|---|---|---|---|---|---|---|---|---|---|---|---|---|---|
| [1173 | 9 | 7] | [62 | 3 | 4] | [−537 | 3 | 0][f] | [117 | 2 | 2] | [1664 | 19 | 5] |
| 1571 | 16 | 5 | 220 | 8 | 6 | −941 | 3 | 11[f] | 375 | 2 | 7 | 1387 | 0 | 7 |
| 361 | 0 | 0 | 0 | | | 0 | | | 0 | | | −29 | 0 | 0 |
| 1932 | 16 | 5 | 220 | 8 | 6 | −941 | 3 | 11[f] | 375 | 2 | 7 | 1358 | 0 | 7 |
| 287 | 10 | 0 | 0 | | | 0 | | | 208 | 0 | 0[h] | 367 | 0 | 0 |
| 1185 | 18 | 0 | — | | | — | | | 128 | 8 | 0 | 1617 | 9 | 3 |

[e] For Nowell's assets see Table 37, page 171.
[f] Plus £77 reinstated after 1686. See Table 37.
[g] House sold.
[h] Interest rates shift from 8% to 6%.
i Capitalized gifts or income, less capital availed of — comparable with line (1) just above.

*Table 36. Growth of "Admitted" Assets, Related to Individual Gifts and to Operations, Harvard College, 1636 to 1712*[a]
*(see also Figure 6, page 175)*

| | 1636–1652 | | | 1652–1654 (largely incl. in other periods) | | | Oct. 1654–June 1669 | | | Feb. 1669–June 1669 (incomplete) | | | June 1669–1682 | | | 1682–1686 (incomplete) | | | 1686–1693 | | | 1693–1712 | | | Sum | | |
|---|---|---|---|---|---|---|---|---|---|---|---|---|---|---|---|---|---|---|---|---|---|---|---|---|---|---|---|
| | £ | . | *d.* | £ | *s.* | *d.* | £ | *s.* | *d.* | £ | *s.* | *d.* | £ | *s.* | *d.* | £ | *s.* | *d.* | £ | *s.* | *d.* | £ | *s.* | *d.* | £ | *s.* | *d.* |
| (1) Current individual gifts[b] | 1162 | 14 | 8 | | | | 732 | 5 | 7 | | | | 1631 | 10 | 4 | 40 | 0 | 0[c] | 100 | 0 | 0 | 1046 | 18 | 0 | 4713 | 8 | 7 |
| (2) Current gifts availed of | 1162 | 14 | 8 | | | | 258 | 17 | 2 | | | | 445 | 12 | 4[d] | 40 | 0 | 0 | 0 | | | 0 | | | 1907 | 4 | 2 |
| (3) Current gifts capitalized | 0 | | | | | | 473 | 8 | 5[e] | | | | 1185 | 18 | 0 | 0 | | | 100 | 0 | 0 | 1046 | 18 | 0 | 2806 | 4 | 5 |
| (4) Other income capitalized | 0 | | | | | | 0 | | | | | | 0 | | | 0 | | | 28 | 8 | 0 | 570 | 11 | 3[f] | 598 | 19 | 3 |
| (5) Capital availed of | (53 | 11 | 6)[g] | | | | 0 | | | | | | 0 | | | 474 | 19 | 8 | 0 | | | 0 | | | 474 | 19 | 8 |
| (6) Change in "admitted" assets[h]: (3) + (4) − (5) in theory | | | | | | | 473 | 8 | 5 | (−1 | 17 | 6 | 1173 | 9 | 7 | (−474 | 19 | 8) | 117 | 2 | 2 | 1664 | 19 | 5 | 2952 | 2 | 5[i] |
| (7) Change in capitalized rents and annuities | 292 | 16 | 4[j] | 0 | | | 320 | 0 | 0 | 0 | | | 361 | 0 | 0 | 0 | | | 0 | | | 131 | 0 | 0 | 944 | 16 | 4 |
| | | | | | | | | | | | | | | | | | | | | | | −160 | 0 | 0 | | | |

[a] Including only those assets received on the books and including neither capitalized rents and annuities, nor bequests, interest, and rent due or overdue (see note e). Includes some old bills known to be worthless. *Does not include buildings given.* Individual gifts do *not* include government-sponsored subscriptions, government grants, or the ferry. Mowlson fund is considered an annuity.

[b] From Tables 25 and 31, Receipts and Disbursements.

[c] Additional gifts may have been received from Ashurst and J. Browne and possibly others.

[d] Extra expense of part of 1680 President's House (probably £160).

[e] Danforth received interest and rent on his books as it came due, which later Treasurers did not, though they listed amounts due as assets. Here we have taken out amounts due. There is an adjustment of £5 10*s.* for difference in value of Keayne house as received and as valued when an asset.

[f] £160 Keayne house sold and transferred from rent; £165 13*s.* 10*d.* gain on heavy money sold; £244 17*s.* 5*d.* from other income (Newgate, Pennoyer, and Pelham back income was collected, some in Nov. 1711, and not yet spent).

[g] From Table 25, not carried along because, as Table 25 note h says, it must have been advanced from the next period, and because we cannot include it in actual capital in Table 35.

[h] Line (6), brought here from Table 35 line (1), should theoretically equal lines (3) + (4) less (5) here. See p. 165, note * for possible reasons for discrepancy.

[i] "Admitted" assets in 1712.

[j] Including Mowlson.

NOTE: Shillings and pence are quoted not because the figures are exact, but to facilitate balancing.

subscription promoted by the Country, from 1654 to 1669 there was for the circumstances a sizable surplus of receipts (including gifts) over expenses for operation. In Danforth's fifteen years as Treasurer, £732 5*s.* 7*d.* came in gifts, plus the subscription for building repairs; £259 of this was spent for current expenses and £473 established the "College Stock."[11]

In evaluating this £473 of Stock, hindsight reveals that a £22 bond (and its £6 8*s.* interest) from the Ward legacy was worthless, the Corporation later voted to cancel Denison's £20 bill (and £8 interest) in compensation (investment expense) for his work about the College's unsuccessful Pequot lands claim, Richards wrote down about £40 of the value of the cattle, and so far as we know no very noticeable amount was ever paid on the principal of the Jewett and Willoughby bills of £60 and £168 respectively (or their £33 interest). With these considerations, the £473 of Stock comes down to no more than £163.*

The assets that were delivered to Treasurer Richards with ceremony on June 3, 1669, listed £287 of bonds (among which were now £200 of Deputy-Governor Willoughby and £60 of Jewett), plus £162 of bills or obligations payable in country pay. Danforth may have acquired these latter in payment of debts to the College, or he may have lent produce received — to be repaid in produce. By the end of the next three years Richards had eliminated about half of the country pay securities and had a cash balance of over £100. (The country pay "security" may have gone into the students' stomachs.) Thomas Brown had taken over Daniel Shedd's bill for £14 of wheat; this obligation, later of Thomas Brown's sons "Icabod and Ebenezer," was still running along in 1696, and it may be that the mortgage of William Brown in 1712 was the old bill rewritten, with a sizable addition and several payments to its credit in the intervening years.

The Jewett boys were paying on their father's 1660 obligation of £60 (he died in 1661); by 1682 they had paid in a total of £57, but the principal of the bill, plus more interest, was still outstanding. Perhaps the sons thought that the £57, with interest paid to Dan-

* Mr. Danforth could hardly have expected that these two leading citizens, or their estates, would prove to be so delinquent.

Danforth's account ends in February 1669; he took over the Stewardship. There is an hiatus with only slight changes until Richards became Treasurer in June 1669.

forth, covered the obligation of their father's estate, but Harvard did not see it that way.

During these years John Hull, the mint-master, made a gift of £100. Legacies of £100 from Joseph Browne and £128 N.E. (New England) from Henry Ashurst were recorded; they were paid, *if* they were paid, only by Nowell's time. The Reverend Edmund Browne's legacy came due, though it was not then listed and was still unpaid in 1715. Country Treasurer Richard Russell's executors turned over £31 13*s.* 4*d.* in country pay to the carpenter of the 1680 President's House; the balance of this personal bequest of £100 was still considered an outstanding obligation due in 1715. Willoughby's executors paid £106 9*s.* 4*d.* for interest, but £156 accrued, so their account stood at £249 in 1682.

By far the outstanding receipt in Richards' years as Treasurer was Sir Matthew Holworthy's £1234 N.E., the bequest which for the first time (possibly excepting the occasion of the brief surplus of gifts in the late 1650's) gave Harvard College any substantial sum to invest. Richards very quickly "lett it out" at 8 per cent interest, and the bills so acquired form practically his entire list of what we call "admitted" assets in 1682. At that time his Stock account included £1193 of Holworthy bills and Hull's £100 (later taken over by a note of Man), and also £333 of bills dated 1667 or before, plus £293 in legacies due but not yet received. (Of these legacies we know £193 had not come in by 1715, and whether the £100 due from Joseph Browne's estate ever was received is not clear.) Richards' assets listed, too, £141 in due or overdue rent and interest, 61⅔ bushels of malt valued at £12, and £7 6*s.* in cash.

Because of Sir Matthew Holworthy, receipts in these thirteen years of Richards' Treasurership did exceed disbursements, and Richards was able to capitalize £1186 of the gifts not availed of for expenses. Without the Holworthy donation the Stock in good "securities" would have evaporated completely (much of it because the 1669 "good" bonds were no longer so good in 1682).* Assets

* Did Richards and his fellow-members of the Corporation "dissipate" the Stock, or the Holworthy gift, or other current gifts? Mr. Morison, *HCSC*, p. 438, speaks of the Holworthy gift's having been "gradually dissipated," for "It was ordered drawn upon for salaries as early as December 1683." I can find no place where Holworthy money as such is ordered drawn upon. The only authority quoted for this is Sibley II,

in June 1669, excluding interest due and the worthless Ward legacy note, had been £449 10*s.* 11*d.*; in 1682, omitting also bequests due, they were £1623. The increase in assets received on the books was thus £1173, which represents the current gifts (or other income) capitalized.*

Treasurer Richards had been elected an Assistant of the Colony in May of 1680, and in 1682 when he "went for England" on a mission for the Colony the faithful Danforth (the Deputy Governor of the Colony) records in College Book III that "the Colledge Estate" was "delivered by the Worshipfull Captain John Richards

---

458–459, who in turn cites a Corporation salary vote (*CSM* XV, 254) of December 5, 1683, which says that "what the Income from the Ferry at Charlstowne and Mr. Glover's gift doth come short of this summe shall be made up *out of the money received in England by the honored Treasurer of the College, Major Richards*" [italics added]. I submit that the italicized expression is the same as, or very similar to, wording often used to describe Pennoyer income. For example, *CSM* XV, 257 (twice): "out of Mr. Pennoyer's mony received by and now in the hands of . . ."; and see also 259, 262 (twice). Moreover, the vote of December 5, 1683, ordered money to Fellows Andrew and Cotton which appears to be that listed as paid to them by the Pennoyer account (*CSM* XV, 75). Major Richards was *in* England about this time and no doubt collected Pennoyer money personally. Holworthy money came to Richards in Boston. Further, a letter of Richards to Mather in England in 1688 (4 *Coll. MHS* VIII, 502; also quoted in part by Mr. Morison in *HCSC*, p. 438) speaks of the Holworthy money's being "put out at interest, and profitts improved towards the maintenance of Fellowes, Schollars of the House, etc." I think perhaps the Corporation considered it was spending the Stock or other current gifts, as had been the previous practice, and that it thought of keeping the principal of Holworthy money at least for the present. Spending Stock continued, as we shall see, in Nowell's time, but many of the Holworthy bonds remained to form the basis of Brattle's growing permanent endowment. I quibble about this point now only because of its possible relevance to uses of the money in the next few years, on which we have all too little evidence.

* The amount as shown in line (3) of Table 36, £1185 18*s.*, for cash gifts capitalized, does not exactly match line (6) or the increase in any particular portion of the asset account of Table 35. Richards did not leave us a balance sheet, or a reconciliation of expenses, disbursements, and assets as Danforth did. There is no evidence that Richards ever thought exactly in those terms. The £1186 does correspond sufficiently closely for practical purposes, however, to the change (£1173) in assets excluding bequests, rent, and interest due. Exact correspondence here and in later cases is impeded by the practice of capitalizing interest without putting it through receipts, by our possibly misreading hand-writing and our separation of principal and interest in a sometimes arbitrary fashion, by entries referring to Nowell's actions, by the known weakness of some bonds, and by the write-off, without complete record, of some such items as grain or livestock. (We have succeeded in making the capitalization of real estate and annuities consistent throughout Tables 35 and 36, but this was not true of the original accounts.)

In order better to show the operating picture, we have subtracted invested principal which was received back and "lett out" from accounts as Richards left them, to get the receipts and disbursements shown in Tables 25 and 31, and thus their derivatives in this chapter.

unto the Deputy Governor." Samuel Nowell took over the accounts the next March 5, and College Book III shows the record, in Danforth's hand, of his transfer of accounts to Nowell. Richards' accounts begin again on April 8, 1686. Because the decade 1683 to 1693, with its changeover from Colony to Province, has general historical as well as particular Harvard interest, we shall dwell on it at some length.

The assets which we shall call "admitted" are bonds and mortgages, produce, and cash, and do not include interest and rent and bequests due.* On this basis the "admitted" assets had increased by £62 3*s*. 4*d*. during Danforth's eleven months, going from £1645 6*d*. to £1707 3*s*. 10*d*., as shown on Table 35.[12]

The activity of Nowell's Treasurership has been a mystery for over two hundred years. The fact that has attracted attention is that the *total* "assets," as listed at the beginning of the three years in College Book III and at the end by Richards in his book, fell from £2357 11*s*. 8*d*. in March 1683 to £1189 19*s*. 3½*d*. in October 1686.[13]

This fact in itself is startling, and so is the following quotation from Tutor Henry Flynt's "Catalogue of Benefactions":

> The President [President Leverett is probably intended] Says, That Mr. Dudley and Mr. Stoughton, and Major Richards and himself made up Accounts with Mr. Nowell, and they found Several Persons broke that money was Let to, To one in Cambridge one hundred pounds; The rest Mr. Nowell could give no Account of, But the College Estate lost and Sunk to the amount of eleven hundred pounds, in the hands of a good, but unfortunate Gentleman, who Sunk his own Estate also by ill management.

President Quincy in his *History* quotes Tutor Flynt without comment, but his quotation shows a significant difference in the last line: ". . . in the hands of *that* good, but unfortunate gentleman, . . ." [italics added].** Sibley, in turn, in his biography of

* They include the Ward £22, though we know now that it was never paid. One reason for omitting interest is the great inconsistency with which it is quoted as due.

** Tutor Flynt's Catalogue, made about 1720, is not now extant. *HCSC*, p. 43 n. 1. His paragraph comes from Andrew Eliot's MS. "Donations Book I," 49, made up by Eliot in 1773. Eliot apparently had access to Flynt's lost catalogue when he made up his book. The insert in brackets appears in parentheses in Eliot's book and seems to have been Eliot's comment.

*CSM* XVI, 476 (College Book IV), as of October 3, 1722, mentions Flynt's "Ac-

Nowell cites Quincy to the effect that "from various causes the College lost and sunk £1,100 during his administration, and he also lost his own property."[14]

Treasurer Nowell kept accounts but they were perhaps a bit casual.[15] Record-keeping was not one of the duties set forth in President Rogers' instructions to him:

Honored Sir.

You being by the President and Fellows of Harvard College Elected Treasurer pro tempore in the absent of Captain John Richards, you are hereby requested and ordered, as followeth:

1. forth with to take care of the provision for the President, as to out houses, fences and what is necessary to the finishing his lodgings.
2. Of the Colledge as to all necessary repayers from time to time, and in speciall that the rooffe be railed about for the indemnity of such as shall have occasion to go therupon.
3. You are to gather in forth with all debts due upon bill or account that make not allowance to the Colledge and *to renew your security of all debts that are above three year old* [italics added].
4. You shall pay Mr. Danforth the balance of his account.
5. You shall provide twelve new buckets for the Colledge uses and barr of Iron for the chimneys.

(s) John Rogers, President

Cambridge March 5, 1683[16]

Richards left for England on April 10, 1682, and on March 5, 1683, Nowell took charge. Richards was back and *both* he and Nowell attended a Corporation meeting on March 17, 1684, and Richards attended an Overseers' meeting July 1, 1684, and acted as Clerk of the meeting. Richards alone, *as Treasurer*, attended the meeting on July 21, 1684.[17] Yet Richards' accounts state that on October 22, 1686,

I tooke Care againe of the Colledge Stocke per persuation of mr. Dudley mr. Stoughton and mr. Increase Mather, and received of mr. Samuell Nowell, the late Treasurer, the Severall Papers underneath

count of Sundry Donations" and says that it should be entered in "the College Book." I do not find it there. On page 447, under date of November 16, 1719, the Corporation had appointed a committee to make the list, but Flynt seems to have done it himself, no doubt consulting others. Flynt's diary in HUA starts after this date. Leverett's diary for this period adds nothing.

Quincy's quotation, *History*, II, 232, follows immediately after his statement that Danforth delivered £2357 of "satisfactorily invested" estate to Nowell, and that the next record we have shows £1530 in 1693.

written; and am ordered to now make all the Obligations morgages etc., and *take them in myne owne name* [italics added]. . . .[18]

This account is not certified by the Corporation as are most such pages in the College Books or in Richards' or Brattle's Books. One wonders why Richards waited so long before he took back the accounts.*

This is all we know of Nowell's accounts. Of Mr. Nowell himself it is worth noting here that he was a highly respected minister and magistrate. Samuel Sewall, Overseer and close friend of officers of the College, was intimately acquainted with the affairs of Harvard, and throughout the years 1684 to 1686 he repeatedly speaks of Nowell with respect, and of Nowell's participation with him, Richards, and others in funerals, meetings, and such occasions. Sewall records how on October 21 and 22, 1685, the Magistrates with the consent of the Deputies chose Samuel Nowell Treasurer of the Colony. "So after Lecture Mr. Nowell took his Oath as Treasurer, having first made a worthy Speech. . . ."[19] Sewall speaks also of the very large votes Nowell polled in elections for the offices of Assistant and Commissioner of the United Colonies, both of which he held throughout this period, in April 1686 receiving more votes than any other candidate. Sibley tells that in May 1686 Nowell was made chairman of the committee which had charge of safeguarding the Charter Papers; one can hardly imagine a position of more responsibility in the Colony which was at this time engaged in such a fierce struggle to keep its charter alive.**

* Richards' naming of the three men who supervised this transfer makes one wonder if "the President" mentioned by Tutor Flynt (page 166 above) could possibly have been President Mather, who lived until 1723.

On September 25, 1682, Richards wrote Mather from England, suggesting Nowell be appointed to replace him (and Danforth) as Treasurer. At that time Richards said, "I shall not accept that trouble againe." (4 *Coll. MHS* VIII [1868], 496–497.) On April 20, 1683, he suggested, "Put them [the Corporation] in mind of chuseing a new Treasurer, if it be not already done. . . ." (*Ibid.*, p. 501).

On July 2, 1688, Richards wrote Increase Mather in London, "I am not yet dismissed from my Treasurer's place; but of late some orders have come from the Governor to me to act in severall particulars. What is intended I cannot yet gather. . . ." (*Ibid.*, pp. 502–503).

** Sibley, I, 339–341. We mention here only happenings *after* Nowell was Treasurer of Harvard. He had many honors and positions before that time. In December 1687 Nowell went to England and in the next year there joined President Mather in a mission concerning the Colony Charter. Nowell died in London in September 1688; Increase Mather was one of the bearers at his funeral.

There is a slight possibility that the "good, but unfortunate gentleman" of Flynt's memorandum was not intended to be Mr. Nowell — the memorandum is not absolutely definite — but succeeding generations seem to have assumed Flynt meant Nowell. Whatever the interpretation of this report, an analysis of the assets at the beginning and the end of Nowell's College office throws some light on the composition of that £1100.

College Book III gives a 1683 total of £2357 11*s.* 8*d.*, but the accounts listed there add up to £2362 6*s.* 2*d.*[20] The 1683 account includes Mowlson, which our Table 35 Stock analysis lists below under annuities and Richards' 1686 account omits; £2362 6*s.* 2*d.* less Mowlson and plus Edmund Browne's 1678 bequest of £100 (omitted in both 1683 and 1686 but listed in 1693) leaves the £2299 9*s.* 10*d.* of Tables 35 and 37.

For 1686 Richards lists £1170 10*d.* securities and £19 18*s.* 5*d.* interest due, in all £1189 19*s.* 3*d.* To this, to make it match 1683, we must add Edmund Browne's £100 and Russell's £68 6*s.* 8*d.* legacy, making £1358 5*s.* 11*d.* If now we forget Table 35 and look at the excerpts in Table 37 we see that when the two years are made comparable, the "loss" comes down to £941 3*s.* 11*d.* Table 37 attempts to show that there might be an explanation for all but £373 12*s.* 8*d.* of the loss.

If Richards, and Mather, Stoughton, and Dudley, inquired of Nowell what had become of certain bonds turned over to him in 1683, one way Nowell might have answered would have been to produce an exhibit somewhat like the following:

| | Received 1683 | | | Released 1686 | | | Change | | |
|---|---|---|---|---|---|---|---|---|---|
| | £ | *s.* | *d.* | £ | *s.* | *d.* | £ | *s.* | *d.* |
| (1) Accounts on books in 1683 and {old | 559 | 14 | 6 | | | | | | |
| (2) not 1686, including interest {recent | 924 | 2 | 6 | | | | | | |
| (3) New accounts, including interest | | | | 684 | 6 | 10 | | | |
| (4) Continuing accounts, including interest | 637 | 6 | 2 | 505 | 12 | 5 | | | |
| (5) Not on 1686 list and should be | 241 | 3 | 0 | | | | | | |
| (6) Totals in *existing accounts* | 2362 | 6 | 2 | 1189 | 19 | 3 | 1172 | 6 | 11 |
| To the above: | | | | | | | | | |
| (7) Add Russell and Mowlson and Newgate (omitted 1686, but outstanding) | | | | +241 | 3 | 0 | | | |
| (8) Dubious, including interest | −559 | 14 | 6 | | | | | | |
| (9) | 1802 | 11 | 8 | 1431 | 2 | 3 | 371 | 9 | 5 |

Thus, if *all* (which is doubtful) of the very dubious old bills and their interest were defaulted, and none of the recent or their interest (also doubtful), Nowell's unexplained decrease would have amounted to about £371, plus the proceeds of the bequests of Joseph Browne and Henry Ashurst, *if* the College ever collected these two sums.

A third view of this mystery is contributed by a scrap in Richards' writing pasted on folio 63 of his book — opposite the list of securities totaling £2141 17*s.* 8½*d.* which Richards left with Danforth. The scrap shows only:

| | | | |
|---|---|---|---|
| Fisher | 17 | 00 | 0 |
| Hawkins | 22 | 00 | 0 |
| Brown | 100 | 00 | 0 |
| Stoughton | 100 | 00 | 0 |
| Lane | 90 | 00 | 0 |
| 113 35 [?] | 329 | 00 | 0 |
| Now | 1170 | 00 | 10 |
| | 1499 | 00 | 10 |
| 2141 17 8½ | | | |
| 1499 00 10 0 | | | |
| 642 16 10½ | | | |

This was apparently a rough calculation of the difference in Stock between the time Richards left the books and took the £1170 10*d.* back again. However, we do not know why he listed the five items he did, or even what the last two represent.[21] Hawkins' bond was known to be worthless. This difference, if that is what it is, should be reduced at least by Mowlson and Russell moneys (omitted from the 1686 list) to £411 13*s.* 10½*d.* and probably further by some of the interest (also unlisted in 1686).

Nowell was Treasurer in a time that was disrupted because of many factors. Income from Mowlson and Piscataqua had stopped, and other accounts were not infrequently delayed in payment. No one knew what was going to happen to the Colony or to the College. To spend £370 or somewhat more from undesignated funds for current expenses would not have been nearly so

*Table 37. Samuel Nowell's Assets, 1683 to 1686*

| | 1683 | | | 1686 | | | Decrease | | | Comment on decrease | Equivalent loss unexplained | | |
|---|---|---|---|---|---|---|---|---|---|---|---|---|---|
| | £ | *s.* | *d.* | £ | *s.* | *d.* | £ | *s.* | *d.* | | £ | *s.* | *d.* |
| Principal | 1344 | 0 | 4 | 1170 | 0 | 10 | 173 | 19 | 6 | Unexplained | 173 | 10 | 4 |
| Old bills | 363 | 3 | 6 | | | | 363 | 3 | 6 | Only £13 14*s.* 6*d.* of this showed as new bonds in 1686. | 13 | 14 | 6[a] |
| | | | | | | | | | | The rest except £21 was dated before 1669 and might well have defaulted. | 21 | 0 | 0 |
| Bequests | 340 | 6 | 8 | 168 | 6 | 8 | 172 | 0 | 0 | £100 J. Browne doubtful | | | |
| | | | | | | | | | | £40 paid and capitalized | 40 | 0 | 0[a] |
| | | | | | | | | | | £32 Scarlett *temporarily* written off[b] | | | |
| Interest | 251 | 19 | 4 | 19 | 18 | 5 | 232 | 0 | 11 | £10 Newgate later paid[b] | | | |
| | | | | | | | | | | £82 11*s.* 6*d.* due on old bills | | | |
| | | | | | | | | | | £49 new *bond* in 1686 | 49 | 0 | 0[a] |
| | | | | | | | | | | £35 rent probably picked up *after* 1686[b] | | | |
| | | | | | | | | | | £75 7*s.* 10*d.* may have been good | 75 | 7 | 10 |
| | 2299 | 9 | 10[c] | 1358 | 5 | 11 | 941 | 3 | 11 | | 373 | 12 | 8 |

[a] Though items totaling this amount were themselves *on* the list in 1686, their equivalent in principal was missing. (*They* were in the £1170 10*d.* principal above.)

[b] Scarlett £32, Newgate £10, and rent £35 were all later paid or reinstated.

[c] 2362 6*s.* 2*d.* less Mowlson (£162 16*s.* 4*d.* — listed on Table 35 in annuities) plus *E.* Browne (£100) gives £2299 9*s.* 10*d.*

*CSM* XV, 251–252 (College Book III) gives the 1683 sum as £2357 11*s.* 8*d.*, but the addition comes to £2362 6*s.* 2*d.*

Edmund Browne's 1678 bequest of £100 was omitted from both 1683 and 1686 accounts. We add it to both, though it does not affect this analysis. It was first listed by the Treasurers only in 1693.

startling as to get rid of £1100; nor was it too different from earlier Corporation practice in using gifts.* Also, it was only provident to streamline the investment portfolio in the face of the imminent arrival of a new titled Englishman to be Governor of the Colony and President of the Board of Overseers. Moreover, the tuition raise in 1686 may have been recognition of the fact that this rate of spending from Stock could not continue. (I have no evidence that the raise was caused by inflation.)

We suggest, then, that Nowell presided over a decrease in Harvard's assets,** but there is a possibility that a good part of the decrease may have been brought about by quite justifiable writing

* See above p. 164 and note

** See Figure 7, p. 176; the lowest line may exaggerate the possible correction, but the truth must lie considerably below the amount in the "Stock" line for 1682–1686.

down of the value of assets which were known to be of no value. The long-standing slurs against Treasurer Nowell, though they may have some basis, have, at the least, exaggerated the "loss."

Richards picked up the accounts, stripped down now to their bare bones. But for several years he operated in an almost hopeless political atmosphere, with continuous insecurity and dispute the order of the day, with first Dudley, then Andros, then a committee, in control of the "Country," and with President Mather in England or otherwise very much engaged most of the time. Under Leverett and William Brattle and Richards the College continued to function, but it is a tribute to the quality of these men that it did not lose ground.

Contemporary criticism of Harvard's finances comes down to us from the end of the decade of the eighties, as well as from the beginning. The talkative Edmund Randolph wrote on August 5, 1687, and again on March 29, 1688, to the effect that the President and Fellows, now called the Rector and Tutors, were

> calling upon such persons who had any of the Colledg money in their hands to bring it in and take new Security; whereupon about £1200 which was putt out in the Colledge's name is now altred and putt out in the names of Dudley, Stoughton, and Mather and made payable to them and their heires. . . .[22]

There is ample confirmation of the fact that at least some of Harvard's approximately £1200 of securities, when they were renewed, were issued in the names of individuals, though Richards himself is the only such individual of whom there is definite evidence in our records. The Treasurer wrote in his book that he had instructions to "take them in myne owne name"; he subsequently entered on August 1, 1687, "Paid I. A. for making new bonds," and he named the debtors. On that day he rewrote about half the total list of assets.[23] The year 1687 has several such entries.

There are samples of these mortgage deeds complete with all their endorsements in the College Archives. Early in 1687 William Smith and Martha his wife rewrote their £58 mortgage deed "unto the said John Richards his heires and Assignes for ever."[24] There is no mention whatsoever of Harvard College or of Richards' official position. The back of the instrument gives its history (Plate 9). Thomas Dudley, Clerk of Suffolk County, recorded it on July 10,

1687. On December 28, 1694, Anne Richards, John Foster, and Benjamin Alford, Executors of the Estate of John Richards, assigned all rights to Thomas Brattle, Treasurer of Harvard College.

This form of mortgage was not peculiar to the Andros period. A practically identical instrument was signed on June 29, 1693, by Seth Perry. On December 28, 1694, John Richards' executors assigned Perry's deed also to Thomas Brattle, Treasurer of the College. Brattle apparently did not use this type of protection.

For two years the Royal Governor and his deputies kept watch on the College Stock, ordered sundry payments, made appointments — thus taking over some of the functions of the Corporation. Richards and the other College officers seem to have communicated as little as possible of College business to the government officers. The College was slow in making payments, and payments due the College were slow or not paid at all. When in July 1689 Andros was ordered to England, Richards was among the surviving Province Assistants reinstated after the local "revolution," and matters returned more nearly to normal in 1690. Yet, with all this confusion and uncertainty, the Treasurer managed a small gain in "admitted assets," as Table 36 shows. The bulk of this gain was from the one gift, a £100 bequest of William Browne, which had been given for permanent endowment.

The growth in this period after Richards' return was not impressive (with the few gifts), but for the first time the expenses were covered by receipts other than gifts, and a small amount of operating income was capitalized — or at least a balance was left over and was an asset temporarily in "Stock."*

At the time Thomas Brattle became Treasurer, political affairs had settled down into a pattern that did not suit the Massachusetts citizens, but nevertheless was to continue for almost another century. Some people thought the position of the College charter under the Province was ambiguous, and this ambiguity may have interfered with the major factor in the growth of Stock —

* See Table 36. There is no reason to expect such an operating surplus ever to be very large unless there is a deliberate policy of capitalizing investment income or setting up reserve or depreciation funds. Unless the apparent surplus is a temporary working balance, it may well represent the receipt of funds which are earmarked for expenses in the next accounting period. Obviously, also, there is no requirement that all current gifts be added to capital, but line (5) of Table 36, "Capital availed of," must be kept down or the Stock will disappear.

the receipt of gifts. The Corporation on November 9, 1696, voted that

> . . . Considering that whilst the Colledge continues as at present, an unhappy Settlement of it may be feared, and that donations to the Society are obstructed, and that the present Stock is endangered.
>
> That therefore an humble Address and petition may be drawn up to be presented to the King, praying his Majesty to grant us his Royall Charter for the incorporating of the Colledge.[25]

Their authority seemed sufficient to do business, however, and Treasurer Brattle assiduously invested and reinvested the College funds, and vigorously pursued the delinquent debtors. The Stock which he acquired from Richards amounted to £1270 7*s.* in bonds, bills, and mortgages, £277 18*s.* 10*d.* due and overdue interest and rent, £16 6*s.* in cash lately paid in by John Bunker, and memoranda of £168 6*s.* 8*d.* in legacies due.[26] Little more than £100 of the bonds involved individuals whose indebtedness originated in Richards' early period or before, and all such old bills had been rewritten and acknowledged again with current dates. Richards had put affairs in order.

We find that Brattle's excess of receipts over disbursements totals £1617 9*s.* 3*d.* The comparable figure for gain in Stock from comparison of the Stock accounts of Table 35, ignoring interest and bequests due, is £1664 19*s.* 5*d.* (In 1712 Brattle was no longer listing interest due as an asset, so from this point on the Treasurer's practice is the same as we have adopted throughout our discussion: that is, he uses what we have been loosely calling "admitted assets.") Brattle's excess receipts include £1046 18*s.* of gifts, £165 13*s.* 10*d.* gain on exchange of heavy for light pieces of eight, £160 added to this part of the Stock account by the sale in 1696 of the rent-producing Keayne house, and an operating surplus of £244 17*s.* 5*d.* Part of this "operating surplus" was a payment of over £50 Pennoyer income which had come in just before July 1, and no doubt there had been other, similar income which the College had not yet had time to spend.

Figure 7 and the top section of Table 35 show the increase in listed securities and cash — the "College Stock." The items with asterisks in the table are our "admitted" assets. Lines (1) and (2) of the bottom section of Table 35 give the changes in these

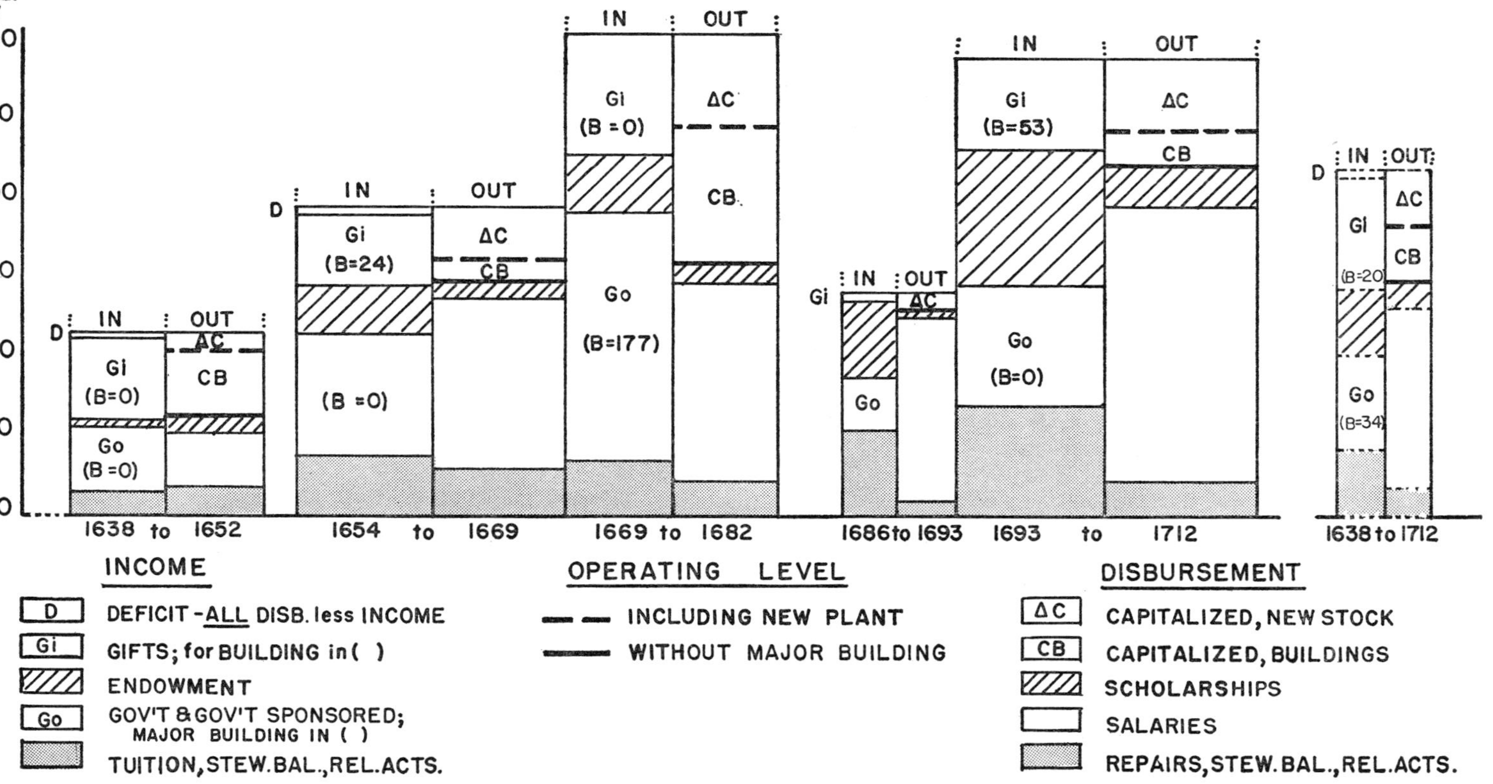


Figure 6. *Income and disbursements, 1638 to 1712, showing relation to Stock and major buildings. An increase in Stock is possible for 1638–52 despite a deficit because the new Stock was not liquid, and for 1654–69 because years of deficit and surplus are combined. Attribution of the deficit to operations would be unsuitable because of the indefinite terms of gifts and grants. There was an operating deficit of about £120 a year, 1682–86, not shown here. From Table 32; see also Table 36.*

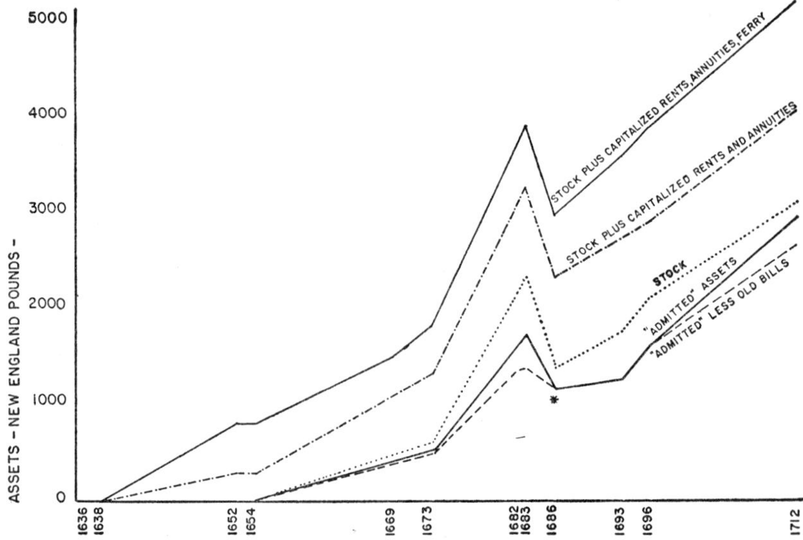


Figure 7. *Growth of financial assets, 1638 to 1712, not including plant.* **To 1686 we might add £77 later reinstated (see p. 171–Table 37, note 6). From Table 35.*

assets. We see that during Danforth's Treasurership about £500 of Stock accumulated, and another £1200 or £1500 under Richards (including the Holworthy legacy of over £1200 in 1681). The assets decreased under Nowell (1683 to 1686), but rose by over 100 per cent under Brattle, coming by 1712 to £2675 in good bonds, mortgages, and cash.*

In addition to the securities we have just discussed, income-producing real estate and annuities accumulated. In order to be able to appreciate their growth, we have in Tables 21 and 35 arbitrarily capitalized these gifts at amounts which are based broadly on interest of 8 per cent if it was first paid before 1693, and on 6 per cent if they became active after that date.

Table 35, as well as Figure 7, shows clearly how these income-

* When Brattle died in May 1713, President Leverett wrote in this diary:

"Thomas Brattle Esquire Treasurer of Harvard College died. He was a Gentleman by his Birth and Education of the first Order in this Country. He had his Education in the aforesaid College was admitted to all the honors of it, and arrived at uncommon accomplishments. . . . His probity and religion was very Conspicuous, and his faithfullness in all his Services very peculiar, and peculiarly to be acknowledged. . . . Affairs of the College . . . under his prudent management have been restored and advanced very considerably . . . . If we may hope the vacancy can ever be filled, it is because *Deo omnia Sunt possibilia.*" (HUA, MS. Diary, p. 76.)

producing assets grew and the relation they bore to the "securities." The ferry is obviously an extremely important factor, in 1652 having more weight than all other categories. In Danforth's time other assets caught up and passed the ferry, but rents and annuities were still more important than securities and produce. Under Richards, with the Holworthy gift, securities grew to more than the capitalized value of rents and annuities. Under Brattle, rents and annuities held fairly constant; the decrease from the sale of the house was offset in large part by the acquisition of several small properties. The value of the ferry rent jumped when (since the amount was so large) we shifted the interest basis from 8 per cent to 6 per cent according to the law of 1693. With all this, in 1712 the securities totaled £3120, and we value the income-producing property, including the ferry, at £2145. The income from annuities and rents was by no means entirely reliable, but it compared favorably with the income effectively received from securities, and the property itself was in almost all cases secure. The obvious great exception to this was the ferry, which in a later century ceased to pay income to the College.

Harvard in the Puritan Period made up no balance sheets. I have made one for July 1, 1712, and show the summary of assets and liabilities in Table 38.

Harvard Treasurers did not put a value on their plant, and they still do not publish such a figure; in view of the possible variations in value and the lack of accuracy in conclusions that may follow from unrealistic valuations, there is justification for omitting this formality.

### POLICY

Almost all of the investments shown as securities in a 1712 listing of assets were bonds. This represents the culmination in our period of a gradual shift from commodities, to bills, and then to bonds and mortgages.

Perhaps the terms of the loans held the secret of the practicality of bonds; if there was no mortgage the Treasurer ordinarily required two signers on each bond. When one signer died, the Treasurer found another: "David Demming of Cambridge became bound with Joseph Mason of Watertown for £21 4*s.* the 16th next, in the room

*Table 38. Balance Sheet for Harvard College, July 1, 1712*

**Assets[a]**

| | £ | s. | d. | £ | s. | d. |
|---|---|---|---|---|---|---|
| Cash | | | | 330 | 1 | 1 |
| Investments[b] | | | | | | |
| 1 Bill (may be bad debt) | 8 | 2 | 0 | | | |
| 38 Bonds (£67 2*s.* may be bad debts) | 2234 | 9 | 4 | | | |
| 6 Mortgages (£201 16*s.* may be bad debts) | 379 | 10 | 0 | | | |
| | | | | 2622 | 1 | 4 |
| Real estate (capitalized income) | 409 | 0 | 0 | | | |
| Annuities (capitalized income) | 535 | 16 | 4 | | | |
| Ferry (capitalized income) | 1200 | 0 | 0 | | | |
| | | | | 2144 | 16 | 4 |
| Accounts receivable | | | | | | |
| Rents and interest due[d] | | | | | | |
| Bequests due | | | | 168 | 6 | 8 |
| Plant and inventory (at cost) | | | | | | |
| President's House | 260 | 0 | 0 | | | |
| Harvard College | 2000 | 0 | 0 | | | |
| Stoughton College | 1020 | 0 | 0 | | | |
| (No inventory available) | | | | | | |
| | | | | 3280 | 0 | 0 |
| | | | | 8545 | 5 | 5 |

**Liabilities**

| | £ | s. | d. | £ | s. | d. |
|---|---|---|---|---|---|---|
| Permanent endowment | | | | | | |
| Scholarship funds: | | | | | | |
| Mowlson-Bridges | 162 | 16 | 4 | | | |
| Pennoyer[c] | 100 | 0 | 0 | | | |
| W. Browne | 100 | 0 | 0 | | | |
| B. Browne | 200 | 0 | 0 | | | |
| Stoughton | 52 | 0 | 0 | | | |
| | | | | 614 | 16 | 4 |
| Other permanent funds | | | | | | |
| Newgate | 63 | 0 | 0 | | | |
| Glover | 60 | 0 | 0 | | | |
| Webb | 160 | 0 | 0 | | | |
| Pennoyer[c] | 150 | 0 | 0 | | | |
| | | | | 433 | 0 | 0 |
| Ferry | | | | 1200 | 0 | 0 |
| Expendable funds (balance) | | | | 3017 | 9 | 1 |
| Funds expended for plant (*contra*) | | | | 3280 | 0 | 0 |
| | | | | 8545 | 5 | 5 |

[a] Includes *capitalized* annuities and rents; principal of annuities was not held by the College.
[b] For detail see *CSM* XVI, 416–419.
[c] Pennoyer is split 3/5 for salaries and 2/5 for scholarships, as it was used in this period.
[d] No longer listed as an asset.

of Joseph Webb late of Boston deceased, the said Mason and Webb's bond being cancelled and delivered up unto the said Mason."[27] In the few cases where a single signer was allowed, the bond was sometimes made for twice the amount of the debt, following the English practice. This would have had the added virtue of covering accrued interest. But even this practice did not always prevent loss.

Treasurer Richards speaks disparagingly of one of Mr. Nowell's mortgages: Richards took a bond of Shattuck and Stratton for £16 New England money, "and delivered Mr. David Church's morgage cancelled. It was an imperfect instrument and not recorded and entangled by other deeds. Wherefore I was willing to change."[28] Ordinarily he registered mortgages promptly and recorded them in the Treasurer's book, giving the Register book and page number. Annuities, too, were recorded. The College was a little delinquent in recording the Newgate instrument, made in June 1650 but recorded by the Registrar of Deeds of Suffolk County only on April 1, 1703.[29]

Such safeguards undoubtedly helped in the collection, but still it was not always simple. We spoke of Nowell's suing to collect on a bond. Brattle has left several pages in the front of his journal filled with dunning letters he wrote to debtors. One of the better series is that which he sent to Edward Pelham "of Road Island" who in April 1684 had borrowed £280 from Nowell on security of land in Cambridge. The interest due was capitalized from then on with the exception of payments for 1688, 1689, and 1690, and when Brattle took over there was £341 4*s*. covered by bonds plus £74 8*s*. of unsecured interest. Pelham made occasional partial payments but in 1700 the Treasurer found it necessary to write that "being frustrated in my expectations of Seeing you at my Lodgings when you were in Town," he (Brattle) "thought good" to write Mr. Pelham that he owed "upwards of four score pounds, which I pray your care to pay me with what Speed you can." By February 1708 the letter said, "My treatment of you has been all along with so much Civility and Respect, which you seemed to be very Sensible of and were please to acknowledge to me, that I could not have thought you would have dealt so Unhandsomely by me as you have done." Captain Pelham had been to town, received £100 which those who paid him expected he would pay to Brattle, but "it seems you went away with it. . . . I must needs tell you that you have Sunk your Credit somewhat with me, but I hope you will fetch it up again. . . ." This goes on, politely but forcefully, October 1708, February 1710, February 1711, May 1711, until, on November 27, 1711, Brattle finally received the money, £341 4*s.* — and the £185 9*s.* interest.[30]

Again, Brattle writes to Mr. Dickson,

> These are to Acquaint you that I take it very unkindly that I have not heard from you all this time and received that money that I lent yourself and Thomas Andrew with the interest which was due 19 April last. I do not care to deal with persons that mind no more their obligations, wherefore I expect your Speedy payment of the money. Otherwise I shall take a course with you, and that within a few dayes. But I hope you will prevent all further trouble; and I rest your Loving friend, Thomas Brattle, College Treasurer.

After a copy of another letter, Brattle writes, "I writ in the very same words to Mr. Symon Crosby, and Mr. Joseph Hill" (page 4). Apparently the writing was effective, for these bonds were not outstanding in the next listing of assets.

A large number of debtors seemed to require similar treatment, and Brattle's ingenuity in expressing himself might well give lessons to modern bill collectors: Mr. Warren borrowed £60 two years ago, "which you seem by your action to have utterly forgot, or at least not to take any notice of . . ." (page 9). John Jackson, with whom Richards had early done business, owed in 1703 seven years' interest on £37. "My patience and forbearance with you so long has been very extraordinary, and so has your carelessness and neglect in the matter." If no money is forthcoming, "I must and will Sue out your mortgage" (page 6). To Edward Goffe: "Thirty pounds 12*s.* at 8*s.* per ounce for interest of £150 three years . . . I cannot let that matter run any longer or higher" (page 6). To Burgess, Hood, Potter, and Ingolls, whose bonds covered rent on the Coggan marsh: If the debt is not paid, you "may certainly look to hear from me after another manner." To Captain Holbrook, when his co-signer Paine refused, "You must excuse me if I Sue" if payment is not made.

Richards sued, and Brattle sued, on occasion. Richards records that a £50 Goffe bond, signed by Samuel and his son Edward, was paid by the Treasurer's "taking land" from them. Yet the Goffes continue to turn up on the books. In 1694 they mortgaged more land to Brattle. Goffe was the executor also of the delinquent Edmund Browne bequest. And in 1711 a suit against Goffe was dismissed on payment of the debt and charges.[31]

In May 1700 Brattle disbursed six shillings, "paid Jno Bull for his attendance on the Court severall days when I sued said Holmes" (page 61). Then, in October 1705, "for what more charge I was at in suing said Holmes I paid Mr. Leverett who was my Attorney in full . . . £1" (pages 61 and 86).

Examples of these actions recur over and over again, and the small fees involved reached a sizable sum. Brattle was certainly vigilant. In October 1710 Jonathan Ward paid £25, which was the principal he owed, but not until the following March, when he paid the £1 interest due, was "his bond delivered him up" (page 109).

Sometimes bonds and mortgages were sold, such as the mortgage (with its interest due) of the deceased Richard Way (page 119).

The Treasurers were not always tough, and bonded debtors were not the only ones who were careless. There is the well-known instance of Increase Mather's letter to Samuel Crisp in London concerning the Pennoyer account: "To my best remembrance I had of you £42 at one time £13 at another time, and it runs in my mind that I had Something more at another time, but I have perfectly forgotten how much it was. My receipts and your accompts will clear the matter, So that no wrong will be done. . . ."[32]

The Treasurers, so ordered by the Corporation, sometimes forgave sums due from widows of their original debtors. Enoch Greenliffe had rented the Webb house ever since it had come into the College's possession in 1660. In April 1693 there was about five years' rent due — £58 5*d*. The Corporation ordered Richards to forgive this amount to the Widow Greenliffe if he saw cause, and he apparently did. The house was then rented to Enoch Greenliffe, Junior, son of the widow.[33]

The College "lett" money to all types of people, and throughout New England. Edmund Quinsey and Captain Samuel Sewall signed together on a bond in 1701. Members of the College community borrowed: Increase Mather £50 in 1678, Fellow Daniel Gookin £10 in 1681, Treasurer-to-be Samuel Nowell (former Fellow) £50 in 1682.[34] These bonds were all paid off promptly. Mr. Richard Wharton, who later defaulted on his bond, was a leading merchant. Debtors included also people who, instead of being called by a military title or "Mr.," or even "Gent.,"* had after their names "blacksmith," or "carpenter." These skilled workmen sometimes took one loan after another, having each time paid off the last loan, and over the years some workmen progressed to the status of being called "Mr."[35]

With all this variety in clients, capital losses specifically reported on the books are few, though default in the full payment of a legacy was not rare, and grants of land worked out poorly. Here we must mention again the "lost" bonds of Mr. Nowell's regime. Some were *surely* lost, such as the Hawkins bill for payment of the final £22 of the Ward legacy; but how many of the other securities which disappeared from the books at that time were actually lost it is impossible to say.

One of the new bonds which appeared in Richards' list of receipts from Nowell was that of Richard Wharton. Professor Bailyn says of him that he "became one of the biggest operators in New England commerce and real estate."[36] Wharton must have taken a few too many risks, for his estate paid only thirteen pence on a pound of Wharton's debts in 1699, and Brattle collected only £8 3*s.* 6*d.* on his double bond for £158 1*s.* 3*d.*, including interest.**

Besides the Wharton £100, Treasurers Brattle in 1712 and 1715 held £177 in other instruments labeled, "may be bad debts."

Thus a few losses show definitely, and there may have been some others.

The Corporation, having chosen a Treasurer with the Overseers' consent, left certain phases of the business largely in his hands. For example, in the usual case it seems to have been up to

* Pelham.

** Brattle, 55. Many merchants went bankrupt under Andros because of the strict enforcement of the acts of trade. "Wharton, with all his wealth, was almost impoverished." He died in 1689 before having had a chance to recoup his losses. Viola F. Barnes, "Richard Wharton, a Seventeenth Century New England Colonial," *CSM* XXVI (1927), 265, 268.

him to determine to whom loans should be made. When the large Holworthy bequest was paid, Richards was told "to dispose of the money sent out of England, either by letting it out or makeing some purchase therewith, as hee shall Judge will be most conduceing to the advantage of the Colledge."[37] On the other hand, practically all expenditures were made by order of the Corporation, and we also find the Treasurer consulting the Corporation on many doubtful small investment matters and getting their approval particularly of actions which might entail some loss. In the sale of real estate he always had Corporation orders.

Though there seems to have been no definitely laid-out policy of the College concerning investment in real estate, few lands or buildings were purchased in this period, and the fairly valuable Keayne house was sold. Michael Spencer's tenement in Cambridge next to the College was mortgaged to the Corporation in 1695 and in 1697 sold to them for £70.[38] In 1706 the Corporation appointed the Treasurer and Mr. Wadsworth and Mr. White to "take a view of the house of Mr. Webb's Gift whither it be best to have it repaired or pulled down and another built in the room of it. . . ." They decided to make some repairs, "digg a well, and put a pump into it, for the use of Said House. . . ." This they did and then rented the house to Mr. William Payne on a 99-year lease.[39] They could not dispose of the property, according to Mr. Webb's will.

So far as the records show, the College acquired or sold no other income-producing real estate in this period.

After Danforth's first Treasurership the College did not list any appreciable amount of livestock or produce among its assets. The growing colony and economy came to afford outlets for investment involving less risk and bother, and with the arrival of the money from Sir Matthew Holworthy the Treasurer had enough so that he could more effectively make loans.

At least until the end of Brattle's era very little cash was kept as working assets. When money came in the Treasurer very promptly either invested it or used it for expenses. The feeling of a hand-to-mouth existence which we get still in Richards' first years seems, however, to be largely gone under Brattle. Salaries were paid on a more dependable schedule, and there was regular income coming in to care for small expenses. Yet the officers were far from spending wildly: "Voted, . . . That six leather Chairs be forthwith provided for the use of the Library, and six more before the Commencement in Case the Treasury will allow of it."[40]

Practically speaking, there seems to have been a policy of capitalizing most gifts received under Brattle, and as many as possible earlier. In many cases there was nothing to have prevented the Corporation from spending current gifts for current expenses; yet, conceivably by the inferred wish of the donors, they continued to add many such gifts to Stock.* In Brattle's capitalizing gain on heavy money exchanged for light there is perhaps the beginning of a policy which would make a vast difference to the institution over the troubled years ahead. Unless some such policy as this is followed in years of inflation, the relative value of the Stock will not hold up.**

From the earliest days the integrity of the permanent endowment of the College was scrupulously respected, though permanent endowment as such was never separately listed. The only fund actually menaced was the Mowlson-Bridges gift, which, had it not

* It is arbitrary on our part to say that it was the *gifts* which were added to Stock; the addition could have been thought of as coming from other income, such as that from investments. However, the relation between the amount of gifts and the gain in Stock shown in Table 36 makes it not illogical to speak as we do here.

** The value in 1961 of the permanent funds listed in Table 38 as of 1712 is:

| | |
|---|---|
| Mowlson | $ 9,019.63 |
| Pennoyer | 19,185.60 |
| Browne | 5,526.58 |
| Stoughton | 105,221.01 |
| Newgate | 403.33 |
| Glover | 8,604.05 |
| Webb | 164,604.79 |
| | $312,564.99, which in 1712 was just about £1000. |

The present Browne fund above includes also a £100 bequest from another William Browne in 1716, and £150 from Samuel in 1731, as well as the £100 bequest of William in 1687 and £200 from Benjamin in 1708. The Webb value shown includes the buildings now on the property.

Professor Harris points out that some of these funds (not Webb) were lost track of in periods such as the Revolutionary War, but they were reconstituted and continue now safely on the books.

*Sources: Endowment Funds of Harvard University* (Cambridge, 1948), pp. 135, 142, 92, 157, 211, 50. *Financial Report to Board of Overseers of Harvard College, 1960–1961*, pp. 179, 180, 165, 185, 217, 149, 35 (in the order of the above list).

been for the persistence of the Corporation, might have disappeared entirely into the Country's treasury.

In concluding the discussion of assets, the rather obvious inference is possible that having some assets greatly facilitated the running of the College: they provided annual income and in emergencies their unrestricted principal could be used. The efforts of the officers to accumulate funds seemed to pay off in improvement toward the end of the Puritan Period, but whether the increase in assets was the major cause of the improvement is an open question. In saying this, it is desirable also to make two other limiting statements: First, despite all attempts to pin down what happened to Harvard's finances, there certainly are possibilities that the picture given here — especially of the earlier years — is not absolutely complete. One factor which contributes to this is expressed by W. T. Baxter in his essay on colonial accounting, "Clearly, there would be small point in . . . talking about realized gains and losses; debts were apt to turn into pork rather than cash."* A second limitation is that, though this chapter has dealt with the growth of assets and has thereby inevitably emphasized their importance, it may well be that in particular situations the importance of growth, or even maintenance, of assets is overshadowed by other educational values which quite justifiably would lead to a temporary reversal of the upward trend in Stock.

* A. C. Littleton and B. S. Yamey, ed., *Studies in the History of Accounting* (Homewood, Illinois, 1956), p. 281.

To try to estimate *yield* on securities in the Puritan Period would be a dubious effort at best. Among the reasons are: (1) the questionable value of some securities and of interest received in commodity pay; (2) the possibly incomplete listing of interest received; (3) the practice of capitalizing interest; (4) the often long-delayed payment of interest; (5) lack of knowledge of investment expense; (6) the possibility of unknown losses. Certainly affairs moved so slowly and spasmodically that to give an *annual* return would make no sense, and the accuracy of any average over a period of years suffers from unevenness of the growth of the basic capital. From Tables 24 and 35 we could make the calculation that the interest in our accounts is 4.5 per cent of average *admitted* assets from 1693 to 1712, but this figure may be one or two per cent off in either direction from the true yield.

# ❧ IX ❧

## *OVERVIEW*

An overview of the first eighty years of Harvard College indicates that the major forces then bearing on the College's administration and finance may be divided into those coming from without and those coming from within:

*External*

Religion
Politics
Economics
Higher education of the time

*Internal*

The Overseers
The Corporation
The officers
The student body
(and parents and alumni)
The educational program

We can now see some of the outstanding ways in which these forces affected and were affected by the economics of the College.

### EXTERNAL FORCES

Religion, at Puritan Harvard, as in the Massachusetts Bay Colony, was all-pervasive, though not all-inclusive: Religion was not the only force at work, but there were few facets of the College which were not subject to some religious influence. Religious considerations were a major motive in the founding, and a major motive in attendance: If the student was not to be a minister, he was at least to be enabled, through his studies, to lead a more "saintly" life. The College President was usually a minister, and almost all of the Tutors became ministers. Many of the Overseers and practically all of the Corporation members were, became, or had been ministers. Much of the financial support came from persons who wished to further religious objectives. While there was no direct financial aid from any church, practically speaking there was for at least the first fifty of our eighty years only one church (though not centralized), and the College had the wholehearted and vigorously voiced support of the ministers.*

But in our period we see a change in the nature of the religious emphasis. By 1713 the following statement in Thomas Brattle's obituary was not startling:

> In the Church he was known and valued for his Catholic Charity to all of the reformed Religion, but mor especialy his great Veneration for the Church of England, although his general and more constant communion was with the Nonconformists.[1]

The religous thinking of Brattle's colleague, Fellow and President John Leverett, was in many ways more "radical" than that of the ousted President Dunster, but by 1700 the time was right.

The College was founded by the General Court. The Court established the Charter and thus the form of the College government (though President Dunster may have drawn up the draft); and the Court, we have seen, provided a very important part of the College's income, both by making grants and by urging and enforcing individual gifts. The Court's ability to set the amount of his salary gave that body a decisive vote in the choice of a President. Besides the ferry and the salary, the Court was largely in control of building outlays, both for new buildings and for major repairs.

In thinking about the large influence of the Colony and Province government, we must remember that throughout these years there were interlocking directorates between most organizations. The Governor of the Colony was President of the Board of Overseers, which by the laws of the Colony consisted of the Governor,

* William B. Weeden, in *Economic and Social History of New England, 1620 to 1789* (Boston, 1894), p. 50, says, "The rule of the minister and pastor, of elder and magistrate, was as firm as that of a feudal baron."

the Deputy Governor, and "all the magistrates of this jurisdiction, together with the teaching elders of the sixe next adjoyning townes, . . . and the president of the colledge. . . ."[2] It helped that Overseers were on the General Court, and very often they or other Harvard alumni were the ones appointed to committees concerned with the College. The exchange worked the other way too: When John Leverett was nearing the end of his Fellowship, Josiah Cotton recorded in his diary: "Obliged to recite at five o'clock in the winter mornings that Mr. Leverett might seasonably attend the General Court at Boston, being Representative for the town of Cambridge."[3] Not only were church, College, and government so intertwined, but the same men appear on the lists of commissioners of such organizations as the Society for Propagating the Gospel among the Indians.[4]

Thus when the Colony was disrupted by dispute and maneuverings over *its* charter, and when the old Puritans were making their final efforts to remain in power, this struggle was duplicated in the College where not only the *form* of the charter, but that there should *be* a charter, seemed important.

In these various dealings and negotiations, when the upper and lower houses of the Court differed, it was necessary for the College President sometimes to walk the fence between the two factions. The College was fortunate in the Royal Governors, for though they took a great and often detailed interest in College affairs, on the whole they were fair. Bellomont, for example, on July 15, 1700, the occasion of an address to the King requesting a Royal charter, wrote to the Board of Trade in England:

> I joined with the assembly in this addresse, not because I approve at all of their church government, but out of a principle of moderation. For tho' I have all my life been of the Church of England, yet I have ever thought the Protestant Churches in the wrong to quarrel about the modes of worship and the externals of it.[5]

The President was careful to consult with the Governor and other members of the Court in advance of decisions in which they might have an interest. In contrast to the fairly satisfactory dealings with the English Royal Governors (when they could be reached at all), Harvard's own Joseph Dudley proved quite troublesome. He was a long-standing friend of President Leverett and was instrumental in Leverett's confirmation as President, but in 1713 we find Leverett writing to Province Secretary Isaac Addington: "I See the Countenance is not towards me as in times past; I shal endeavor to do my duty and pay all the Regards that my Station obliges me to, but I can be no body's Slave."*

We have spoken of the effects of American politics. We must also not forget the great influence of the political situation in England on College finances, for to the ebb and flow of Puritan strength in the mother country Harvard in New England owed support which was very important to its early years. Moreover, the repercussions of the political situation in England on the government of New England obviously mattered very much to Harvard, either because neglect made independence possible or direct interference eliminated the College's legal standing and favored a change in its religious emphasis.

When Harvard College was founded it was to be a part of a planned society. If there were not blacksmiths, blacksmiths were subsidized.[6] If education was lacking, it should be provided, for a need was felt for education. The society of which the College was a part was a very primitive one, and very small. The economy did, however, progress from the very primitive original state to a fairly comfortable condition. With the changes, demand for education on the college level did not seem to increase appreciably.

Whereas lack of currency and dealing with "country pay" was a serious problem in the earliest years, this problem was less important, though still present, in later years. At the end of our period the currency problem was about to shift to dealing with paper money and inflation, an entirely different matter. Since so far as we can see there was nothing like a three per cent a year inflation in the seventeenth century, but rather a price level remarkably stable in the long run, it was not until the first part of the eighteenth century that our Treasurers had to cope with maintaining the value of their endowment.

Thus the economic state of the Colony affected the number of students, possibly the availability of faculty, the form in which transactions took place, the type of investment opportunities, the

* The "Countenance" of Dudley. Letter of 18 September, 1713, in Leverett Saltonstall MSS., copy in S. E. Morison's files.

income from investments. Economic conditions bore also on the amount received in gifts and grants. We have suggested that the dearth of gifts after 1684 may have been due to political unsettlement, but here we may say also that though the merchants of the late 1680's and early nineties may have *wished* to support the College, few were in a position to do so, for various interruptions in their trading caused many bankruptcies in that period.[7]

Since Harvard College was the only institution of higher learning in English America almost to the end of our period, Harvard set its own pattern. The organizational plan for the new college was based very much on its English counterparts, among which there were some variations.[8] Though the institution of Overseers was new (perhaps replacing the King's visitor), the New England Cambridge had the same types of officers, its customs were similar, and its curriculum had the same basis. The fact that the Harvard degree of Dunster's time was recognized by the English universities attests that the New England program was not materially different from that offered by the predecessors in Old England.

Thus between 1636 and 1715 there was a great change in the external conditions, and we certainly cannot say that the early Harvard College operated independently of its environment. That we can see now. The influence of ecology on a college is perhaps more easily realized when we look back at it after the passage of time. We should say, too, to borrow the phraseology of statistics, that the direction of the causal influence is not necessarily all one way; though the major vocation of Harvard graduates was not, in our period, broad economic activity, there were for the size of the institution an amazingly large number of Harvard men who were influential in colonial affairs; probably the outstanding example is Increase Mather, whose activities, apart from his Presidency of the College, had a wide effect in his century. Moreover, in the small, closely knit community we are discussing, it is obvious that there was much interaction between our varying influences. Clearly they cannot be neatly evaluated and added together, but they nonetheless were major determinants of the College's course.

There is a force affecting the College which bridges the gap between the external and the internal influences. That force is the alumni body. We have seen the importance of alumni in the College's relations with its community, and we find that alumni were equally prominent in internal affairs.

### INTERNAL FORCES

Another group which straddles the line between being an external and an internal force is the Board of Overseers, who according to the Laws of 1642 were ministers and members of the General Court, as we have seen. By the Charter of 1650 the Overseers have the power to confirm the Corporation's choice of the President, the five Fellows, and the Treasurer, who together constitute the Corporation. The Corporation is empowered to make orders and by-laws for the College, "provided the said orders be allowed by the Overseers." The Overseers are to give "direction in all emergent occasions, . . . in great and difficult cases, and in cases of nonagreement. . . ."[9] An appendix to the charter, passed by the Court in 1657, permits the Corporation's acts to go into effect, but the Overseers can later alter them if they see fit.

The Corporation met much more frequently than the Overseers and transacted the business of the day, including electing officers and ordering payments, but when the Overseers did meet they confirmed orders and elections and occasionally voted some expenditures. One gets the impression that when the Overseers met, any business of the day was brought before them, and they always did meet to confirm appointments. However, it was to the *Corporation* that the Treasurer ordinarily looked for orders to pay. When payments involved members of the Corporation itself, the order was sometimes, but not always, referred to the Overseers.[10]

Mr. Morison states that initiative rested with the Corporation rather than with the Overseers. By the Charter and its Appendix and by practice this was usually the case; however, the Appendix does say, "And in case the corporation shall see cawse to call a meeting of the overseers, or the *overseers shall thinke goode to meete of themselves. . . .*"* (Italics added.)

In some instances the power of the Overseers stemmed not necessarily from their being Overseers, but from their place on the

* *HCSC*, pp. 12–13. The Charter is reproduced in *HCSC*, opposite p. 8; the Appendix is printed in *HCSC*, pp. 11–12. The provisions of the Charter of 1650 were in force with the exception of the period of political difficulties, and it was reinstated in full in 1707.

General Court: President Leverett went to Boston to see the Governor, who, he says, "was pleased to advise the proceeding to repair Old College: . . . it was then Concluded not to give the Overseers the trouble of an unnecessary Meeting" but the Governor himself (Joseph Dudley) would go to Cambridge next Wednesday on the subject.[11] There was nothing in the Charter about the Overseers having cognizance of buildings, but if there was any sizable sum to be spent on repairs, or if a new building was required, it would be the Court which provided the funds; for this reason it was often logical to appoint committees of the Overseers to consider building repairs. But in this matter, too, there was no consistency of practice.

Some of the functions were so difficult to perform that the Corporation and the Overseers were obviously happy if any responsible person would undertake them. An example is the choosing of a President, after repeated unsuccessful attempts. On June 30, 1679, the Corporation

> Voted that the Worshipfull Mr. Stoughton bee desired and empowered to Provide a President for this Colledge, and that the honored Overseers concurring herewith, the Reverend Mr. Oakes bee intreated to write to Mr. Stoughton accordingly, *in the name of the Corporation.*[12] [Italics added.]

There is no indication that I have seen after Dunster's time of anything but the best of relations between the Corporation and Overseers. The Corporation was often made up of young men — the Fellows were very young — but they acted with power in many cases. When the Corporation was weak the Overseers stepped in,[13] a procedure which could lead to poor administration, but under normal circumstances both Overseers and Corporation seem to have performed most of their statutory functions, and many in the service of the College beyond the call of statute.*

The members of the Corporation acted in their capacity as Corporation members and also in the capacities of their individual

* The relation of the Overseers and Corporation is a complicated question, and a brief summary cannot do it any justice. The Overseers were inactive from 1686 to 1707, and the Corporation, or its substitute, acted. There is a detailed account of charter provisions in *CSM* XV, xxxii–lxvii. See also *HCSC*, pp. 18–21, 304, 309, 575, for Dunster's troubles, which were mixed up with the extraordinary circumstances of his having been asked to resign. Of course, it is in extraordinary circumstances that the allocation of powers is often most important.

offices. Especially since the College was so small and the administration so closely knit, the character and performance of the few officers directly affected the economics of the institution.

We need hardly say that all the Presidents were strongly religious. The Reverend Henry Dunster was a scholar and apparently a person whom people loved and readily followed. He can be credited with taking an embryo college, providing buildings, collecting students, establishing organization, doing much of the teaching, and prevailing upon the General Court to give the permanent charter which was a necessity if the institution was to have any educational and financial standing. While thus establishing a college, he managed the only press in New England, cared for the Indian youths whom optimistic Puritans sent to him for education (and clothing and washing), and brought up a very numerous family including his own and stepchildren. Mr. Dunster had financial troubles with his wife's estate which certainly indicate that he was no business man, even by the standards of the day. As one writer puts it, he "went on rather more trustingly than wisely — not with the wisdom of a business man."*

In contrast to Dunster, Charles Chauncy, whose sixty-second birthday almost coincided with his inauguration, sounds rather dull, but he was an eminent scholar and a successful minister. During his regime — possibly it was the temper of the times — the number of students went from around fifty to the point where there were no graduates of the class of 1672, and four, two, and ten, in the next three classes respectively. (Chauncy died in February, 1672.)

The next President to hold office for any length of time was Increase Mather, whom many people admired exceedingly and many people hated equally heartily. The peripatetic President Mather was unquestionably a brilliant man of great influence, and

* HUA, Dunster Papers (1803–1857), letter of February 4, 1854, from Joseph Willard (?).

His biographer says that, on religious subjects, "Mr. Dunster, . . . a learned Orientalist, felt there was something more to be known, and opened his eyes to the light." (Jeremiah Chaplin, *Life of Henry Dunster* [Boston, 1872], p. ix.) Whatever we may classify as light, it was Dunster's questioning the details of the accepted religious practice, coming to his own conclusions, and then, whatever the cost, courageously, and perhaps unnecessarily loudly, holding to his conclusions, that cost the College its devoted first president.

though we may not care for some of his ideas, there is no doubt that his strength was a great asset to Harvard College in the very difficult period of adjustment to the new political regime. Mather was not a man to be dealt with lightly. As a business man he was definitely casual. There is no proof that Mather failed to turn over any of the small funds he collected for Harvard, but there is room to wonder what he did with some of the money entrusted to him.*

John Leverett and William Brattle, the two popular Fellows who taught from 1685 to 1697, can, if compared with Mather, be called "liberal," though the liberalism of their day was the conservatism of the next.** Under either description, as you may choose, President Leverett was at the head of Harvard College when the more independent Puritan regime faded and what might be termed the "colonial" period became well established.

Leverett was a member of a magisterial family, and his familiarity with the law and the General Court stood him in good stead as President of the College. Anyone who peruses the hundreds of pages of his meticulously kept notes and records is well aware that one of President Leverett's strong points was an inclination to good hard work. And it is this systemizing of the administration of the College which stands out in the first part of his term of office. It was well that after the years of changing or traveling Presidents the institution should be led by a man of these solid tendencies.

There were, practically speaking, only three Treasurers of the College in the 59 years from 1654 to 1713. Especially under Richards, Presidents and Fellows came and went, but the Treasurer

* One of Mather's troubles was that he undertook his mission to England for the Country (and the College) in 1688 when Andros was in power, and he found it necessary to embark secretly. Then in 1689 Andros was replaced by the Council for Safety which, having doubtful legal status, had also little liquidity of funds. While he was in England Mather used the College's English income for his own subsistence — another case of the College's "accommodating" the Country with funds — and the major question about Mather's use of money is whether or not these accounts were ever entirely adjusted. The government subsequently voted Mather some compensation for his services as Country agent in England, and they also voted to pay back some money which, through him, the College had lent to the Country. Mather's casual record-keeping did not facilitate the adjustment. (See *A&R* VII, 428, 452, 48–49.)

** One might think that the two men's friendliness toward the Church of England and willingness to deal with the supporters of the Royal government was subservience to those in control, as England began to assert more power in Massachusetts. But the Fellows' dislike of the witch trial procedures, and many others of their actions, give evidence that they had the courage to support their independently reached convictions.

gave continuity to the administration. The Treasurers were all men of stature and experience.* Danforth was a man of ample means who had a notable career in politics. Richards and Brattle were leading merchants, the first active in politics and a representative of the Colony in England, the latter a leader in "liberal" religion and an outstanding mathematician and astronomer.

No one of these officers, Presidents or Treasurers, was a nonentity. They were men of the world, traveled for their century. They felt the temper of the times and also affected it.

Although there was a great turnover among teaching Fellows of the Corporation, and among Presidents from 1672 to 1685 — the fact that the Presidents were so often only "acting" was also a weakening factor — study of Figure 8 shows that there was continuity provided not only by the Treasurers, but also by the *non*-teaching Fellows of the Corporation. From 1650 to 1692 there was remarkably little change in this latter group. Five nonresident Fellows of the Corporation served for lengthy periods: Jonathan Mitchell served eighteen years, Thomas Shepard twenty-one years, Increase Mather ten years, John Sherman seven years, and Nehemiah Hobart eleven years (and later fifteen more). Mather's total service on the Corporation, including the time he was President, covered twenty-six years. Leverett and William Brattle, with an hiatus at the issuing of the Charter of 1700, held some office from 1685 to their deaths in 1724 and 1717 respectively; and at the end of the century several other notably long terms of service began. We must, therefore, not let the recorded changes in officers blind us to the stability provided by the Corporation.**

* It is gratifying to find Danforth described as not "as narrow-minded as most of his party"; he defended the praying Indians at the time of the 1675 war, and condemned witchcraft trials in 1692. (*DAB*. This is James Truslow Adams' faint praise.) The same remark applies to Thomas Brattle, who condemned the Salem trials as "ignorance and folly" (*DAB*).

** The larger Corporation which functioned from 1692 to 1707 was not quite so substantial as it looks in Figure 8. Mr. Albert Matthews' analysis of attendance at Corporation meetings in this period (*CSM* XV, cxlvii–cli) shows that some members were faithful in attendance, but others were very seldom there. The larger Corporation could, however, perhaps have stirred up additional interest in the College, especially since there were no functioning Overseers.

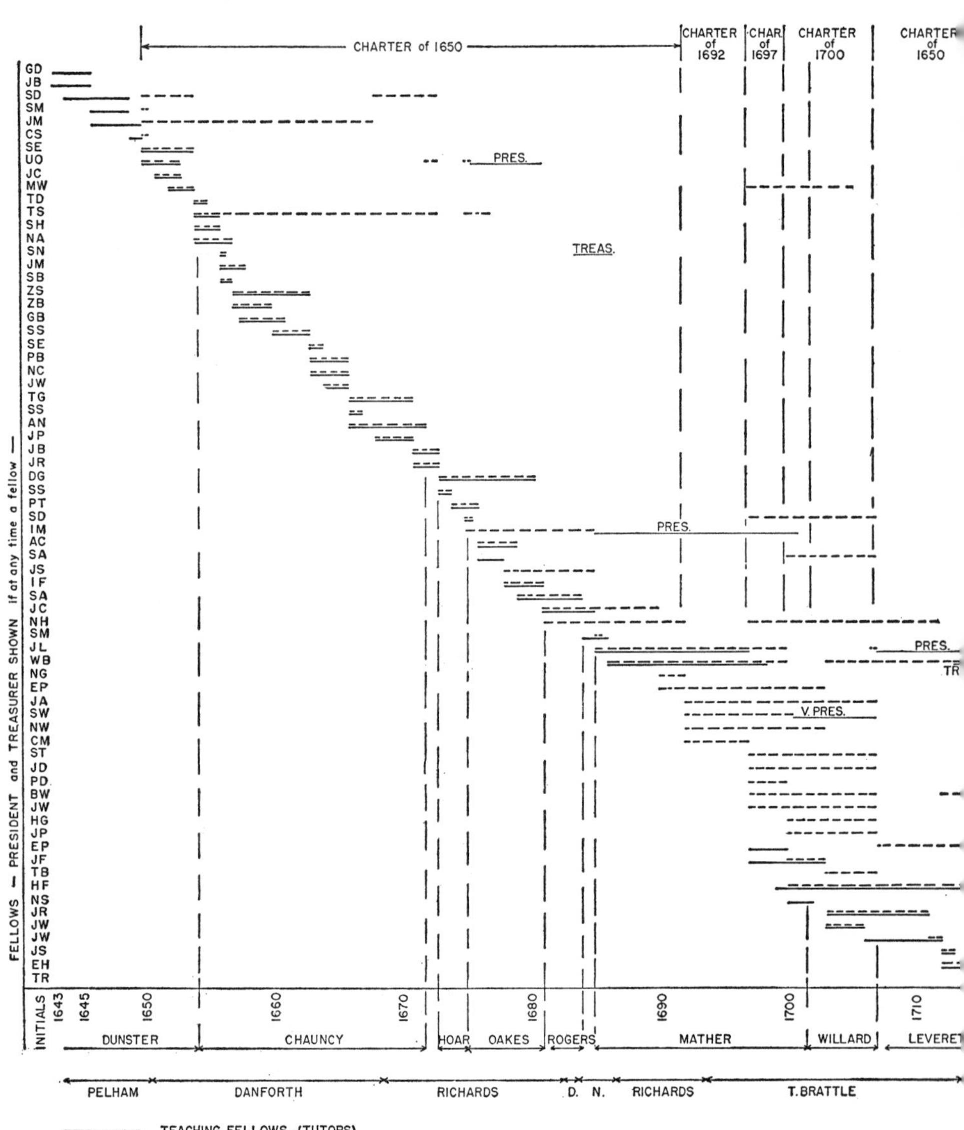


Figure 8. *The terms of service of the Harvard Corporation and Tutors, to 1715.* Source: *Dates from* CSM *XV, cliv–clix.*

## THE FINANCIAL ADMINISTRATION

The general effectiveness of financial management of seventeenth-century Harvard is difficult if not impossible to evaluate at this distance and in a limited study such as this, for two reasons:

(1) Considerations of educational program may temporarily outweigh considerations of finance. No educational institution *need* have an operating deficit, but the carrying-out of reasonable aims of the institution may dictate a deficit for one or more years. No institution can decide to run deficits very long. Also implicit in a decision to have a deficit is a choice between spending on present program and providing for future security, flexibility, and growth — the economic choice which may determine long-run progress. Evaluation of Harvard's educational program is beyond the scope of this study.

(2) Barring some flagrant mismanagement and having no comparable institution with which to contrast early Harvard's finance, we can only assume that since the College survived and grew and turned out useful graduates, and since we find no very serious complaint recorded, the financial management served its purpose — to provide means for carrying out the primary aims of the institution. If more money had been available, possibly the results might have been better; this may have been especially true of scholarships and faculty salaries It appears, however, that there were no lines of students waiting for admission, and many who could have afforded to attend chose other paths. The remarkable thing is that, in a day when matters of the moment seemed so compelling, so many students chose the rigorous four- or seven-year course of learning at the College. No general educational reform was in the air here in Massachusetts Bay which might have attracted more students or introduced other aims; Harvard had in some respects changed the English university system to meet what seemed American needs.

Though we do not, therefore, attempt any general evaluation of Harvard's financial practice in this period, we can recall a few practices which appeared to work out well and some which were less successful. There are, of course, more specific summaries at the end of each section in earlier chapters.

Administration could not be ideal in periods of changing or

part-time presidents, but the College in 1650 established detailed written rules for the running of its day-to-day business. The minor officers knew what was expected of them. So far as we can tell, though the Corporation occasionally concerned itself further in details, ordinarily it allowed its subordinates to run their own affairs, with periodic "careful" reports and audits required. "Old Mary" apparently did not always do a good job on the students' rooms, and (hardly on the same level of seriousness) the Steward in 1669 had to be replaced by Thomas Danforth, but otherwise we hear of few difficulties in this respect. Exactly what caused President Hoar's troubles we do not know.

*Expense.* Especially in the early years, expenses were often incurred only as *contra* income came in. Dependence upon tuitions for the payment of a large part of the Tutors' salaries was convenient for the Treasurer, but the great variation in amount caused by changes in the number of students was highly inconvenient for the Tutors. The faculty was expected to teach largely for the privilege of staying at the College, though compensation did improve noticeably toward the end of the century and we see the beginning of the evolution of a salary scale. The turnover of faculty members was greatest when their compensation was least.

The cost-plus arrangement made for a time with the Steward was not conducive to economy.

Practically all scholarships came from specifically designated endowment income. Work-scholarships were an indispensable aid to some students, gave the students early training in taking responsibility, and provided the college with needed assistants.

*Income.* The largest part of the income came from students. Dormitories and feeding were largely self-supporting. Tuition payments were very small compared with cost of board.

With some — though small — fixed overhead to cover, matters were eased considerably when the number of students was up: the faculty received more pay, and the Steward more easily made a profit.

Income from government was both important and influential. Fortunately government, even under the Royal Governors, was usually well disposed to the College; it had a definitely paternalistic concept of its role in, originally, a planned society. Accepting the President's salary and other grants from the Court cost the College much of its independence, but the Court was a flexible source of funds and the amounts so provided did vary with needs — witness the increases in the salary and in building expenditures.

The church's ministers and the Court, who wielded the power in the Colony, were of incalculable assistance in influencing individual givers.

Many gifts came from persons long familiar with the College through having served on committees to aid or investigate the institution; much aid came from friends of such committee members. The process of follow-the-leader was important, and publicizing of gift lists, despite the modesty of donors, seemed to help. Much work on fund-raising paid off many years later and in unexpected places, especially through bequests.

Alumni influence was very helpful, but many gifts came from non-alumni. A major proportion of gifts came from merchants. Is there a parallel in 1962 giving?

Annuities of a fixed sum did not work out well, for the amount of money did not adjust to the times. Do the early gifts of income rather than outright capital, and the lack of such gifts in later years of our period, indicate at all an early lack of confidence in the Corporation's handling the money?

It was important that the College have a secure legal status and administration if individuals were to trust it to use their gifts wisely.

*The growing endowment and its income.* Income from current gifts and from endowment was almost from the beginning of great importance to the College and subsidized about 40 per cent of the College's cost per student. The financial system was at first set up with the expectation of using capital — or perhaps we should say that for the first fifty years there was almost no capital, just income which had not yet been spent. The endowment income grew from practically nothing at mid-century until by the period 1693 to 1712 it reached about £156 a year and provided 27 per cent of the total income excluding Stewards' receipts, or

15 per cent if Stewards' accounts are included. The value of endowment in 1712 was about five eighths of total assets, plant the other three eighths — in all perhaps £8500.

The relatively stable price levels maintained the value of what financial assets there were.

The practice of listing rent and interest due as capital, combined with the incompleteness of our records as well as the variations in accounting, makes it virtually impossible to calculate sensibly any exact yield on investments. Moreover, we have no adequate estimate of investment expense, especially on rental property. For the same reasons it is not feasible in this period to compare the effectiveness of the types of investments: personal bonds, mortgages, and real estate. Since the Treasurers did not buy real estate for investment unless it was indicated by a donor, we must assume that in the seventeenth century they did not think it a good or suitable investment. Real estate values did, however, hold up very well. Obviously the nature of investments must vary with the opportunities of the times.

The ferry, with its income growing with the growth and demands of the society, seemed an ideal source of income.

Many donors directed that their gifts be "improved" for College purposes. The literal following of this direction by taking care that any capital gains be added to endowment helped maintain the purchasing power of the endowment when inflation did set in early in the eighteenth century.

Though land grants by the Court and gifts of land from individuals paid poorly in the seventeenth century, some of these inactive assets later acquired some value.

The possession of some dependable endowment income greatly facilitated planning and therefore administration.

The Press and the activities to aid the Indians made little direct contribution to the funds of the College, but both undoubtedly influenced supporters in the College's favor.

If, in conclusion, we should feel that the College began to fare better financially in the 1690's we would have a hard time to assign any one reason: Too many things changed at about the same time. Among the changes were:

(1) The old charter of the Colony was vacated in 1684; the new Provincial status began in 1691, and direct English influence may then have been stronger than in mid-century. From 1692 to 1707 there were new College charters providing different forms and sizes of the Corporation. To 1686 the government, the Overseers, and the College officers were in sympathy on basic matters of religion and politics, though there were important differences in the degree of their enthusiasm for the most strict Puritan practices. After 1686 there was the split between those who favored the older Massachusetts independence in religion and government and those who tended more to the Church of England and a Royal government.

(2) The Puritan influence was waning. "Political privilege was henceforth to depend on wealth and not on church membership."[14]

(3) The economic condition of the Colony or Province was improving.

(4) Increase Mather became President in 1685. The same year Leverett and William Brattle, the first somewhat permanent faculty, were made Tutors, and they continued influential for the rest of our period.

(5) The number of students increased, but only by a very few.

(6) Thomas Brattle was elected Treasurer in 1693.

(7) The College had acquired its first permanent general endowment.

To whatever force or forces we may ascribe its progress, if we believe the major purpose of a College to be threefold — to educate the young, to maintain intellectual standards and heritage, and to promote scholarly work — surely we can join Cotton Mather in saying, from especially the first two points of view, "A Colledge, the best thing that ever New-England thought upon!"[15] And unquestionably one necessary condition for an effective college is the effective handling of its economic affairs.

*Appendices*

*Bibliography*

*Notes*

*Index*

# *APPENDIX A*

## LIST OF PRESIDENTS, TREASURERS, AND STEWARDS OF HARVARD COLLEGE, 1636 to 1750

(See Figure 8)

### PRESIDENTS

| | |
|---|---|
| (Nathaniel Eaton, Professor | 1637–Sept. 9, 1639) |
| Henry Dunster | Aug. 27, 1640–Oct. 24, 1654 |
| Charles Chauncy | Nov. 27, 1654–Feb. 19, 1672* |
| Leonard Hoar | Dec. 10, 1672–Mar. 15, 1675 |
| Urian Oakes, Acting | Apr. 7, 1675–Feb. 9, 1680 |
| Urian Oakes | Feb. 9, 1680–July 25, 1681* |
| John Rogers | Apr. 10, 1682–July 2, 1684* |
| Increase Mather, Acting | June 11, 1685–July 23, 1686 |
| Increase Mather, Rector | July 23, 1686–June 27, 1692 |
| Increase Mather | June 27, 1692–Sept. 6, 1701 |
| Samuel Willard, Vice-President | July 12, 1700– |
| Samuel Willard, Acting President | Sept. 6, 1701–Aug. 14, 1707* |
| John Leverett | Jan. 14, 1708–May 3, 1724* |
| Benjamin Wadsworth | July 7, 1725–Mar. 16, 1737* |
| Edward Holyoke | Sept. 28, 1737–June 1, 1769* |

### TREASURERS

| | |
|---|---|
| Herbert Pelham | 1643–1650 |
| Thomas Danforth | 1650–1668 |
| John Richards | 1669–1682 |
| Thomas Danforth | 1682–1683 |
| Samuel Nowell | 1683–1686 |
| John Richards | 1686–1693 |
| Thomas Brattle | 1693–1713 |
| William Brattle | 1713–1715 |
| John White | 1715–1721 |
| Edward Hutchinson | 1721–1752 |

### STEWARDS

| | |
|---|---|
| Matthew Day | –1649 |
| Thomas Chesholme | 1649–1660 |
| John Sherman | 1660– |
| William Bordman | –1668 |
| Thomas Danforth | 1668–1682 |
| Andrew Bordman | 1682–1687 |
| Aaron Bordman | 1687–1703 |
| Andrew Bordman | 1703–1747 |
| Andrew Bordman | 1747–1750 |

*Source: CSM* XV, clii, clvi-clvii, clxi.

* President who died in office or within a month of leaving office.

# APPENDIX B

(*See pages 140–141 above*)

## SCHOLARSHIPS AWARDED AT HARVARD COLLEGE

(SELECTED CLASSES)

| Classes (inclusive) | Average number of individuals *per class* who received some aid, including jobs, while in College[a] | Average size graduating class | Per cent of class receiving aid at *some time* |
|---|---|---|---|
| 1650–1660 | 2 | 7 or 10[b] | 25 or 20[b] |
| 1675–1685 | 3 | 6 | 51 |
| 1689–1698 | 3.4 | 13 | 26 |
| 1708–1710 | 7[c] | 13 | 53 |

*Source: CSM* XXXI, Chesholme's Book; XV, 82–91, 373–402, and *passim;* XVI, 859–862; QBB, 1687 on.

[a] Included are Scholars of House and Butler; inclusion of Waiter, Bell-ringer, and Monitor adds very few, for such jobs were held by scholarship students. Figures ignore repeated awards to the same person.

[b] The larger figure includes some nongraduates; during 1655–1658 especially, several students did not take their degrees because of the fight over the length of the course, and these classes were thus larger than the number of graduates would indicate.

[c] All the scholarships in this table include those given to A.M. candidates; in these three years there were only two "graduate students" (out of 20 recipients) who had scholarships who did not have them as undergraduates. Undergraduates often had scholarships continued after graduation.

*This table is subject to limitations explained in the text.*

# *APPENDIX C*

(*See pages 141–143 above.*)

## HARVARD COLLEGE TREASURERS' ACCOUNTS WITH THE STEWARDS, 1687 to 1712[a]

| Steward received | 1687–1693 £ | s. | d. | 1693–1712 £ | s. | d. | Steward paid | 1687–1693 £ | s. | d. | 1693–1712 £ | s. | d. |
|---|---|---|---|---|---|---|---|---|---|---|---|---|---|
| Food charges | 1872 | 7 | 5 | 7784 | 16 | 9 | Food cost | 1810 | 10 | 09 | 7324 | 17 | 8 |
| Rent | 223 | 17 | 0 | 820 | 3 | 0 | Butler | 72 | 0 | 0 | 228 | 0 | 0 |
| Monitor | 20 | 0 | 0 | 95 | 0 | 0 | Monitor | 20 | 0 | 0 | 95 | 0 | 0 |
| Fees | 103 | 9 | 3[b] | 159 | 7 | 0[b] | Repairs & miscellaneous expense[e] | 317 | 2 | 11 | 1211 | 9 | 1 |
| | *105 | 10 | 0[c] | *668 | 14 | 10[c] | | | | | | | |
| Steward received from Treas.[d] | *15 | 0 | 0 | *18 | 15 | 0 | Orders paid[f] | *120 | 10 | 0 | *687 | 9 | 10 |
| | 2340 | 3 | 8 | 9546 | 16 | 7 | | 2340 | 3 | 8 | 9546 | 16 | 7 |

[a] The Stewards' Account would reverse the sides.

[b] Actual fees, less net orders of Treasurer.

[c] Net orders paid, that is, fees allowed the Steward—from Treasurer's memoranda.

[d] There were additional cash payments of Treasurer's bills sent via Steward (cf. scholarships). Figures appear in (d) above only when Steward's balance was negative on settlement.

[e] Of Repairs, £32 5*s.* 10*d.* is College glass 1687–1693; £88 4*s.* 9*d.* is College glass 1693–1712. Balancing item.

[f] Such as for salaries, scholarships, or building brew-house.

* Those Corporation orders or payments that are marked with asterisks come from basic net Treasurer's accounts as I have reconstituted them in Tables 25 and 31.

# *BIBLIOGRAPHY*

A. The Harvard University Archives, manuscript records to 1715
B. Other unpublished material
C. Public documents
D. Articles or extracts from manuscripts, printed in scholarly journals and collections
E. Books

## A. THE HARVARD UNIVERSITY ARCHIVES, MANUSCRIPT RECORDS TO 1715

(There is an inventory of the Harvard University Archives in Appendix F of S. E. Morison's *Harvard College in the Seventeenth Century*, pages 662–681. Arrangement of the papers has been somewhat changed since this inventory was published in 1936, but there is little additional material.)


1. Harvard College Records, "College Books" I, III, IV. (College Book II burned.) Published as Volumes XV and XVI of the *Publications of the Colonial Society of Massachusetts*, edited, with a 153-page introduction, by Albert Matthews, 1925.
   President Wadsworth's Index to College Books I–VI, printed in *Publications of the Colonial Society of Massachusetts*, XV.
   Harvard College Papers
   Harvard College Papers, Supplement
   Harvard College Papers Calendar
   The College Laws
   College Charter Papers
2. Reports to Overseers
3. Corporation Records
   Corporation Papers
4. Presidents' Papers
   Henry Dunster Papers
   Increase Mather Papers
   John Leverett Papers
   John Leverett's Diary, 1703–1723
5. Treasurers' Papers
   Journal and Ledger of John Richards, 1669–1682, 1686–1693
   Journal of Thomas Brattle, 1693–1713, called "College Book V"
6. Steward Chesholme's Ledger, 1650–1659. Printed as pages 19–276 of *Publications of the Colonial Society of Massachusetts*, XXXI, edited with an introduction by S. E. Morison, 1935.

Quarter-Bill Book, 1687–1720, of Stewards Aaron and Andrew Bordman
Ledger, 1703–1731, of Steward Andrew Bordman
Steward's Accounts, Audited, 1713–1731

7. Butlers' Book, 1722–1750
8. Donation Book of Andrew Eliot, Volume I, to 1784
   Gift Lists — S. A. Eliot and Peck
   A. McF. Davis
   A. T. Gibbs
   Benefactors, Volume I
   Wills, Gifts, and Grants
   Gift Papers
   Donations of Books
9. Buildings Papers
10. Land Papers
11. Ferry Papers
    Ferry Papers, Supplement
12. Deeds
13. Disorder Papers, Thomas Danforth, 1676
14. General Court Acts
15. Library Papers
16. Chronological Miscellany
17. Tutor Henry Flynt's Diary.

### B. OTHER UNPUBLISHED MATERIAL

Foster, Margery Somers. "The Economic History of Harvard College in the Puritan Period." Unpublished Ph.D. thesis, Radcliffe College, 1958 (copies at Radcliffe and Harvard University Archives).

Leverett, John. Letter of September 18, 1713, to Massachusetts Bay Province Secretary Isaac Addington. Leverett Saltonstall MSS., Massachusetts Historical Society. Copy in S. E. Morison's files.

Stearns, Raymond Phineas. "Hugh Peter." Unpublished Ph.D. thesis, Harvard University, 1934.

Wiedner, Donald Lawrence. "Coins and Accounts in West European and Colonial History, 1250–1936." Unpublished Ph.D. thesis, Harvard University, 1958.

### C. PUBLIC DOCUMENTS

1. *Records of the Town of Cambridge, Massachusetts, 1630–1703*. Cambridge: by order of the City Council, 1901.
   *Register Book of the Lands and Houses in the "New Towne."* Cambridge: by order of the City Council, 1896.
2. *General Laws and Liberties of Massachusetts Colony*. Cambridge: Samuel Green, 1672. Reproduced Boston: Rockwell and Churchill, 1890.
   *The Laws and Liberties of Massachusetts*. Reprinted from the copy of the 1648 edition in the Henry E. Huntington Library, with an Introduction by Max Farrand. Cambridge: Harvard University Press, 1929.

*The Acts and Resolves of the Province of the Massachusetts Bay.* 21 vols., including Appendices. Boston: Wright and Potter, Printers, 1869–1922.

*Records of the Court of Assistants of the Colony of the Massachusetts Bay, 1630–1692.* 3 vols. Boston: The County of Suffolk, 1901–1928.

*Records of the Governor and Company of the Massachusetts Bay in New England.* Edited by Nathaniel B. Shurtleff, M.D. 5 vols. Boston: William White, 1854.

Records of the President and Council of the Territory and Dominion of New England. *Proceedings of Massachusetts Historical Society,* 2nd Ser., XIII (1899–1900), 222–286.

3. *Records of the Colony of New Plymouth, in New England.* 12 vols. Edited by Nathaniel B. Shurtleff and David Pulsifer. Boston: William White, 1855–1861.

4. *Acts of the Commissioners of the United Colonies of New England.* 2 vols. Volumes IX and X in *Records of Plymouth Colony* (above). Edited by David Pulsifer. Boston: William White, 1859.

5. *Documents Relative to the Colonial History of the State of New York.* 15 vols. Procured by John Romeyn Brodhead, Esq. Albany: Weed, Parsons and Company, Printers, 1853.

6. *Report of the Record Commissioners of the City of Boston* (Boston Records), 39 vols. 1881–1909. Vols. II, 1634–1660 (1902, 3rd ed.); VII, 1660–1701 (1881); XI, 1701–1715 (1884).

### D. ARTICLES OR EXTRACTS FROM MANUSCRIPTS, PRINTED IN SCHOLARLY JOURNALS AND COLLECTIONS

(and not in Harvard College Records or in books below)

Barnes, Viola F. "Richard Wharton, a Seventeenth Century New England Colonial." *Publications of the Colonial Society of Massachusetts,* XXVI (1925), 238–270.

Baxter, William T. "Accounting in Colonial America." *Studies in the History of Accounting,* ed. A. C. Littleton and B. S. Yamey, pp. 272–287. Homewood, Illinois: Richard D. Irwin, 1956.

——— "Credit, Bills, and Bookkeeping in a Simple Economy," *Accounting Review,* XXI (1946), 154–166.

Browne, Edmund. Letter to Sir Simonds D'Ewes. *Publications of the Colonial Society of Massachusetts,* VII (1902), 75.

Clapp, Clifford B. "The Gifts of Henry Ashurst and Richard Baxter to Harvard College." *Publications of the Colonial Society of Massachusetts,* XX (1918), 192–203.

Cotton, Josiah. Extracts from his Diary. Edited by Albert Matthews. *Publications of the Colonial Society of Massachusetts,* XXVI (1925), 277–280.

Crandall, Ruth. "Wholesale Commodity Prices in Boston during the Eighteenth Century." *Review of Economic Statistics,* XVI (1934), 117–128, 178–183.

Danforth, Samuel. "An Almanack for 1649," the page reproduced in Winthrop (1908 ed.) II, 340.

Danforth, Thomas. "Danforth Papers." 2nd Ser., *Collections of the Massachusetts Historical Society*, VIII (1826), 46–112.

Davis, Andrew McFarland. "Certain Considerations concerning the Coinage of the Colony and the Public Bills of Credit of the Province of the Massachusetts Bay." *Proceedings of the American Academy of Arts and Sciences*, XXXIII (1898), 190–212.

de Roover, Raymond. "The Development of Accounting Prior to Luca Pacioli according to the Account-Books of Medieval Merchants." *Studies in the History of Accounting*, ed. A. C. Littleton and B. S. Yamey, pp. 114–174. Homewood, Illinois: Richard D. Irwin, 1956.

Dexter, Franklin B. "Estimates of Population in the American Colonies." *Proceedings of the American Antiquarian Society*, new series, V (1887), 22–50.

Dudley, Thomas. "Letter to the Countess of Lincoln," March 12, 1631. In *Chronicles of the First Planters of the Colony of Massachusetts Bay*, ed. Alexander Young, pp. 301–341. Boston, Charles C. Little and James Brown, 1846.

Dunster, Henry. Letter to Christianus Ravius, February 1648 (?). 4th Ser., *Collections of the Massachusetts Historical Society*, I (1852), 251–254.

Felt, Joseph B. In *Collections of the American Statistical Association*, I (1843–1847): Part I, "Statistics of Towns in Massachusetts," pp. 1–100, 111–116; Part II, "Statistics of Population in Massachusetts," pp. 121–216; Part III, "Statistics of Taxation in Massachusetts, including Valuation and Population," pp. 221–596.

Foster, Margery S., "The Cost of a Harvard Education in the Puritan Period." *Publications of the Cambridge Historical Society*, XXXVIII (1959–1960), 7–22.

Goffe, Colonel William. Extracts from his Journal, 1660. *Proceedings of the Massachusetts Historical Society* [1st Ser.] VII (1863–1864), 280–283.

Gookin, Daniel. *Historical Collections of the Indians in New England*, written in 1674. 1st Ser., *Collections of the Massachusetts Historical Society*, I (1792), 141–229.

Hudson, Winthrop S. "The Morison Myth concerning the Founding of Harvard College." *Church History*, VIII (1939), 148–159.

James, F. G. "Charity Endowments as Sources of Local Credit in Seventeenth- and Eighteenth-Century England." *Journal of Economic History*, VIII (1948), 153–170.

Lyttle, Charles. "A Sketch of the Theological Development of Harvard University, 1636–1805." *Church History*, V (1936), 301–329.

Master, James, Esq. "A Booke of my Expences," in Appendix of *The Flemings in Oxford; Being Documents Selected from the Rydal Papers in Illustration of the Lives and Ways of Oxford Men 1650–1700*, ed. John Richard Magrath (Oxford Historical Society Series). Oxford: 1904.

Mather, Cotton. "Some Considerations on the Bills of Credit." In *Colonial Currency Reprints*, ed. A. McF. Davis. 4 vols. Boston: Prince Society, 1910–1911.

Mitchell, Jonathan. "A Modell For the Maintaining of students & fellows . . ." (1663?). *Publications of the Colonial Society of Massachusetts*, ed. S. E. Morison, XXXI (1935), 303–322.

Morison, Samuel Eliot. "Precedence at Harvard College in the Seventeenth Century." *Proceedings of the American Antiquarian Society*, new series, XLII (1932), 420–424.

Richards, John. Letter from Boston to Increase Mather in London, July 2, 1688. 4th Ser., *Collections of the Massachusetts Historical Society*, VIII (1868), 502–503.

Scull, G. D. "The Society for the Propagation of the Gospel in New England and the Rev. Thomas Welde." *New England Historical and Genealogical Register*, XXXIX (1885), 179–183.

Seybolt, Robert F. "Scholomasters of Colonial Boston." *Publications of the Colonial Society of Massachusetts*, XXVII (1927–1930), 130–156.

Shepard, Thomas. Letter to Hugh Peter, December 27, 1645. *American Historical Review*, IV (1898), 105–107.

——— "The Autobiography of Thomas Shepard." *Publications of the Colonial Society of Massachusetts*, XXVII (1927–1930), 343–400.

Shipton, Clifford K. "Immigration to New England, 1680–1740." *Journal of Political Economy*, XLIV (1936), 225–239.

Simpson, Sophia Shuttleworth. "Two Hundred Years Ago." *Publications of the Cambridge Historical Society*, XVI (1922), 29–68.

Sumner, William G. "The Spanish Dollar and the Colonial Shilling." *American Historical Review*, III (1898), 607–619.

Ware, Horace E. "Was the Government of Massachusetts Bay Colony a Theocracy?" *Publications of the Colonial Society of Massachusetts*, X (1905), 151–180.

Welde, Thomas. "Rev. Thomas Welde's 'Innocency Cleared.' " With comment by G. D. Scull (see also "Scull" in this section above). *New England Historical and Genealogical Register*, XXXVI (1882), 62–70.

Winship, George P. "A Document concerning the First Anglo-American Press." *Transactions of the Bibliographical Society* (London, 1939), pp. 51–70 (reprint).

## E. BOOKS

Bailyn, Bernard. *The New England Merchants in the Seventeenth Century*. Cambridge: Harvard University Press, 1955.

Batchelder, Samuel Francis. *Bits of Cambridge History*. Cambridge: Harvard University Press, 1930.

Baxter, William T. *The House of Hancock*. Cambridge: Harvard University Press, 1945.

Beer, George L. *Origins of the British Colonial System, 1578–1660*. New York: Macmillan, 1908.

Bowditch, Charles P. *An Account of the Trust administered by the Trustees of the Charity of Edward Hopkins*. Privately printed, 1889.

Brown, Richard. *A History of Accounting and Accountants*. Edinburgh: T. C. and E. C. Jack, 1905.

Bullock, C. J. *Essays on the Monetary History of the United States*. New York: Macmillan, 1900.

Channing, Edward. *A History of the United States*. 6 vols., 1905–1925. New York: Macmillan (reprinted 1948).

Chaplin, Jeremiah. *Life of Henry Dunster*. Boston: James R. Osgood, 1872.

Cole, Arthur Harrison. *Wholesale Commodity Prices in the United States, 1700–1861*. Cambridge: Harvard University Press, 1938.

Davis, Andrew McFarland. *Currency and Banking in the Province of the Massachusetts Bay*. 2 vols. New York: For the American Economic Association, by Macmillan, 1901.

Davis, Andrew McFarland, ed. *Colonial Currency Reprints, 1682–1751*. 4 vols. Boston: The Prince Society, 1910.

Dewey, Davis R. *Financial History of the United States*. 10th ed. New York: Longmans, Green, 1928.

*Dictionary of American Biography*. New York: Charles Scribner's Sons.

*Dictionary of National Biography*. London: Oxford University Press.

*Documents relating to the University and Colleges of Cambridge*. 3 vols. Published by direction of the Commissioners appointed by the Queen to inquire into the State, Discipline, Studies, and Revenues of the Said University and Colleges. London: Longmans, Brown, Green, and Longmans, 1852.

Dorfman, Joseph. *The Economic Mind in American Civilization, 1606–1865*. 2 vols. New York: Viking Press, 1946.

Douglas, Charles H. J. *The Financial History of Massachusetts, 1628–1775*. (Vol. I, No. 4, of "Studies in History, Economics, and Public Law".) New York: Columbia College, 1892.

Farmer, John. *A Genealogical Register of the First Settlers of New England*. Lancaster, Massachusetts: Carter, Andrews, 1829.

Felt, Joseph B. *An Historical Account of Massachusetts Currency*. Boston: Perkins and Marvin, 1839.

Gardiner, Samuel R. *The First Two Stuarts and the Puritan Revolution, 1603–1660*. London: Longmans, Green, 1913.

Harvard University. *Endowment Funds of Harvard University, June 30, 1947*. Cambridge: 1948.

Harvard University. *Financial Report to the Board of Overseers of Harvard College for the Fiscal Year 1960–61*. Cambridge: by the University, 1961.

Hayes, Carlton J. H. *A Political and Cultural History of Modern Europe*. 2 vols. New York: Macmillan, 1933.

Johnson, E. A. J. *American Economic Thought in the Seventeenth Century*. London: P. S. King & Son Ltd., 1932.

Johnson, Edward. *Wonder-Working Providence*, ed. J. F. Jameson (Original Narratives Series). New York: Charles Scribner's Sons, 1910.

Johnson, Edward. *Wonder-Working Providence*. Edited with a 114-page introduction by William Frederick Poole. Andover, Massachusetts: Warren F. Draper, 1867.

Jordan, Wilbur K. *Philanthropy in England, 1480–1660*. New York: Russell Sage Foundation, 1959.

Kaye, P. L. *English Colonial Administration under Lord Clarendon, 1660–1667*. Baltimore: Johns Hopkins Press, 1905.

Keynes, John Maynard. *The General Theory of Employment, Interest and Money.* New York: Harcourt, Brace, 1936.

Littleton, A. C. *Accounting Evolution to 1900.* New York: American Institute Publishing Company, 1933.

Littleton, A. C., and B. S. Yamey, Editors. *Studies in the History of Accounting.* Homewood, Illinois: Richard D. Irwin, 1956.

Mather, Cotton. *Magnalia Christi Americana* (1704). In seven books, Vols. I and II. Hartford: Silas Andrus & Son, 1855.

Miller, Perry. *The New England Mind: The Seventeenth Century.* Cambridge: Harvard University Press, 1954.

——— *The New England Mind: From Colony to Province.* Cambridge: Harvard University Press, 1953.

Mitchell, Broadus, and Louise P. Mitchell. *American Economic History.* Boston: Houghton Mifflin, 1947.

Morison, Samuel Eliot. *Builders of the Bay Colony.* Boston: Houghton Mifflin, 1930.

——— *The Founding of Harvard College.* Cambridge: Harvard University Press, 1935.

——— *Harvard College in the Seventeenth Century.* 2 vols. Cambridge: Harvard University Press, 1936.

——— Text of *Historical Markers of the Massachusetts Bay Colony.* Commonwealth of Massachusetts, 1930.

——— *The Puritan Pronaos.* New York: New York University Press, 1936.

——— *Three Centuries of Harvard, 1636–1936.* Cambridge: Harvard University Press, 1936 (reprinted 1946).

Mullinger, James Bass. *The University of Cambridge.* 3 vols. Cambridge, England: Cambridge University Press, 1873–1911.

Murdock, Kenneth Ballard. *Increase Mather, The Foremost American Puritan.* Cambridge: Harvard University Press, 1925.

Nettels, Curtis P. *The Money Supply of the American Colonies before 1720* (University of Wisconsin Studies in the Social Sciences and History, No. 20). Madison, Wisconsin: University of Wisconsin, 1934.

Osgood, Herbert L. *The American Colonies in the Seventeenth Century.* 3 vols. New York: Macmillan, 1904–1907.

Pacioli, Luca. *Treatise on Double Entry Bookkeeping.* Section IX, Treatise XI, from *Summa de Arithmetica, Geometria, Proportioni & Proportionalità* (1494), trans. P. Crivelli. London: The Institute of Bookkeepers, Ltd., 1924.

Paige, Lucius R. *History of Cambridge, Massachusetts, 1630–1877.* Boston: H. O. Houghton and Company, 1877.

Peirce, Benjamin. *A History of Harvard University.* Cambridge: Brown, Shattuck, and Company, 1833.

Quincy, Josiah. *The History of Harvard University.* 2 vols. Cambridge: John Owen, 1840.

Savage, James. *A Genealogical Dictionary of the First Settlers of New England.* 4 vols. Boston: Little, Brown, 1861.

Scott, William Robert. *The Constitution and Finance of English, Scottish and Irish Joint Stock Companies to 1720.* 3 vols. Cambridge, England: Cambridge University Press, 1910–1912.

Sewall, Samuel. *Diary of Samuel Sewall, 1674–1729* (not continuous). 3 vols. Boston: Vols. V, VI, and VII of Fifth Series, *Collections of the Massachusetts Historical Society*, 1878, 1879, 1882.

Shannon, Fred Albert. *America's Economic Growth.* New York: Macmillan, 1940.

Shipton, Clifford K. *Sibley's Harvard Graduates. Vol. IV, Biographical sketches of those who attended Harvard College in the Classes 1690–1700.* Cambridge: Harvard University Press, 1933. . . . *Vol. V, the Classes 1701–1712. . . . Vol. VI, the Classes 1713–1721.* Boston: Massachusetts Historical Society, 1937 and 1942.

Shuckburgh, E. S. *Emmanuel College* (University of Cambridge, College Histories). London: F. E. Robinson, 1904.

Sibley, John Langdon. *Biographical Sketches of Graduates of Harvard University.* Vol. I, Classes of 1642–1658. Vol. II, 1659–1677. Vol. III, 1678–1689. Cambridge: Charles William Sever, University Bookstore, 1873–1885.

Smith, S. F. *History of Newton, Massachusetts.* Boston: American Logotype Company, 1880.

Stearns, Raymond Phineas. *The Strenuous Puritan.* University of Illinois, 1954.

Sutherland, Stella H. *Population Distribution in Colonial America.* New York: Columbia University Press, 1936.

Toppan, R. M. *Edward Randolph.* 7 vols. Boston. The Prince Society, John Wilson & Son, 1909.

Trevelyan, G. M. *English Social History.* London: Longmans, Green 1942.

Waters, Henry F. *Genealogical Gleanings in England.* 2 vols. Boston: New England Historic Genealogical Society, 1901.

Weeden, William B. *Economic and Social History of New England, 1620–1789.* 2 vols. Boston: Houghton Mifflin, 1894.

Wiener, Norbert. *The Human Use of Human Brings.* Boston: Houghton Mifflin, 1950.

Winthrop, John, Esq. *The History of New England from 1630 to 1649*, ed. James Savage. Vol. I, Boston: Phelps and Farnum, 1825; Vol. II, Boston: Thomas B. Wait and Son, 1826.

——— *The History of New England from 1630 to 1649*, ed. James K. Hosmer (Original Narratives Series). New York: Charles Scribner's Sons, 1908 (reprinted 1953).

Young, Alexander. *Chronicles of the First Planters of the Colony of Massachusetts Bay.* Boston: Charles C. Little and James Brown, 1846.

# *NOTES*

## CHAPTER I: THE GENERAL SETTING

1. William Robert Scott, *The Constitution and Finance of English, Scottish and Irish Joint Stock Companies to 1720* (Cambridge, England, 1910–1912), II, 315.

2. Samuel Eliot Morison, *The Founding of Harvard College* (Cambridge, 1935), p. 359 *et seq.*

3. *The Laws and Liberties of Massachusetts* (1648 ed.; Cambridge, 1929), p. 47.

4. Samuel Eliot Morison, *Harvard College in the Seventeenth Century* (Cambridge, 1936), p. 562.

5. John Winthrop, Esq., *The History of New England from 1630 to 1649*, ed. James K. Hosmer (New York, 1908), II, 211. There are three main editions of Winthrop's *History:* James Savage's of 1825–1826 and 1853, and Hosmer's of 1908 (reprinted in 1953). Though I am more fond of Savage's first edition, unless otherwise indicated reference will be to page numbers of the 1908 volumes, since they may be more readily available.

6. Winthrop I, 143–144. See also Winthrop I, 210: The ministers advised the Court and "did all agree . . . ," and Horace E. Ware, "Was the Government of Massachusetts Bay Colony a Theocracy?" in *Publications of the Colonial Society of Massachusetts* (Cambridge, 1905), X, especially pp. 169, 173.

7. Winthrop I, 160; II, 23. On December 27, 1645, Thomas Shepard addressed a letter to Peter as "Minister of Christ everywhere." *Am. Hist. Rev.* IV (October 1898), 106.

8. R. P. Stearns, *The Strenuous Puritan* (University of Illinois, 1954), p. 75, and R. P. Stearns, " Hugh Peter" (Harvard University unpublished thesis, 1934), p. 180, quoting Hugo Visscher, *Guilielmus Amesius*, which, on pp. 74–75 cites an extract from a March 29, 1632, resolution of the Council of the City of Rotterdam. Eventually Peter returned to England, was very prominent in the Civil War and under the Protectorate, and was executed after the Restoration in 1660. *Dictionary of National Biography* (London, 1917–      ), "Peters."

9. *FHC*, pp. 201–202.

10. *Records of the Town of Cambridge, Massachusetts, 1630–1703* (Cambridge, 1901), p. 33.

11. *FHC*, pp. 215–216.

12. Samuel Danforth, "An Almanack for 1649," the page reproduced in Winthrop (1908 ed.) II, 340. (Cited by *FHC*, p. 220.)

13. Thomas Danforth in *CSM* XV, 171; Cotton Mather, *Magnalia Christi Americana* (Hartford, 1855) II, 10; Edward Johnson, *Wonder-Working Providence*, ed. J. F. Jameson (Original Narratives Series, New York, 1910), p. 187.

14. Winthrop I, 310.

15. Dunster's Memorandum to the Commissioners, December 1653, Harvard University Archives, Dunster MSS. Printed in *FHC*, p. 448.

16. Winthrop II, 84.

17. *CSM* XV, 174.

18. *DNB*, "Peters." Albert Matthews, *CSM* XV, Introduction, xxxiii.

19. *CSM* XV, 175.

20. *DNB*, "Pelham."

21. Danforth in *CSM* XV, 181.

22. HUA, Harvard College Charter, reprod. in *HCSC*, p. 8.

23. *Mass. Bay Recs.* III, 343–344.

24. *CSM* XV, 208–210 (Danforth's copy of the inventory taken by the President and Fellows on December 10, 1654).

25. This and subsequent summaries of English history in Chapter I are based, unless otherwise indicated, upon Samuel R. Gardiner, *The First Two Stuarts and the Puritan Revolution* (London, 1913); Carlton J. H. Hayes, *A Political and Cultural History of Modern Europe* (New York, 1933), Vol. I; P. L. Kaye, *English Colonial Administration under Lord Clarendon 1660–1667* (Baltimore, 1905); G. M. Trevelyan, *English Social History* (London, 1943).

26. Among much other evidence we have President Dunster's letter to some friends in Lancashire, undated but written about December, 1651: "Truly wee are all [*sic*] one heart (I mean the Godly) with the parliament and Army, And see that Christ hath carried them . . . in all they have . . . by his impulse in a sort been driven to do. If they had ever found Charles pliable to terms of piety and righteousness in sincerity . . . he had been King to this day. . . ." Later: "For the monarchy: Man's wickedness as the meritorious Cause, and God's Providence and mighty hand as the efficient Cause hath dissolved [it]. . . ." (Jeremiah Chaplin, *Life of Henry Dunster* (Boston, 1872), Appendix, pp. 283–6.)

Again — the two fugitive regicide judges, Colonel Goffe and Major-General Whalley, in 1660 lived openly for a time in Cambridge with Daniel Gookin, who was an Overseer of the College. General Goffe's journal records: "Sup't at Mr. Chauncey's; the good old servant of the Lord, still expressing much affection, and telling us, he was perswaded the Lord had brought us to this country for good both to them and orselves." (*Proc. MHS* VII, 281–283.)

27. "Report of the King's Commissioners concerning Massachusetts, etc.," in *Documents Relative to the Colonial History of the State of New York*, III, 112.

Much of the substance of this and the preceding paragraph comes from Kaye, p. 128 and *passim*.

28. Danforth Papers, p. 99. (Cited by Kaye, 136.)

29. *HCSC*, p. 330.

30. *CSM* XV, 218.

31. *HCSC*, pp. 394–395.

32. *HCSC*, pp. 418–421.

33. For this period of English History see Hayes, especially pp. 451–453.

34. Benjamin Peirce, *A History of Harvard University* (Cambridge, 1833), p. 83, quotes a letter of Increase Mather's which attributes this expression to Dudley.

35. For this period see Edward Channing, *A History of the United States* (New York, 1948), II, Chaps. VI to X, *passim;* Herbert L. Osgood, *The American Colonies in the Seventeenth Century* (New York, 1907), III, Chaps. X, XIII, XIV. For dates I have often used Mr. Albert Matthews' tables in the Introduction to *CSM* XV.

36. Council Records of the Dominion of New England, ii, 52–53, in 2 *Proc. MHS* XIII, 257. Cited by *CSM* XV, xxv.

37. *CSM* XV, xxv; XVI, 827–828.

38. Mather's letter of December 16, 1698, to Lieutenant-Governor Stoughton, quoted in Samuel Sewall, *Diary of Samuel Sewall, 1674–1729*, 5 *Coll. MHS* (Boston, 1878), V, 493.

39. *HCSC*, p. 490.

40. *A&R* VII, 312, 703.

41. *CSM* XV, 380.

42. Judge Sewall tells that as early as August 1710 Thomas Brattle's health was in a "very low and languishing" state. With a "thigh no bigger than my wrist," he had no strength at all to receive visitors. *Diary of Samuel Sewall, 1674–1729*, 5 *Coll. MHS* (Boston, 1879), VI, 286.

## CHAPTER II: HARVARD FINANCIAL RECORDS IN THE SEVENTEENTH CENTURY

1. For the list of the relevant contents of the Harvard University Archives, see Appendix F of *HCSC*. The Archives have been rearranged and renumbered somewhat since publication of *HCSC* in 1936, but there have been few if any acquisitions notable for our period. For the major College records which are printed, see Mr. Albert Matthews' Introduction to *CSM* XV. Thanks largely to Thomas Danforth, we have many records of the Corporation and Overseers; they are published in *CSM* XV and XVI. General Court and Council votes may be found in *Mass. Bay Recs.* and *A&R*.

2. Also printed in *CSM* XXXI.

3. Richards' MS. accounts (HUA), pp. 1, 42, 49, 50.

4. A. C. Littleton, *Accounting Evolution to 1900* (New York, 1933), p. 211. The business records of the outstanding American merchant Thomas Hancock and his nephew John a century later than those we are studying were little if any more advanced in their method than seventeenth-century Harvard documents. (See W. T. Baxter, *The House of Hancock* [Cambridge, 1945], pp. 35–38.) For background see A. C. Littleton and B. S. Yamey, ed., *Studies in the History of Accounting* (Homewood, Illinois, 1956).

5. Richard Brown, *A History of Accounting and Accountants* (Edinburgh, 1905), p. 106.

6. Littleton, p. 214.

7. Fred Albert Shannon, *America's Economic Growth* (New York, 1940), p. 28.

8. Richards, p. 21.

9. *CSM* XV, 212.

10. Richards, p. 8.

11. *CSM* XV, 18. Shepard was in charge of the College Stock after Eaton left; see page 6 above.

12. *CSM* XV, 17–19.

13. Brattle's MS. Journal (HUA), p. 32.

14. HUA, Corporation Papers, 1636–1660.

15. Brattle's Journal, letter to Mr. Edward Pelham, February 12, 1708.

16. Richards, pp. 67b, 68.

17. Mr. Irwin K. French, formerly Business Manager of Middlebury, tells of seeing such transactions recorded in the Middlebury books.

18. Cotton Mather, "Some Considerations on the Bills of Credit," in *Colonial Currency Reprints*, A. McF. Davis, ed. (Boston, 1910–11), I, 190. Cited by E. A. J. Johnson, *American Economic Thought in the Seventeenth Century* (London, 1932), p. 162.

19. F. G. James, "Charity Endowments as Sources of Local Credit in Seventeenth- and Eighteenth-Century England," *Jour. Econ. Hist.*, VIII (1948), 153.

20. Richards, pp. 61, 17, 13.

21. To make up to the College a loss of four shillings. Brattle, p. 44.

22. Brattle, p. 50.

23. Richards, p. 49.

24. See *CSM* XV, 54, 216.

25. HUA, the Bordmans' Quarter-Bill Book (1687–1720), regularly for years from 1690 on. According to Professor Raymond de Roover, the practice of signing "Sauf erreurs et omissions" is still common on the continent of Europe.

26. William T. Baxter, "Credit, Bills, and Bookkeeping in a Simple Economy," *Accounting Review*, XXI (1946), 160.

27. Richards, pp. 13, 17.

28. *CSM* XXXI, 61. In the Steward's accounts, Sir Ince had in 1651 on three occasions money "Alowed him by making up the Colledge accounts," £1, £2, and £1 10*s*.

29. *CSM* XVI, 830. This payment covered not only writing but auditing and negotiating.

30. *CSM* XV, 32, 45, 259.

31. QBB.

32. R. N. Toppan, *Edward Randolph* (Boston, 1909), VI, 225, 245.

33. His letter of September 18, 1643, to the Colony Treasurer, printed in *FHC*, 298.

34. Cf. *Documents relating to the University and Colleges of Cambridge*, published by direction of the Commissioners appointed by the Queen to inquire into the State, Discipline, Studies, and Revenues of the Said University and Colleges (London, 1852) I, 107–295. This account is in Latin.

35. See Littleton, pp. 260–264.

36. Fra Luca Pacioli, *Summa de Arithmetica, Geometria, Proportioni & Proportionalità* (1494 ed.). Section IX, Treatise XI, transl. P. Crivelli (London, 1924).

37. Littleton, p. 151.

## CHAPTER III: ECONOMIC VALUES IN PURITAN NEW ENGLAND

1. Franklin B. Dexter, "Estimates of Population in the American Colonies," *Proc. Am. Antiquarian Soc.*, n.s., V (1887), 24–27; Fred A. Shannon, *America's Economic Growth* (New York, 1940), p. 14; John Winthrop, Esq., *The History of New England from 1630–1649*, ed. James Savage (Boston, 1825 and 1826), II, 331 n.; *FHC*, p. 360.

2. John Winthrop, Esq., *The History of New England from 1630 to 1649*, ed. James K. Hosmer (New York, 1908), II, 31.

3. William B. Weeden, *Economic and Social History of New England, 1620–1789* (Boston, 1894), p. 202.

4. Clifford K. Shipton, "Immigration to New England 1680–1740," *Jour. Polit. Econ.*, XLIV, April 1936.

5. Dexter, 3–6; Edward Channing, *A History of the United States* (New York, 1948), II, 222 and n.; Shannon, pp. 18, 61.

6. Winthrop I, 161, 331.

7. Weeden, pp. 114, 208–212.

8. Sophia Shuttleworth Simpson, "Two Hundred Years Ago," *Publications of the Cambridge Historical Society*, XVI (1922), 40.

9. *Historical Markers of the Massachusetts Bay Colony*. Text by Samuel Eliot Morison. Published by the Commonwealth of Massachusetts in 1930.

10. Weeden, p. 100.

11. Weeden, p. 99.

12. Shannon, p. 57.

13. Weeden, pp. 226–228; *Mass. Bay Recs.* I, 126, 243–244, 274.

14. George L. Beer, *Origins of the British Colonial System, 1578–1660* (New York, 1908), p. 267.

15. G. P. Winship, "A Document concerning the First Anglo-American Press," *Transactions of Bibliographical Society* (London, 1939), p. 55.

16. Winthrop II, 17.

17. Winthrop II, 23–24.

18. Winthrop II, 31.

19. E. A. J. Johnson, *American Economic Thought in the Seventeenth Century* (London, 1932), p. 11.

20. Cited from Mitchell's "Nehemiah Sermon" of May 15, 1667, by E. A. J. Johnson, p. 15.

21. John Maynard Keynes, *The General Theory of Employment, Interest and Money*, notes on mercantilism (New York, 1936), p. 340.

22. William Robert Scott, *The Constitution and Finance of English, Scottish and Irish Joint Stock Companies to 1720* (Cambridge, England, 1910–1912), I, 168; E. A. J. Johnson, p. 181; William T. Baxter, *The House of Hancock* (Cambridge, 1945), p. 298; C. J. Bullock, *Essays on the Monetary History of the United States* (New York, 1900), pp. 2–4, 14.

23. *Mass. Archives, Pecuniary I* (May 19, 1680) quoted by Joseph B. Felt, *An Historical Account of Massachusetts Currency* (Boston, 1839), p. 44. For detailed discussion of Massachusetts and other Colonial currency, see also Andrew McFarland Davis, *Proc. AAAS*, XXXIII (1898), 191–211; Andrew McFarland Davis, *Currency and Banking in the Province of the Massachusetts Bay* (New York, 1901), Vol. I; Curtis P. Nettels, *The Money Supply of the American Colonies before 1720* (Madison, Wisconsin, 1934); William B. Sumner, "The Spanish Dollar and the Colonial Shilling," *Am. Hist. Rev.*, III (July 1898); and see the extremely interesting unpublished thesis of Donald Wiedner, "Coins and Accounts in West European and Colonial History, 1250–1936," (1958) HUA.

24. Scott I, 347–352, 466, 467.

25. *CSM* XV, 67.

26. *CSM* XV, 81.

27. Brattle, pp. 50, 64, 71, 77.

28. Brattle, p. 79.

29. *CSM* XVI, 426.

30. Davis, *Currency*, pp. 8–9.

31. Davis, *Currency*, pp. 389–390.

32. *Mass. Bay Recs.* IV, ii, 463.

33. Page 26.

34. Brattle, p. 113.

35. Miss Ruth Crandall, who was for many years assistant to Professor H. H. Burbank and now assists Professor Arthur H. Cole, has very generously made available to me some valuable material she has collected and not published which helps give a picture of the growth of Boston, using the Suffolk County Deeds as sources. See M. S. Foster, unpublished thesis, HUA and Radcliffe Archives, pp. 103, 104, for more detail.

36. Weeden, Appendix A, pp. 877–890, lists scattered prices current from 1630 on, but he, like other writers, is cautious about constructing any series.

37. See Winthrop I, 112, 200; Weeden, pp. 106, 107, 879, 142, 203; Shannon, pp. 58, 71.

38. *Mass. Bay Recs.* II, 174, 213; III, 298, 426; IV, i, 367; IV, ii, 43, 367, 564; V, 138, 408.

39. Richards, p. 9.

40. Richards, p. 12. See also above, pp. 25–26.

41. Winthrop II, 139.

42. Lucius R. Paige, *History of Cambridge, Massachusetts, 1630–1877* (Boston, 1877), p. 229.

43. QBB.

44. Broadus Mitchell & Louise P. Mitchell, *American Economic History* (Boston, 1947), p. 101.

45. Shannon, p. 64.

46. Shannon, p. 76.

47. These salary quotations are from Weeden, p. 221.

48. *Boston Records* II, 99; VII, 30, 171; XI, 4. Cited by R. F. Seybolt in *CSM* XXVII, 136–138.

49. William Frederick Poole in his introduction to Johnson's *Wonder-Working Providence* (Andover, 1867), p. xxvii n. 1. Cited by Jeremiah Chaplin, *Life of Henry Dunster* (Boston, 1872), p. 83, n. 2.

50. Winthrop II, 250.

51. "Mitchell's Modell," in *CSM* XXXI, 321.

52. *HCSC*, pp. 332–333.

53. Winthrop I, 105, and n. 1 (1825 ed.).

54. Winthrop II, 35n. (1826 ed.).

55. Davis, *Currency*, p. 375.

56. Figures for England are from F. G. James, "Charity Endowments as Sources of Local Credit in Seventeenth- and Eighteenth-Century England," *Jour. Econ. Hist.*, VIII (1948), 169.

57. A composite from various sources including Weeden; Shannon, pp. 81–87; Winthrop II Appendix, 1826 ed., pp. 376–379; the Steward's books. For Harvard salaries, see Chapter VII below.

58. *HCSC*, pp. 336–337.

59. Weeden, p. 109.

60. Weeden, pp. 213–214.

61. Weeden, pp. 214–215.

62. Winthrop I, 89.

63. Winthrop II, 23.

64. Scott I, 185, 204; 264 (citing *Political Survey of Ireland*, London, 1719, Appendix, pp. 3–9); 316; 265; 275 (citing Pepys' *Diary*, p. 176); 254 (citing the Rawlinson MS., Bod. Lib., A., 195a, f. 241); 277.

65. James, pp. 168–169.

66. Wilbur K. Jordan, *Philanthropy in England, 1480–1660* (New York, 1959), p. 118.

67. *CSM* XVI, 409.

68. Richards, p. 74; Brattle, p. 30.

## CHAPTER IV: INCOME FROM STUDENTS

1. References for statements about student payments in the Puritan Period are, unless noted to the contrary, the Steward's Book of Thomas Chesholme (published in Vol. XXXI of *CSM*), the Quarter-Bill Books of Aaron and Andrew Bordman (unpublished), and College Books, I, III, and IV of the College Records (Vols. XV and XVI of *CSM*). All the originals are in the Harvard University Archives.

In this section, material on cost to the student is taken in large part from my paper read April 28, 1959, at the Cambridge Historical Society, published in Vol. XXXVIII of their *Publications*, and reproduced here with their permission.

2. *CSM* XV, 5–13.

3. *CSM* XXXI, 139–140, 85–144 *passim*.

4. *CSM* XXXI, 332; XV, 14–15, 213–215.

5. *CSM* XV, 65.

6. *CSM* XXXI, 335.

7. Printed in *CSM* XXXI, 340. All three of the offenders subsequently graduated. *HCSC*, p. 120.

8. College Orders of 1650, *CSM* XV, 33–34.

9. *CSM* XV, 193.

10. Laws of 1655, *CSM* XXXI, 335.

11. Laws of 1655, *CSM* XXXI, 331–332.

12. *CSM* XV, 35.

13. *HCSC*, pp. 70, 300, 328.

14. Laws of 1655, and ordered 1667; *CSM* XXXI, 332, 342.

15. *CSM* XXXI, 265, 207.

16. *CSM* XV, 212–217.

17. Figures are from HUA, Corporation Papers, 1636–1660, Dunster's accounts.

18. Danforth's figures come from *CSM* XV, 213–215. The College Laws of 1655 state: "The Students that now have Studyes in the Colledge shall pay for them the accustomed Rent, but all [who] are hereafter admitted shall pay Rent to the Colledge quarterly for their Chambers and Studyes as they shall be valued by the President & Fellows." (*CSM* XXXI, 332.) This excerpt, plus the schedule of purchase prices and rents of the various studies that is shown in *CSM* XV, 14–15, and the Steward's Book, gives quite conclusive evidence of the time and nature of the change from purchase to rents.

19. *CSM* XV, 260.

20. Richards, p. 21.

21. *CSM* XV, 389; XVI, 407.

22. *CSM* XV, 47.

23. *HCSC*, p. 96, n. 1.

24. *CSM* XV, 258.

25. *CSM* XV, 262.

26. *CSM* XV, 361, 421, 433, 447; XVI, 832. QBB, p. 150; Steward's Book 1703–1731, p. 31.

27. *HCSC*, Appendix, p. 570.

28. Page 59, above.

## CHAPTER V: GOVERNMENT AID

1. June 6, 1639, *Mass. Bay Recs.* I, 263. Peter proposed Marblehead as the site before the Court chose Newtown.

2. Corporation Papers, 1636–1660; *Mass. Bay Recs.* II, 28, 42.

3. *Mass. Bay Recs.* II, 70, 84; the £150 was to be paid out of money collected in England, and in payment of the £400. The vote of £100 is recorded in *Mass. Bay Recs.* II, 176.

4. *FHC*, p. 296. Mr. Matthews, in *CSM* XV, cv, says, "There is no evidence that this money was ever received by Dunster."

5. *Mass. Bay Recs.* II, 200–201.

6. *Mass. Bay Recs.* III, 331. Again, we can only assume that this was done. One Cambridge rate at that time was about £50. Only one rate was assessed in 1650. Cf. *Records of the Town of Cambridge, Massachusetts, 1630–1703* (Cambridge, 1901), p. 353.

7. *Mass. Bay Recs.* III, 214. This appears to include the amount in the September order; or perhaps it just covers the interest, though more than this amount seems to have been due.

8. HUA, Corporation Papers, 1636–1660.

9. *Records of the Colony of New Plymouth, in New England*, IX (Acts of the Commissioners of the United Colonies of New England I), ed. David Pulsifer (Boston, 1859), pp. 20–21. Volumes I and II of the Acts of the Commissioners are printed as IX and X of the records of Plymouth Colony.

10. This expression is used in a 1647 petition to the Commissioners, *Plym. Col. Recs.* IX, 93.

11. A draft "abridgment" of College accounts prepared for the Court. In HUA, Corporation Papers, 1636–1660. See *FHC*, pp. 315–318, for details of collection.

12. *Plym. Col. Recs.* IX, 93–96.

13. *Plym. Col. Recs.* IX, 216–217.

14. *Mass. Bay Recs.* III, 279–280.

15. HUA, Corporation Papers, 1636–1660, "Dunster Account."

16. This last document was bought at auction for $2000 and presented to the Library by an alumnus of the Class of 1897.

17. Committee Report, printed from the Dunster MSS., HUA, in *HCSC*, pp. 570–573.

18. *CSM* XV, 206. *Mass. Bay Recs.* IV, ii, 535. This provision was also written into the Laws; cf. *General Laws and Liberties of Massachusetts Colony* (Cambridge, 1672; reproduced Boston, 1890), p. 30.

19. Mr. Morison's account of this gift is in *HCSC*, pp. 373–376. *CSM* XV, n. 2, gives Mr. Albert Matthews' account.

20. *Mass. Bay Recs.* IV, ii, 433. Joshua Moody was chosen President of the College in 1684, but he declined the honor. (*CSM* XV, 256–257.)

21. Richards, pp. 2, 4, 5, 8.

22. HUA, Harvard College Papers, I, Item 18.

23. HUA, Harvard College Papers, I, Item 19; Richards, p. 57.

24. *Mass. Bay Recs.* III, 208.

25. On pp. 184–185 of *CSM* IV, Danforth gives a list totaling £250 5*s.* 6*d.* labeled for repairs, which included £104 from Richard Saltonstall and £20 from the Reverend John Wilson in addition to the approximately £127 15*s.* 6*d.* shown in Danforth accounts in *CSM* XV, 213–214, as given in 1654 for repairs. Since the Saltonstall and Wilson Gifts, and more, are shown in the page 213–214 accounts as being without designation as to purpose, it may well be that they were

not designated for buildings by the donors. Whether or not the gifts were designated, Danforth says £337 11*s.* 1*d.*, which was far more than the £250, was *spent* on repairs over the next nine years.

26. *CSM* XV, lxxv, citing *Mass. Archives,* lviii, 32–33. Or see *HCSC,* Appendix A, p. 577.

27. *HCSC,* pp. 376–378, 423–430. *CSM* XV, 220–221, lxxxv–xc.

28. *CSM* XV, 222–223, has a list of towns subscribing in 1672, but the list should probably be dated 1677; see 1678 list in *HCSC,* pp. 647–650, and apparent promises of £3028 9*s.* 6*d.* See also Stewards' 1682 report *HCSC,* pp. 650–653.

29. The total tax levied by Massachusetts was £1299 in 1674, £14,051 in 1675, £21,090 in 1676, £10,471 in 1677, £3494 in 1678. J. B. Felt, "Statistics of Taxation in Massachusetts," *Coll. Am. Stat. Assn.,* I, iii (1847), pp. 251, 256–257, 275.

30. *Mass. Bay Recs.* IV, ii, 537. *HCSC,* p. 398.

31. *CSM* XV, cvi, cvii, cviii, quoting *Mass. Archives,* lviii, 103a.

32. *CSM* XV, cvii, cviii, citing *Mass. Archives,* lviii, 103, which bears a date of "10:4:1680," normally interpreted as June 10, 1680. The next document in *CSM* is from 103a and is dated June 9, 1680; it provides that the Country Treasury pay not over £100 of the expense, but the deputies did not consent to this action of the magistrates. It looks to me as if the first document may have passed both branches after the document quoted second failed to pass, and thus the Court authorized spending up to £200. Mr. Morison feels (*HCSC,* p. 437, n. 1) that £100 was authorized and that "the only College stock known to be then in the Colony treasury was the Mowlson-Bridges scholarship fund. . . . Probably the balance of £160 over the £100 granted was paid out of this fund: but fortunately the General Court did not discover that when they settled accounts with the College in the next century." I do not entirely follow Mr. Morison's reasoning here. The Court may have meant to use Stock in *Richards'* hands. Moreover, we have no evidence that the College received £260 from the Country.

Richards' book shows clearly that exactly £260 was spent to build the house. Of this amount, at least £91 13*s.* 4*d.* had been received by the College Treasurer; it was not Country money. None of the balance shows on the receipt side at all, but the way of entering payments indicates that some of it, though not necessarily all, may have come from the Country. We are left not knowing whether the Country's contribution was £168 6*s.* 8*d.* or some smaller amount.

33. *A&R* VII, 275, 671–672, 697

34. *Mass. Archives,* lviii, 265, as cited in *CSM* XV, cxii. *A&R* IX, 79, 105. *Mass. Archives,* lviii, 270, 273, 274, cited in *CSM* XV, cxiii.

35. *Mass. Bay Recs.* I, 323.

36. May 8, 1662, HUA, Supplement to Ferry Papers, 1646–1785; *FHC,* pp. 301–302. The official rate in 1654 was £40, but according to Dunster's letter to the Colony Treasurer (September 18, 1643, printed in *FHC,* pp. 298–299, from *Mass. Archives,* CCXL, 58), the receipts were down to £30 a year. Yet the Committee of 1654 debited him with £40 received for each of 11 years, and Dunster himself in his 1653 letter to the Commissioners (MS copy in HUA) intimates that the rate was £40. Wadsworth's index of the lost College Book II has an entry of renting the Ferry in 1654 for £40 (*CSM* XV, xxi). The "Briefe

Information" of 1655 lists the Ferry as an asset, but says, "Though we have the Ferry, yet what the produce of it will be, we have no certainty. . . ." (*HCSC*, Appendix, p. 577).

37. Rent figures mostly from Treasurer's records; 1702 from Brattle, 69.

38. HUA, Land Papers, I. *CSM* XV, 51, 52, 53, 60, 275–277. *HCSC*, pp. 31–34.

39. *Records of the Town of Cambridge, Massachusetts, 1630–1703*, p. 33. Harvard College Papers, Suppl. to Vol. I, Item 2. The Peyntree House had already been purchased for the College.

40. *Records of the Town of Cambridge, Massachusetts, 1630–1703*, p. 82.

41. It was sold in 1775 with the permission of the General Court (*FHC*, p. 324).

42. Cf. the copy of the Weld-Peter accounts given to the Corporation for Promotion and Propagation of the Gospel of Jesus Christ among the Indians in New England. (*NEHGR* XXXIX (1885), 179–182.)

43. Winthrop II, 309 (1646). See also Charles H. J. Douglas, *The Financial History of Massachusetts, 1628–1775* (New York, 1892), pp. 35, 39, 40, 54–55. Douglas gives evidence of a continual failure to keep or to present anywhere nearly complete records of the Colony Treasurers' receipts and expenditures.

## CHAPTER VI: INCOME FROM GIFTS AND FROM ENDOWMENT, AND SUMMARY OF ALL INCOME

1. John Winthrop, Esq., *The History of New England from 1630 to 1649*, ed. James K. Hosmer (New York, 1908), II, 31.

2. Weld's final account, of which there is a manuscript copy in the Harvard University Archives, is printed in *CSM* XIV, 123–126, and in *NEHGR* XXXIX, 179–182. Weld's defense of his accounting is in *NEHGR* XXXVI, 62–70.

3. *CSM* XV, 172, 209. Henry F. Waters, *Genealogical Gleanings in England* (Boston, 1901), I, 508, quotes Bridges' will which bequeathed "the summe of fiftie pounds towards the enlargement of a colledge in New England for students there." Cited by *FHC*, p. 307, n. 2. Thus it is not certain that the whole £162 16*s*. 4*d*. was originally designated for scholarships.

4. Sibley records this story under Nathaniel White, a student from Eleuthera. John Langdon Sibley, *Biographical Sketches of Graduates of Harvard University* (Cambridge, 1873), I, 137–140. See also *CSM* XV, 200, and *HCSC*, pp. 39–43.

5. The "Modell" is printed in *CSM* XXXI, 309–322. The story is told in the introduction to those pages and also in *HCSC*, pp. 370–373.

6. *CSM* XVI, 835–836.

7. *CSM* XVI, 837.

8. *CSM* XV, 39.

9. Richards, p. 55.

10. HUA, original deed of gift.

11. HUA, Harvard College Papers, I, 46; Brattle, pp. 24, 32, 47, 84. Copies of receipts by Thomas Brattle to Col. Samuel Shrimpton wherein £4 money is taken instead of £5 produce — in HUA, Land Papers (original owned by Grenville Norcross).

12. *CSM* XXXI, 51–52; XV, 286.

13. Richards, pp. 50, 51; Brattle, p. 24; *HCSC*, pp. 36, 380.

14. *HCSC*, pp. 383–384, 439.

15. Richards, Brattle, and *CSM* XV, all *passim.*

16. Daniel Gookin, *Historical Collections of the Indians in New England*, written in 1674, 1 *Coll. MHS*, I (1792), 176. Cited by *CSM* XV, lxxxiii. This account comes largely from *CSM* XV, lxxxii–lxxxiv, citing votes of the Corporation printed in the same volume, pp. 346, 352, 358, and the Inventory of 1654, p. 208.

17. *CSM* XV, xciv–xcv, 345, 357–358, 360, 391; Brattle, pp. 55, 61; *HCSC*, pp. 518–521. Plans had first been drawn up in 1693 or 1694.

18. *CSM* XVI, 847, 851.

19. 4 *Coll. MHS*, I, 254.

## CHAPTER VII: ANALYSIS OF DISBURSEMENTS

1. We do have record, including Mather's signed receipt in Harvard University Archives, that Mather did have some salary payments from the Province.

2. Dunster's 1647 Petition to the Commissioners of the United Colonies, *Plym. Col. Recs.* IX, 94.

3. *CSM*, XV, 194.

4. From at least 1703 on, Tutors sometimes received the study rent of one pupil. (QBB, 1687–1720, pp. 139, 142, 161; Steward's ledger, 1703–1731, p. 30.) This would indicate that students were taken into the Fellows' quarters.

5. Students of Harvard history may wonder at these results, for Mr. Morison, in *HCSC*, p. 52, n. 4, refers to the discontented Tutors' calculations (made about 1721) of their predecessors' salaries and from that concludes that Leverett and Brattle received over £125 apiece in total compensation. The old memorandum is in HUA, Harvard College Papers, I, 124; see also Harvard College Papers Calendar I. Harvard College Papers, I, 51 and 55, give the detail of the computation of this amount, and it looks to me, though I hesitate to differ from an almost contemporary account, as if it contains some misconceptions: First, it adds £25 salary, £25 ferry, £20 Pennoyer, and £56 tuitions. From Corporation votes it would seem that the Pennoyer money, which did not regularly amount to £20, was *included* in the flat £25 allowed as "salary." Then the £56 tuition seems to have been calculated by saying that the graduating classes averaged 14 each (and the estimation of the average is shown), that each of two Tutors had two classes, and that each student paid £2 a year; 14 × 2 × 2 gives £56. One might think this would be a conservative estimate, for there were a few students who did not graduate. However, referral to the Steward's records and actual summation of the tuitions received and paid quarterly to the Tutors shows that this factor is much more than offset by the fact that many students who graduated did not attend College for all four quarters, and some attended very little, and paid detriments and half-tuition. The actual tuition received, while it did vary widely over the years, averaged from October 1693 to August 1702 (the classes 1693 to 1701 were used in the Tutors' average) £94 11*s.*, or £47 each for two tutors. A shift to a period three or four years earlier or later reduces these figures; the average for the period 1693 to 1712 was £89, or £44 10*s.* each. The sum, then, of the £25 salary,

£25 ferry, and £43 tuition (average July 1687 to July 1697, all but two of the years of Leverett's and Brattle's teaching fellowships) indicates that their average receipt was £93 to 1695, when the ferry rate went up, and £98 after that time — and not £125 apiece.

6. Richards, pp. 55, 74, 80.

7. *CSM* XV, 345; Brattle, p. 33, *et passim; CSM* XVI, 408.

8. *CSM* XV, cxliii note; *HCSC*, p. 54, n. 6.

9. Chesholme's Book, *CSM* XXXI, *passim;* College Orders, *CSM* XV, 46.

10. See pp. 79–80 above.

11. *CSM* XV, 46, 259.

12. *CSM* XV, 10, 50. This money was ordered for "Taylor the Butler." In *HCSC* p. 55, n. 4, Mr. Morison speaks of John Taylor, who "after serving as college carpenter since the early part of Dunster's administration, . . ." "was appointed Butler about the year 1671." He cites Sibley, II, 288. On page 288 Sibley says of Joseph Taylor, 1669, "His father was Butler of the College." On page 109 of *HCSC*, it says, "For many, possibly most, of the years prior to 1672, the college butler was a student . . . ," and note 2 lists "the five student-butlers of whom there is record," the fifth being Edward Taylor (1671-poet). The first four were mentioned in Steward Chesholme's book, which stops as of 1660. "Taylor" was described in the College records as Butler for 1670–1671, and Edward Taylor recorded in his diary that he was Butler all the $3\frac{1}{4}$ years he was at College, from July 1668 on (Sibley, II, 398). There were two student Taylors — Joseph (1669) and Edward (1671). It seems to me, despite Sibley and his references, that John Taylor, the old carpenter and father of Joseph, was not likely to have been the Butler; I have found no contemporary evidence that he was. Moreover, there was a series of student Butlers after the five listed by Mr. Morison, including Edward Payson (1677) in April 1675, R. Wadsworth (1679) in October 1677, N. Russell (1681) in October 1679, and so on. See *CSM* XV and XVI, 63, 65, 67, 74, 77, 81, 85, 829, 339, 356 (2), 366, 388, 390, 422; Richards, p. 12.

13. *CSM* XXXI, 60–61, 222, 241, 251; XV, 46, 262; Steward's ledger 1703–1731, 33.

14. *CSM* XV, 46, 48, 262, 65.

15. Richards records paying him £3 in August 1690, and on August 24, 1691, ordered the Steward to pay £3. The Steward also paid £3 in August 1692. (Richards, p. 80; also *CSM* XVI, 829, 831; back of the QBB.) *HCSC*, p. 288, says somewhat erroneously that "the first recorded salary was £5 . . . in 1693." Occasional amounts were also paid out before this time for library services such as moving books.

16. *CSM* XV, 210, 344, 348, 357, 361, 366, 368, 370, 373, 374, 376, 377, 378, 389, 392, 396; XVI, 405, 421, 423. Brattle, *passim.*

17. See p. 88 above — Shepard's proposition.

18. *Plym. Col. Recs.* IX, 94–96.

19. See above, p. 112.

20. Butler and Bell-ringer, see above, pp. 67, 80, 137–138; Monitor, above, p. 70, *CSM* XXXI, 173 and 335; QBB of 1687 on; for "wayting in the hall," *CSM* XXXI, 250. The Monitor's pay probably should not be considered a *direct*

College expense, any more than specifically endowed scholarships, for the money to pay the Monitor was collected by the Steward each quarter by the device of "putting it on the heads" of the students — dividing the cost among the students.

21. HUA, Leverett's MS. diary, p. 55.

22. See above, pp. 73–74; QBB, College Account, p. 2; *CSM* XVI, 830.

23. *FHC*, pp. 273–274.

## CHAPTER VIII: ASSETS

1. Corporation memorial to the General Court, June 14, 1697. Josiah Quincy, *The History of Harvard University* (Cambridge, 1840), I, 497.

2. Governor Thomas Dudley's letter of March 12, 1631, to the Countess of Lincoln in Alexander Young, *Chronicles of the First Planters of the Colony of Massachusetts Bay* (Boston, 1846), p. 324.

3. Letter of the Reverend Edmund Browne (Harvard donor) to Sir Simonds D'Ewes in *CSM* VII, 75. Date of the letter according to Matthews in *CSM* XV, lxx n. 4.

4. Letter of July 2, 1688, to Increase Mather in London. 4 *Coll. MHS* VIII, 502–503.

5. Wilbur K. Jordan, *Philanthropy in England, 1480–1660* (New York, 1959), p. 38 *et passim.*

6. William Robert Scott, *The Constitution and Finance of the English, Scottish and Irish Joint Stock Companies to 1720* (Cambridge, England, 1912), especially I, 318, 347–389, 443.

7. See E. A. J. Johnson, pp. 84, 91, 92, 213, 215, 219, 266, 267, citing, among others, C. Mather, *Durable Riches*, II, 2, and I. Mather, *Excellency of Public Spirit*, p. 11.

8. *A&R* I, 113.

9. The substance of this paragraph on English endowments comes from James, pp. 155–156, 158, 160–165, 169 (citing numerous authorities), supplemented by Scott, 238. For further discussion of the availability of money, see above, p. 40 and following.

10. *CSM* XV, 186; £225 4*d.* in the Steward's account, less £8 4*s.* 9½*d.* owed to Mr. Dunster, £30 owed on the church gallery rent, and £85 owed to students for study construction.

11. This Stock is made up of the £862 11*s.* from correctly adding Danforth's Stock on p. 216 of *CSM* XV, and deducting Mowlson, Keayne, *and* £73 17*s.* of due or overdue rents and interest.

12. Danforth's accounts, shown in *CSM* XV, 245–249, cover a short interim period and he obviously kept them only to fill in until Nowell took over; he may well have postponed payment on some items, and he omitted recording others. Nowell's expenses may have been somewhat larger than normal because of this.

13. Folio 16. Richards' book came to light only about 1865, but College Book III records of Stock in April 1693 or earlier made the change apparent. *CSM* XV, 255.

14. Sibley, I, 340.

15. Richards records some of Nowell's transactions retroactively: "To money due on former account as Mr. Nowell enforms . . . ," "To forbearance due per Mr. Nowell's account . . ." (folio 70). Brattle records that a debtor says Nowell sued him and he paid the debt, "which if true, the abovesaid 45*s.* would be in full of his bond. . . ." Brattle seems to have had no records of Nowell's to refer to (Brattle, p. 30). Again, £25 was received from the Glover annuity, which had been paid to date in 1686, "she says." (Brattle, p. 30. "She" was the Glover heir.)

16. Photocopy in HUA, Presidents' Miscellaneous Papers. Original the property of Charles F. Rogers, Jr.

17. Richards, p. 45; *CSM* XV, 254, 256, 75, 76. N.E.H.G.R. VIII, 19, says that John Richards and Joseph Dudley arrived back on October 23, 1683, having been absent one year and five months.

18. Richards, 16. On folio 68 Richards speaks of April 8, 1686, "when I received the account from Mr. Nowell," but this seems to refer only to the last entry in that particular account.

19. Sewall, *Diary* (5 *Coll. MHS*), I, 77, 100, 101, 132, 137.

20. *CSM* XV, 251–252.

21. "Stoughton" may be the Mason mortgage which Richards said Stoughton was holding. (Richards, p. 63. *CSM* XV, 247.)

22. R. N. Toppan, *Edward Randolph* (Boston, 1909), VI, 225, 245. Randolph's editor, Toppan, in a note to this entry admits that the transfer may have been just a routine to trustees, but it looks odd, he thinks.

23. Richards, p. 18. Isaac Addington, Secretary of the Dominion, received a shilling a bond.

24. Original in HUA, Deeds.

25. *CSM* XV, 355–356. See also an address of the Fellows to the General Court, in HUA, Harvard College Papers, I, 18.

26. *CSM* XV, 409–411, and Brattle's book. Edmund Browne's legacy was also still due, though not listed in this account.

27. Brattle, p. 57.

28. Richards, p. 19.

29. Brattle, p. 30.

30. Richards, p. 70; Brattle, pp. 4, 6, 113.

31. Richards, p. 17; Brattle, pp. 30, 81, 109, 112.

32. Brattle, p. 1.

33. Richards, p. 72. See also p. 64 above.

34. Brattle, p. 68; Richards, pp. 10, 56, 59, 61.

35. Cf., Mr. Thomas Atkins (formerly carpenter). Richards, pp. 66, 74.

36. Bernard Bailyn, *The New England Merchants in the Seventeenth Century* (Cambridge, 1955), p. 111. Mr. Bailyn quotes Wharton's biographer, Viola F. Barnes, from *CSM* XXVI, 249, as saying that Wharton "enjoyed 'playing the game.' . . . His imagination, power of organization, courage in taking risks, . . . are all characteristic of the successful captain of industry."

37. *CSM* XV, 68.

38. Brattle, pp. 37, 46, 48.

39. *CSM* XV, 376, 378, 388.

40. *CSM* XV, 350 (April 8, 1695).

## CHAPTER IX: OVERVIEW

1. *Boston News–Letter*, no. 475, May 18, 1713, quoted in HUA, John Leverett's MS. Diary, 76–77.

2. *CSM* XV, xxxiv, 42.

3. *CSM* XXVI, 280.

4. Cf. HUA, Harvard College Papers, I, 43.

5. HUA, Charter Papers, 1698–1700.

6. Weeden, p. 80.

7. Viola F. Barnes, "Richard Wharton, a Seventeenth Century New England Colonial," in *CSM* XXVI, 265.

8. For a discussion of English universities, see *FHC*, pp. 40–107; *HCSC*, pp. 298–300. See also J. B. Mullinger, *The University of Cambridge* (Cambridge, England, 1911), III, especially p. 200: "The records clearly establish the fact that . . . the initiative . . . was taken at Harvard by Cambridge men alone . . . [*They*] retained, for the most part, the traditions of their past academic life and the methods of their former teachers."

9. Charter of 1650, MS. in HUA. *Facsimile* in *HCSC*, p. 8.

10. There are innumerable instances: "Ordered by the Corporation that endowment income be spent as follows," "that payment be made to Tutors, etc." (*CSM* XV, 224, 226, 227, and so on, 64, 65, and so on.) In June 1669 the *Overseers* ordered Danforth to transfer his accounts to Richards, but in April 1682 the *Corporation* ordered Richards to turn over his papers to Danforth; in January 1683 the Corporation elected the Treasurer. (See also above, p. 167, and *CSM*, XV, 218–219, 245, 57, 60, 72.)

11. Leverett's MS. diary, p. 75.

12. *CSM* XV, 66.

13. See *HCSC*, p. 304n., for an example.

14. Herbert L. Osgood, *The American Colonies in the Seventeenth Century* (New York, 1904–1907), III, 441.

15. Cotton Mather, *Magnalia Christi Americana* (Hartford, 1855) II, 9.

# INDEX

# *INDEX*